D0744575

TOTAL DESIGN

Architecture of Welton Becket and Associates

FEBRUARY 1972

To THE ~~BEST~~ OF FRIENDS.

LOVE, BOB AND JULE

TOTAL DESIGN

Architecture of Welton Becket and Associates

WILLIAM DUDLEY HUNT, Jr., FAIA

McGRAW-HILL BOOK COMPANY

New York   St. Louis   San Francisco   Düsseldorf   Johannesburg
Kuala Lumpur   London   Mexico   Montreal   New Delhi
Panama   Rio de Janeiro   Singapore   Sydney   Toronto

TOTAL DESIGN: Architecture of Welton Becket and Associates

Copyright © 1972 by McGraw-Hill, Inc. All Rights Reserved. Printed in the United States of America. No part of this publication may be reproduced, stored in a retrieval system, or transmitted, in any form or by any means, electronic, mechanical, photocopying, recording, or otherwise, without the prior written permission of the publisher. *Library of Congress Catalog Card Number 70-178928*

07-031298-2

1234567890   HDAH   75432

This book was set in Optima by York Graphic Services, Inc.,
printed by Halliday Lithograph Corporation, and bound by A. Horowitz & Son.
Color printing by The Longacre Press, Inc.
The designer was William Dudley Hunt, Jr., FAIA. The editors were
William G. Salo, Jr., Frank Purcell, and Lydia Maiorca.
Stephen J. Boldish supervised production.

*To Welton David Becket, FAIA, whose greatest legacy
is to be found in his architecture,
his architectural philosophy, and in his comrades
he so carefully trained to carry on*

CONTENTS

Preface ix

Part One THE CONCEPTS OF TOTAL DESIGN

1. A Philosophy for Architecture	3
2. Welton Becket and the Office	9
3. Principles of Total Design Today	19

Part Two THE FRAMEWORK FOR TOTAL DESIGN

4. Corporate Organization	31
5. Organization of Offices	39
6. Organization of Design	45
7. Organization of Production	57
8. Organization of Engineering	63
9. Organization of Special Functions	69

Part Three THE BUSINESS OF TOTAL DESIGN

10. Management for Architecture	77
11. Business Development	93
12. Dimensions of the Practice	101

Part Four   THE PRACTICE OF TOTAL DESIGN

13. Administration of Projects   113
14. Research and Other Studies   119
15. Design and Schematic Development   129
16. Preliminaries and Production   147
17. Services during Construction   157

Part Five   A PORTRAIT OF A TOTAL DESIGN

18. The Clients and Their Problems   167
19. Establishment of Feasibility   171
20. Studies and the Problems Solved   183
21. Production of Drawings and Specifications   201
22. Design Translated into a Building   209

Part Six   THE FUTURE OF TOTAL DESIGN

23. A Look Ahead at Total Design   221
24. A Look Ahead at the Practice   227

Index of Buildings   237
Index of Photographers   241
Index   242

PREFACE

Why another book about architecture? Or about architects? Or about these architects?

During the more than three years while it was being written, questions of this sort were frequently asked about this book by those who heard about it.

There is no single, simple answer. Perhaps it would be more seemly to let the book speak for itself, through its own pages. In that way, the reader could find his own answers to the questions. And he could make his own judgment of the motivation of the book and the result achieved.

On the other hand, there is something to be said for attempting to answer the questions, as clearly as possible, here. This will expose to the reader the author's reasons for the choice of subject and the methodology of the book. Then the reader will be in a position to judge the results against the stated aims and objectives. And there are some bits of information that might properly be included in the preface but would have no real place in the heart of the book.

In the first place, Welton Becket, who died on January 16, 1969 at the age of 66, was a unique individual. He was a self-made man who lived a most successful life and built a great architectural firm. He became wealthy. He worked hard, played just as hard. His cronies, friends, and acquaintances ranged all over the spectrum, from General Eisenhower, to the movie crowd, to the presidents of great American and foreign corporations. He had earned for himself all of the good things life has to offer and he enjoyed living to the utmost.

He was one of the softest-spoken men around.

Some thought him to be humble, but Welton Becket was not humble. He was proud of himself, of his work, of his sons, of his accomplishments, and of his people, the employees of the firm. He was not humble in the usual sense of that word but he had humility.

Other men have been called "jolly good fellows." Welton Becket could be as "jolly" as anyone, when he played pool betting small sums, when he drank scotch, on the golf course, at work when the occasion was right. But he was never really a jolly good fellow—he had a certain built-in dignity and reserve about him.

He had a way of making his wishes known, mostly by indirection but also with considerable force if necessary. And he had a temper. When asked a deliberately leading question, the type writers sometimes ask, "With all these vice presidents (about twenty at the time), what do you do?" he bristled for about ten seconds, then thrust his jaw out slightly, and said very softly, very convincingly, "I am the president."

Most of all, Welton Becket was an architect. That is what he wanted to do, that is what he wanted to be known as, and that is what he spent almost all of his time being. When asked why he didn't accept more of the speaking engagements constantly pressed upon him, or committee assignments, or other extra-curricular activities, he replied, "I decided a long time ago that it was possible to practice architecture or do other things, not both. What I wanted was to practice, actively and completely."

In all the publicity, in the large number of feature

stories about Welton Becket and his firm over the years—there were many, the magazines *Time, Saturday Evening Post, Newsweek, Fortune* to name a few—a goodly number of attempts were made by writers to pin labels on the man and on his firm. "Businessman's Architect" was one he particularly disliked. The firm, of course, worked and still works for businessmen, but it also does projects for foundations, individuals, and others.

Although Becket never said it, what he really wanted to be known as was an "Architect's Architect." Of course that phrase, when it is used at all, is not applied to the kind of architect Becket was. Maybe to the solitary, or almost solitary, artist-architect who takes one job, or at most a few jobs at a time, and then only from those clients he likes for projects that interest him. Or it might be applied to the great masters, the ones who are sometimes called "form-makers" or something similar.

What Becket would have meant, if he had ever used the phrase—he wouldn't have, it wasn't his style and he would have considered it an arrogance— was that he dedicated his whole life to architecture almost to the exclusion of all else. And odd though it may seem in one who was thought by many to be exclusively a businessman-architect or an executive type, he found it almost impossible even to discuss the business side of the profession for any length of time. What interested him was architecture in the sense of design, function, space, form, art, structure.

Welton Becket was a good businessman, a top-flight executive. The firm he built, the clients he wooed and held on to, the buildings, and the master plans all attest to his success in those areas. But there is an important point here: he was good at those things, but he lived architecture. He would sit at the coffee table in his office discussing the details of office management or some similar workaday subject, and after the major points had been made, sometimes before, he would jump up, move to the great wall of photographs of his buildings in his office, to talk about "architecture," to make some point about design, or detailing, or structure.

One of the most telling facts about this man was the fact that he owned the firm completely and absolutely. No partners, no associates, no stockholders other than himself. It seems impossible in a firm so large and so successful, but it was true until the day he died. No one but his lawyer knew what was in his will, that he would leave the firm to his two sons, his nephew, and his key people, sixteen individuals in all.

Now it may not be too uncommon—even today— for one man to own a company of this size, but for one to own an architectural firm this large is unheard of. Yet Becket was able to command both the respect and the loyalty of his employees in spite of his absolute control of the firm. When he died, 40 percent of the firm's employees were enrolled in the Profit Sharing and Retirement Plan which requires four and a half years of service before participation. And seventy-nine people had been with the firm ten years or more. Quite a record in a firm that had 400 employees at the time.

Why a book about this firm, other than because of the unique qualities of the man who founded and built it? Well, the firm itself is unique. There are two labels, self-imposed, which Welton Becket did believe in and adhere to: "Vision through Supervision," by which he meant creative attention to the necessities of a client's problems, an early motto of the firm; and "Total Design," the current motto which reduced to its lowest possible denominator means that the firm prefers to handle all aspects of architecture: programming, design, engineering, production, interior design, down to the smallest details to produce a building complete in every way. The phrase does not mean that the firm tries to play the role of "Master Builder" in the ancient sense of that phrase. This firm will not even talk about taking on the construction of a building, for example. It sticks to what Welton Becket believed to be "architecture" in the broadest sense of the word, but it will not become involved in services which he believed to be more properly construction, real estate, or financial.

So it would seem that there are reasons enough for this book—in the man who started the firm and built it, in its present structure and practice, and in the future of architecture and of the firm itself. There are other reasons, perhaps of some importance to the reader. One is that the book itself is unlike any other on architecture. There are books in which architects give voice to their philosophies. There are others which record in pictures and words the work of architects. There are "profiles" of architects in magazines or book form. There are hard-bound super-brochures which architects give to their clients.

This book is none of these. Instead, it is an honest effort to delve into the heart and soul of a most successful architectural firm, to probe it for whatever there is of truth and light, and to paint not a sketch but a portrait; not an *esquisse* of an hour but a rendering that is the result of many thousands of hours of toil. Inspiration, perhaps, but toil most definitely. Enlightenment, possibly, and truth, hopefully.

Many articles, even many books, come from a quick exposure of their subjects, following the concepts of the popular, the salable, the titillating, the deliberately provocative or sensational. This book is not any of these (which may disappoint some readers). This is a solid story of an architectural firm that delivers wide-ranging services for a variety of building types. It is the story of how the firm was started, how it grew, what it stands for, and how it operates. From this, it might be assumed that anyone interested in architecture, in any way, can derive some benefit. In any case, this has been the aim of the author.

Finally, it should be said that Welton Becket and his top people all agreed that none of their "secrets" were barred to the author. In the hundreds of hours of taped interviews on which the book is founded, there was a candid revelation of facts, not the withholding of secrets.

William Dudley Hunt, Jr., FAIA
Washington, D.C.

x

OPPOSITE: *Equitable Life Assurance Society of the United States, Los Angeles, California.*

Part One
THE CONCEPTS OF TOTAL DESIGN

Apartments: The Meadows, San Rafael, California. View of Recreation Center and apartment buildings, interior of recreation center.

1
A PHILOSOPHY
FOR ARCHITECTURE

Today, in a time of architectural turmoil and soul-searching, with the future of architecture and of architects clouded and subject to considerable speculation both within and outside the profession, the firm of Welton Becket and Associates might be called by some an anachronism.

In the first place, the key people in this firm seem absolutely sure of where they and their practice of architecture are heading. They believe the philosophy under which they operate to be valid and worthy and salable to clients at a profit to the practitioners—and to the clients—in terms of dollars, yes, but also in terms of quality and intrinsic value to both architects and clients.

In a time when some young people and some who are older appear to be hooked on the "relevance of architecture" and talk about such subjects as "commitment" and "advocacy," the people in this firm are hooked on "architecture," and that is what they talk about.

In a time when architects are exceedingly unsure of their present role, and even more unsure of the future, the people here are dedicated to architecture and its creation.

While they may have some doubts about the exact details of the future of architecture, the people of WB&A have no doubts at all about the availability of great challenges and opportunities in the design of buildings and cities of the future. And they have few doubts about the big principles that will help them seize the opportunities and meet the challenges.

Some may call this approach reactionary, but it is certainly refreshing. And when you get right down to it, what could be more real, more relevant, than architects doing the only thing they are really trained to do, the only things they can really accomplish as professionals—the creation of architecture.

Well that is what this firm is all about—the creation of architecture.

Now some might question the definition of architecture current here, or the way it is practiced, or the resulting buildings and other designs. But it works. And the clients like it. And it is very successful. And it is architecture, unadulterated by excursions into the bypaths of construction and other areas so tempting to many architects today.

The keystone of the philosophy of Welton Becket and Associates is in the phrase "Total Design." This is at once the motto of the firm, its credo, and its working philosophy. The effects of this are to be found in everything the firm does, in the kinds of jobs it takes, in the organizational patterns, in the services offered to clients.

What is total design? In its simplest terms, the phrase connotes both architectural philosophy and practice that embrace all of the services required to analyze any architectural problem, perform the necessary studies and research to solve the problem, and translate the solution into a building or group of buildings complete down to the last detail of furniture, sculpture and other art, landscaping, and furnishings, even to ashtrays, menus, and matchboxes.

Total design, by this definition, includes not only all of the traditional architectural functions and all engineering but interior design, industrial design of objects for the buildings and their surroundings, master planning, space planning, and a host of other functions. But it must be remembered that all of these functions are actually part of the professional aspects of design in the broadest sense of that word and include services during construction to assure its proper execution.

On the other hand, total design does not embrace any activities essentially not of a design nature. Through the years as WB&A continually expanded its staff to include engineers, interior designers, graphic artists, space planners, store planners, and other design-oriented specialists, the firm has scrupulously avoided attempting to act as a realtor or financier or to become involved in construction. The deep-rooted conviction here is that real estate, finance, construction, and the like are nondesign in nature, therefore nonarchitectural and nonprofessional. Because of this conviction, if there has ever been any inclination to get into these areas, it has been successfully resisted.

This is not to say that Welton Becket and Associates does not get deeply involved in research, analysis, or other studies required by its clients in areas of site selection, land assembly, financing, of construction, and things of that sort. There is a great deal of activity in this firm in such areas. But there is a very important distinction to be made in what the firm will or will not take on for a client, and in the manner in which it takes on work related to its major services.

The firm handles feasibility studies of all kinds for numerous clients, some for very large projects, others smaller in scope. In some cases, these studies involve only the financial feasibility of a given project on a site already selected by a client. In other cases, even among large corporations, the firm finds itself faced with performing feasibility studies of considerably larger scope. Sometimes this happens because a corporation with little previous building experience or some other client finds itself in a position to acquire a parcel of land for development or to make some out-of-the-ordinary capital investment in real estate or improvement. Or a potential client may decide to develop land it already holds but has had little experience with such ventures.

In cases like these, WB&A will take on studies in whatever depth is required, analyses of potential sites, location studies, traffic analyses, and many other kinds of research related to the field of real estate. But the firm will not act as realtors for clients, in the actual handling of the purchase or sale of property, preferring to leave such activities to those who are specialists in these fields and know them best.

In a similar vein, WB&A is often called upon for financial counseling of clients, especially by those which have not had great experience in developing buildings, but also by some experienced clients. Here again, the lines of services offered by the firm are strictly drawn. Advice, studies, counseling—yes; but WB&A avoids becoming involved in the actual financing of projects handled for its clients.

Welton Becket and Associates designs leasing brochures for its clients, but it does not perform leasing operations for them.

The firm advises its clients on development, but it does not act as the developer for them or for itself.

The firm oversees and inspects the construction of the buildings of its clients, but it does not act as the contractor for those buildings.

WB&A aids and counsels its clients on speculative or promotional types of projects when required, but it will not become involved in actual project promotions.

WB&A advises its clients on architectural and construction law, from an architectural or construction point of view, but it will not attempt to act as attorney for the clients in drawing up construction contracts and the like.

What all of this adds up to is that over the years, as architecture has become more and more complicated and more involved with a number of things brought on by expanding needs and exploding technology, Welton Becket and Associates has made every attempt to broaden its services to meet the needs and demands of the clients of the day. And, hopefully, of the future. All of this up to a point, and up to now that has always been the point where professional activities or design activities end and where those which are nonprofessional or nondesign begin.

This has worked out very well, up to now, although there have been some false starts, and a bit of re-direction of energies has been required at various times. The trouble with it in the future may well be that what is professional or not, and what is design or not, will become ever harder to define. The easy-to-spot blacks or whites of the past seem to get ever grayer. And those who are the masters of the future of WB&A must be ever alert to foresee the changes, adapt the concepts of total design to its realities.

Bank: Security Pacific National Bank, Tishman Airport Center, Los Angeles, California. View of exterior and of interior banking floor.

Hotel: Hawaiian Village, Honolulu, Hawaii. Views of exterior and interior.

8

2
WELTON BECKET AND THE OFFICE

In one way, the story of the architectural firm of Welton Becket and Associates is the story of Welton Becket himself. In another way, it is the story of the people he attracted to the firm, a great number of whom have stayed on for years.

In any case, without Becket, it goes without saying almost that there probably never would have been a firm like this one. At least no other architect has ever been able to build one like it.

So it is essential to an understanding of Welton Becket and Associates, the practice, to have some insight into Welton Becket, the man, and into the growth he inspired and worked for.

The essential data of his beginning are these. He was born in Seattle, Washington, on August 8, 1902. The son of a builder, he had early dreams of becoming an architect. He graduated in architecture from the University of Washington in 1927 and spent another year studying at the Ecole des Beaux Arts in Fontainebleau. He was known as a talented student but managed not to let his studies prevent him from playing baseball and football while at the University of Washington.

As is often true in this profession, Becket's architectural beginnings were inauspicious, as a designer-draftsman for a small office in Los Angeles in 1929, going back to Seattle for a few years where he did modest buildings, some of them for his older brother, Evro, a builder. Maybe the real beginning of what would eventually become one of the world's largest and most successful architectural firms came when Welton Becket teamed up with his University of Washington classmate Walter Wurdeman in 1933 to form a partnership to practice in Los Angeles.

Two photographs, taken early in their partnership, of Welton Becket and Walter Wurdeman.

1937: *Goetz Residence,
Bel Air, California.*

1938: *Montgomery Residence,
Bel Air, California.*

1940: *Morgan Residence,
Bel Air, California.*

Becket was a man who was fond of a good story and told them with gusto. One of his favorites about his early practice in Seattle concerned a commission to do a house—for a somewhat overprivileged Great Dane. According to Becket, "The doghouse was done in sort of an early Swedish modern with an exposed beam ceiling. It had lights, steam heat, and a swinging door. The owner was so pleased with it, he hired me to do a house for him—in the same style. I guess you could say, in a way, that this was the first of our many repeat clients."

For six years, the two young architects were in a Los Angeles partnership with Charles Plummer, an older man. For the most part, the buildings they did were unspectacular, reflecting their inexperience and the tight money of the depression. Welton Becket often recalled how hard they struggled and how hard they worked, some seventy to eighty hours a week for very little money and even less recognition. Their plight is illustrated by one job, remodeling a cafeteria, for which they took their fees in meals.

In the middle thirties, the hard work began to pay off. In 1934 came their first big break. After working night and day for months on a design, the partners won the big international competition for the Pan Pacific Auditorium in Los Angeles. The fee was small, only $5,000, but the prize brought a wave of publicity that was sorely needed.

Then Walter Wurdeman began to develop good contacts among the top movie stars by using his share of the prize money to join a tennis club frequented by the movie crowd. For several years, the firm almost made a specialty of houses for Hollywood luminaries. This was an era of residential architecture derived from past styles, and the partnership did English cottages, half-timbered mansions, classic homes, and what have you. Among their clients of the time were Robert Montgomery, Cesar Romero, James Cagney, Virginia Bruce, and Jeanne Crain.

During this time Wurdeman and Becket saw the first glimmerings of the philosophy of architecture which they were to develop and eventually call Total Design. As Becket told it, "We made every effort to design these traditional houses with honesty and authenticity. It soon became apparent that the building itself was not enough and we would have to get involved in the interiors. Once we did a house that was mission style, and the owners called in a decorator afterward to furnish it in the worst sort of futuristic 1925 French modern. That did it. From then on, we always tried to get clients to let us do the whole design."

For the most part, in the early years of Plummer, Wurdeman and Becket, the firm operated with the partners doing all, or almost all of their own work. For example, Wurdeman and Becket did all of the design and drafting on the Pan Pacific competition. Working against time and a fast-approaching deadline, they hired a delineator to make the renderings, but at the last minute he imbibed a bit too much and the two partners had to do their own renderings over a weekend to meet the Monday deadline. They both pitched in and the deadline was met.

The Pan Pacific Auditorium job brought with it considerable publicity, and new commissions began to come into the office. And the partners found themselves able to hire draftsmen and other assistants to do part of the work. In 1936, the auditorium won an Honor Award from the Southern California chapter of AIA, generating further publicity for the firm. This was the first of a long list of major awards to be won by the firm over the coming years. Early in 1939, Plummer died, and the partnership was continued under the name of Wurdeman and Becket.

A short time later, an opportunity came along for Welton Becket to go to Manila to consult with the Philippine government on housing for low-income families. Leaving for a three-month stay, Becket landed a commission for a big new Jai Alai Auditorium and stayed two years.

Back in the States, World War II had almost halted private construction, but Wurdeman and Becket soon found their residential experience in demand by the government, which desperately needed housing for military families and war workers. During the next few years, while most other construction was at a standstill, the firm did 14,000 housing units, mostly in southern California. This was not the most satisfying kind of work for a couple of young architects, but it did keep them going and the volume of the work permitted their office to grow. Within a year or two, they had more than forty employees and had already entered the world of big architecture. As Wurdeman put it at the time, "This was spit and matchstick stuff, but it made us build a large organization and helped us not to be appalled at big jobs."

As the war went on, Wurdeman and Becket began to pick up a few nonresidential commissions, most of which had to wait until war's end for construction to start: an addition to the Pan Pacific Auditorium, a country club, a mausoleum, a restaurant, a few stores, a club in Las Vegas.

And they were chosen by builder Fritz Burns to do a very significant project: a prototype for a postwar house, called The House of Tomorrow, which was constructed as an exhibit to whet the appetites of war-weary Los Angelenos for the comforts of the future. Again in this project the firm had obtained a commission with considerable publicity value. It brought the partnership to the attention of the great numbers of people who poured through the house and even greater numbers who were exposed to numerous articles on the house and to publicity issued by the sponsors.

Near the end of World War II, the firm of Wurdeman and Becket was in a good position to capitalize on the coming construction boom, experienced and capable people aboard, a going organization. Becket felt, looking back on the early years, that the success achieved so far had been due to a combination of very hard, dedicated work, with a liberal sprinkling of breaks, or good luck. From here on the partners would continue the hard work, but they would begin to make their own breaks. And even more important, the work they were accomplishing would begin to bring in additional commis-

1941: Pan Pacific Auditorium, Los Angeles, California.

1941: Jai Alai Auditorium, Manila, Philippine Islands.

1943: House of Tomorrow, Los Angeles, California.

1944: Bullock's Department Store, Pasadena, California.

1946: General Petroleum Co., Los Angeles, California.

1947: Prudential Insurance Co., Los Angeles, California.

sions from their former clients, and they would obtain increasing numbers of new clients.

The first big indication of the growth to come took the form of a commission to do an important new department store for Bullock's. The president of this chain, P. G. Winnett, had visited a number of the W&B houses for movie stars, and he wanted a store in Pasadena that would reflect an entirely new concept—a department store designed as if it were a fine residence. And the assignment had another plus: the partnership was retained to do the complete store inside and out.

Bullock's Pasadena opened a whole new area of service for the partners. Since the firm had almost no experience in design for merchandising, a year was spent in research. As Becket put it, "We spent so much time nosing around in other Bullock's stores, people thought we worked there." The research paid off, not only in this very successful store but in establishing a postwar trend in suburban department store design. And it paid off in other ways: since that early building, the firm has done hundreds of department stores for almost all the great chains; in fact, it has done over twenty-five major jobs for Federated Department Stores (which now owns Bullock's).

The Pasadena store had another important aspect—it was a milestone in the developing philosophy of W&B, demonstrating the growing conviction of the partners that architecture is for the client, not for the architect. This was a most important step and one that would be developed to a high point over the ensuing years.

The Bullock's Pasadena job had another very important side effect: it led to the firm's first major office building. And this demonstrates a major principle of the future growth of the firm—new commissions generated by the old. In this case, one of the directors of Bullock's was also a high official in Mobil Oil Corporation, now General Petroleum Corporation. Impressed with the partnership's work on the department store, he was instrumental in its selection for the office building. Although Becket always insisted that this was another big break, by now the breaks were starting to come not from luck but by design.

Becket explained his "break" this way: "The president of Mobil Oil was impressed with our firm, but the thing that finally tipped him into our camp was a story I told him. About 3:00 A.M. one morning, I was driving back to Seattle after a long session on an out-of-town job and ran out of gas. A gigantic Mobil Oil tank truck stopped, but it was empty. The driver told me to hop in and drove me back fifteen miles to the nearest town for a can of gasoline and then back to my car. I was so impressed that ever since I've never carried any other oil company credit card but yours."

And Welton Becket would add than that this broke the ice and the president awarded W&B the commission.

In any case, the partnership now had its first office building, a type in which it would distinguish itself in years to come. At $8 million, it was by far their largest building to date. And they proceeded to design a very flexible building, modular in every detail of plan, with movable partitions. Through careful design, and by persuasion of the Los Angeles City Council, they pioneered the use of lightweight concrete for fireproofing, saving 1,200 tons of steel and $800,000 in construction costs. At the time, most of the other work of the firm consisted of stores, among them two more for Bullock's, two for Buffum's and four for Firestone.

One important exception to the stores was the commission to do another big office building, this time the Western home office of Prudential Insurance Company of America. Another trademark of the firm was in the making, its transformation of Wilshire Boulevard, main artery of Los Angeles, from its pre-war state of smaller, relatively low-rise buildings to the high-rise, cosmopolitan character of the street today. Prudential was important in other ways. Lightweight concrete was again used, with resulting savings in cost and weight. And this was one of the first buildings in the U.S. with horizontal sunshields at each floor to improve the comfort of the occupants and reduce air-conditioning loads.

By the time 1948 rolled around, the partnership was solidly established. It had $121 million in work on the boards, embracing just about every major building type. The partners' income had risen to a level almost never reached by architects in practice, they had eighty employees, and work had begun on a new Wilshire Boulevard office building for the firm itself. Since it was five stories high, some thought they would never fill it with people, but within a year after its completion, in 1949, balconies had to be added in the drafting rooms to take care of the incoming draftsmen.

About this time, another important milestone was reached, the completion of the firm's first shopping center, Stonestown, including the large Emporium Department Store, in San Francisco. In this project, the firm pioneered the concept of the large regional shopping center with stores clustered around a central mall. In years to come, the firm would do many more like this, and the concept would be adopted all over the world.

Important commissions followed quickly, among them a store for Hall Brothers in Kansas City, which led to a series of jobs for Hallmark, an administration building for Hilton, which led to the firm's first hotel, the Beverly Hilton, and to a number of additional hotels for Hilton, Hilton International, and other chains, and to the naming of the firm as master planners for the University of California at Los Angeles, which was to become a major interest of the firm for more than twenty years. During this period, the office building for Standard Federal (now California Federal) was designed with one of the earliest glass curtain walls.

The partnership was now beginning to be recognized all over the country. It began to be noticed by national magazines, and *Time* and others ran features on its work. And awards started to roll in, a pattern that has persisted right up to the present.

And then Walter Wurdeman died an untimely and unexpected death, at the age of forty-six, when everything seemed to be going just right.

1949: Stonestown Shopping Center, San Francisco, California.

1950: California Federal Savings and Loan, Los Angeles, California.

1952: The Beverly Hilton, Beverly Hills, California.

1957: *Ford Division Offices,*
        Dearborn, Michigan.

1959: *Nile Hilton Hotel,*
        Cairo, Egypt.

1959: *Memorial Sports Arena,*
        Los Angeles, California.

Saddened deeply, Welton Becket was determined to keep the firm on track. Though he was friend enough, and sentimentalist enough, to keep Walt Wurdeman's old chair beside the double desk they had shared so many years, Becket did not let his feelings deter him from his goals of making a great firm out of one that was still in its formative years.

Moving as quickly as he could under the circumstances, Becket bought out Wurdeman's heirs and became the sole owner of the firm. From that day, he was to have no partners, to share ownership with no one.

Thus, in 1949, the firm became Welton Becket and Associates, an organization that was actually to become, in 1955, two entities: (1) a California corporation solely owned by Welton Becket, occupying its own building, and offering complete services in all states in which architectural corporations are allowed by law to practice; and (2) Welton Becket, Architect, a sole proprietorship which practiced in states where corporate practice is not allowed, which had no buildings and no employees. The proprietorship would obtain jobs in noncorporation states and assign them to the corporation to perform, with the full knowledge of clients that it intended to do so.

A bright era, one filled with hard work and some considerable accomplishment, had ended with the death of Walt Wurdeman. Another had begun.

Well established now, and with its reputation growing, Welton Becket and Associates continued to expand. And the commissions began to come in regularly, not only for office buildings, stores, and shopping centers, which had been the mainstay until now, but for hospitals, hotels, institutional buildings, and many other types.

Having had an early success with work overseas in the Philippines, the firm now began to receive other foreign work: a bank in Brazil and hotels for Hilton in Havana and Cairo.

Following the death of Walt Wurdeman, Welton Becket was appointed supervising architect for the UCLA campus, a position to which he was to devote much of his personal time during the remainder of his life. In addition, the firm continued as master planner for the campus.

The work on the UCLA master plan proceeded, and the firm started the UCLA Center for the Health Sciences with two years of work on the first building, the basic unit of the hospital and medical school. As the years passed, the firm was to work on this project almost continuously, adding new wings to the original structure and new buildings in the complex in conformance with the master plan. During the years from 1949, when the firm was named master planners for UCLA, it was to do almost forty jobs on the campus, including the Neuropsychiatric Institute, School of Dentistry, School of Public Health, the Marion Davies Children's Clinic, the Jules Stein Eye Institute, the Mental Retardation Unit, Rehabilitation Center, and the Reed Neurological Research Center—all connected with the Health Center. In addition, WB&A did many other buildings on the campus, including the Music Building, Student Union, the Pauley Pavilion, and a number of dormitories and parking structures.

Awards for the work of the firm began to come with some regularity in the fifties. One, of which Becket was quite proud, was the award, in 1950, made to the Prudential Building by the Seventh Pan American Congress of Architects. Another made to Becket himself, and of which he was also very proud, was that of Fellowship in The American Institute of Architects, for design, in 1952. Many other honors were to come to the firm and to the man in the ensuing years, but none were to please him more than these two awarded him by his peers.

The fifties were a productive time in the life of Welton Becket and Associates. Completed during that time (to name only a few of the more important) were the Beverly Hilton Hotel, Capitol Records Tower, Police Facilities Building, the Texaco Office Building, and the Memorial Sports Arena, all in the Los Angeles area. Other significant projects completed were the Ford Division Office Building in Dearborn, Southland Center in Dallas, Hallmark Cards Building in Kansas City, and the Eisenhower Foundation Museum in Abilene. Foreign work included the Havana Hilton, the Nile Hilton in Cairo, and Hawaiian Village in Honolulu.

Each of these buildings was a milestone of sorts for WB&A: its first major hotels were to lead to many others; major civic buildings were the first of many; a manufacturing plant, Hallmark, featured vertical-flow production lines down through the various stories of the building. In addition, there was Henry Kaiser's Hawaiian Village, which led not only to a friendship between the industrialist and the architect, but also to the firm's most ambitious building to date, Kaiser Center in Oakland, California.

In most of these buildings, the principles of total design were applied, WB&A handling the complete design, including the usual architectural and engineering work and in addition the design of interiors and selection of furniture and furnishings. In some cases, such as the Nile Hilton, this extended to the design of many original pieces of furniture and other items, which were then manufactured in Egypt to the firm's specifications. For this job, the firm maintained a project office in Cairo for five years.

If the fifties were great years of growth for Welton Becket and Associates, the sixties were even better. In 1960, Kaiser Center was completed, the largest job the firm had done up until that time. Completely designed by WB&A, inside and out, it was the foremost example of its time of the principles of total design. It also produced one of those stories of which Welton Becket was so fond and which most often placed Becket himself in a supporting role while some other person, usually a client, got the lead.

According to Becket, "We had a long conference on the early schematics for Kaiser Center, in which Henry J. Kaiser kept demanding that we raise our sights as to the size of the building. Finally, after many hours of discussion, we hammered out an agreement on total floor area which seemed more than adequate to me. I happened to glance at Henry J., who appeared to be taking a little nap at the conference table, just as Edgar Kaiser nudged him awake. His first words were, 'Double it.' And we did double the floor area."

1960: Southland Center, Dallas, Texas.

Welton Becket in Los Angeles office late in 1968.

15

During the years, another aspect of the success of Becket and the firm became very apparent: his ability to select and attract talented people and his almost uncanny ability to inspire such loyalty that they stayed with him.

Becket himself attributed this mainly to two things: the working conditions and remuneration were considerably above average for architectural firms, and WB&A policy was to bring in bright young people and give them big, important assignments right from the start. The people he found and brought in agree with this for the most part, although most would say it a little differently. Admittedly the working conditions were fine. But without the very generous profit-sharing and retirement plan and annual bonuses, salaries are actually competitive with those offered elsewhere. These fringe benefits (fringe in name only since they were often equal to or more than a man's basic salary) made work at WB&A considerably more attractive financially.

As to the assignments given to young designers and others in the firm there is universal agreement. Where else could a young graduate, just out of school, act as the designer or project architect for a multi-million-dollar hotel or office building?

On the other hand, say some WB&A employees who have been with the firm for years, one major reason for loyalty was Welton Becket himself. People stayed on for years for many reasons, not the least of which was the kind of man and architect Becket was. They stayed on in spite of the fact that company policy forbade public credit for any individual in the firm, reserving credit only for the firm itself. And they stayed on knowing that Becket intended to share the ownership with no one else as long as he lived.

Over the years, as the firm expanded and projects began to grow in size and number, the average volume of construction put in place steadied to some $100 million or so a year. In time, the firm reached a maximum of some 500 employees in the early sixties. Since that time, the average annual volume of work has grown, but the number of employees has remained about the same. Doing an increased amount of work with the same number of people has been possible through better organization, bigger jobs, and more efficient services.

As time passed, it became apparent that taking work wherever it might be, in this country and often abroad, placed considerable strain on the home office in Los Angeles. Clients could be better served in the Eastern states and other places from offices in closer proximity to the work. Accordingly, an office was established in San Francisco in 1949, to be followed by another in New York a year later and one in Houston in 1960. Now there is a fifth office in Chicago, acquired early in 1970. These are architectural offices offering complete architectural services, performing total design, not just branches of a home office. Each works to obtain commissions on its own, and each produces its own work. All offices cooperate with each other fully, and all of the other offices have close ties with Los Angeles for any specialized help they might need from the Los Angeles office, which now operates as a complete office itself, in addition to its role as corporate headquarters for Welton Becket and Associates.

During the sixties, a great number of large and significant buildings have been accomplished. Office buildings have long been a mainstay of the firm, many of them exploring new directions in structure, planning, or other aspects of architecture. Some of the most important are Humble Oil in Houston; North Carolina Mutual in Durham; Phillips Petroleum in Bartlesville, Oklahoma; Hartford National Bank in Hartford, Connecticut; Xerox Square in Rochester, New York; and Gulf Life Towers in Jacksonville, Florida.

Also completed in the 1960s were a large number of department stores and shopping centers, several world's fair buildings, numerous hotels and hospitals, colleges, civic buildings, and many others. No attempt in this firm to specialize by building type! Some of the milestone buildings were Los Angeles International Airport (in a joint venture), Los Angeles Music Center, Manila Hilton, and the Los Angeles Century City master plan and several buildings on that site. One of the most important buildings was the new five-story office building for WB&A itself, the first structure erected in Century City in 1960. Here four levels (the fifth is rented to Pauley Petroleum, Inc., the company of Ed Pauley, an old friend of Becket's) are occupied by the diverse and complete staff of the Los Angeles office of Welton Becket and Associates.

As the end of the sixties approached, WB&A was beginning another new era that promised much excitement and accomplishment. The firm had its boards loaded with work, much of which was large, complex, and out of the ordinary: the master plan and five resort hotels for the new Walt Disney World, in Orlando, Florida; rebuilding downtown Worcester, Massachusetts; a major building at the U.S. Military Academy at West Point; a new college in Redwood City, California; the Kennedy Cultural Center on Long Island, New York.

A longtime dream of Welton Becket's was under construction, a new wing on the WB&A office building in Los Angeles, to be devoted to architectural research.

The San Francisco office was scheduled to move soon into bright new space in the Aetna Life Building, which the firm had designed. The New York office would also soon move into new and expanded space.

A bright and exciting future for WB&A, the firm, and seemingly for WB, the man. Then, in early 1969, Welton Becket had a heart attack and on January 16 of that year, at age 66, he died. He had been stricken with a heart attack before, but afterward he took good care of himself. In late 1968, he seemed relaxed and healthy, looking forward to great things to come, working hard and playing hard still, but pacing himself. It is sometimes said that a man passed away "at the height of his career." This would not apply to Welton Becket. He was at a height, but he had staked out other, greater heights to scale for himself, for Welton Becket and Associates, and for all of those people who had helped him build the firm.

He had agonized over the succession in the firm for years. In the end he willed it to those who had helped him build it and who could be expected to carry on to the greater heights.

3
PRINCIPLES OF
TOTAL DESIGN TODAY

Shortly before Welton Becket died, he named his nephew MacDonald Becket president of the firm. MacDonald had come up the steps in Welton Becket and Associates. Starting in 1948, while still an architectural student, he had spent the years from then in training for the job he now held, in the drafting room, in economic analysis and land planning, in business development, in design, and in the field. For several years, he had served the firm as Senior Vice President and Chief Executive Officer.

To MacDonald Becket, after twenty-one years of service to his uncle and to the firm, also came a bequest of stock in WB&A. Stock was also left to Bruce, Welton Becket's older son, an architect in the firm, and to his other son, Welton M., who has since graduated from college and joined the firm in business development. Stock was bequeathed to twelve other employees. Thus these fifteen people control

WB&A in the name of the estate and will eventually own the firm.

It seems characteristic of Becket, somehow, that in his will he accomplished what he could never bring himself to do in life: reward long and loyal service by participation in the ownership of the firm.

Asked early in February 1969 about the future of Welton Becket and Associates, the new president, MacDonald Becket, replied in a manner that went directly to the point: "The organization will be kept together, everything that can be done to ensure growth in both quantity and quality will be done, and we will adhere to the philosophy of total design."

What of the other inheritors of WB&A? Who are they and how do they fit in? It has been pointed out that other than Bruce Becket, who is now undergoing the broad and rigorous training his cousin MacDonald experienced, and Welton M. Becket, who

1960: Bethlehem Steel Company,
San Francisco, California.

1962: Humble Oil & Refining
Co., Houston, Texas.

must come to his own decisions as to his future, the others are men of considerable experience, all long-term employees of the firm, and all are now in positions of importance and authority.

In terms of service, Furman Myers is the elder statesman, thirty-six years with Becket and now Senior Vice President and Corporate Director of Administration. Maynard Woodard, Senior Vice President and Corporate Director of Design, until his recent retirement, came to the firm in 1945, one of a number of people Becket hired away from the movie industry during the studio strike of that era. Then there is Paul Sessinghaus, Senior Vice President and Director of Mechanical and Electrical Engineering, Los Angeles, who came to WB&A at about the same time. Jack Beardwood, Senior Vice President and long-time Director of Business Development, now Executive Vice President, joined WB&A in 1953, and also with the firm for a relatively long period of time, Alan Rosen, Vice President and Director of Architectural Production, Los Angeles. Other inheritors of stock in WB&A are Charles B. McReynolds, Dominick Primiani, and Gilbert Thweatt, all Senior Vice Presidents, and Directors of the Los Angeles, San Francisco, and Houston offices, respectively. Others include Donnell Grimes, Senior Vice President and Director of Business Development, Los Angeles; Robert Tyler, Vice President and Director of Design, Los Angeles; and Louis Naidorf, Vice President and Director of Research. Albert Grossman, attorney for the firm, rounds out the list of holders of the original stock.

In the hands of these experienced and capable people, and in those of other key employees, lies the future of Welton Becket and Associates. They must produce now on their own without the guidance of the founder. How will they go about it? Much remains to be seen as time goes on, but the principles of architectural practice already established are strong and workable. And the firm itself has lots of good commissions on the boards and is in a strong position in every way. At this juncture, perhaps it would be helpful if the principles and policies that guide the practice were examined in some detail.

In the first place, it should be stressed that WB&A is engaged in the general practice of architecture, not in handling only specialized building types. This is demonstrated by the fact that the firm currently has on the boards master planning, offices, shopping centers, stores, hospitals, a stadium, college buildings, a courthouse, civic centers, a downtown renewal project, hotels, a convention center, high schools, apartments, airport buildings, theaters, and other types. It should be noted that there are no single-family residences (although the firm sometimes has to do one for a valued client) and at present, there is only a limited amount of industrial work. Other than these, WB&A does all types.

Of course, these statements about general practice do not completely and accurately reflect the facts. WB&A does practice general architecture, but it has a host of people on its staff who have had long and valuable experience in the types named. There have been times when the firm has been tempted by the idea of specialization, going so far at one point as to set up specific departments within its organization to handle specialized types. This did not work well, and the system has been discarded in favor of a more generalized organizational structure.

In lieu of departments specialized by building types, there are departments specialized by function, including the obvious ones: engineering, design, production, and so on. In addition, there are some departments not so obvious required by the dedication to total design: interior design, furnishing and decorating, store planning, graphics.

This brings up the subject of the services offered clients. The overriding principle of this, which the firm calls total design, is that the services WB&A perform for clients include everything that could possibly be required in the design of a master plan, in a building or group of buildings, in its interiors, furniture, furnishings, or graphics. The people here like projects that embrace all of these aspects, but of course they are not always able to persuade every client to accept them all.

Officially, the firm offers its clients services in architecture, engineering, programming, space studies, research, survey and analysis, site selection, master planning, zoning assistance, industrial design, furnishing and decorating, graphics, plan checking, cost control and analysis, and store planning and fixturing. In other words, the services embrace almost anything that could be remotely called professional architecture in the largest sense of that phrase.

The firm will not become involved in any aspects of construction except, of course, the regular architectural services during construction of its projects. And it shuns anything to do with the real estate or finance business. The firm is an investor in real estate to the extent that it owns its own buildings in Los Angeles and Houston, and Welton Becket himself was a real estate investor as a private citizen, unconnected with the practice. However, the conviction has persisted here from the earliest days that no investments should be made in anything that might appear in even the slightest degree as a conflict of interest between the firm or its owner and its clients.

On a very early building, the firm had to take its fee in stock or not get paid at all, but the stock was disposed of as soon as possible. On another occasion, a stockbroker bought some shares of a building-product manufacturing company for Becket without clearing it with him, but Becket sold them immediately upon finding out what had happened. And there is a hard-and-fast rule that no real estate investments are to be made in land or improvements at or near the site of any building on which the firm performs services.

Although WB&A ordinarily shuns the labels pinned on it by overzealous editors or writers, one of these may have some merit in any discussion of the principles and policies under which the firm operates: "Corporate Architects." If that label is intended to indicate that the firm likes to work with corporate clients or other groups such as institutions, it seems appropriate. WB&A does like such clients and has served a good number of them.

The people at WB&A understand such clients—it

1963: Phillips Petroleum Co., Bartlesville, Oklahoma.

1963: North Carolina Mutual Life Insurance Co., Durham, North Carolina.

1963: Cullen Center,
Houston, Texas.

1963: Los Angeles International
Airport, Los Angeles,
California.

1964: General Electric Co.
Pavilion, 1964–65 World's Fair,
New York, New York.

should be remembered that the firm itself has practiced as a corporation for many years. The top administrators at WB&A themselves think like their corporate clients in many respects. The structure of the practice is more similar to that of companies in other fields than it is to most architectural firms. Acting with a board of directors, a president, vice presidents, executive committee, and department heads in its corporate structure, and with five complete offices at the operative level, WB&A finds itself very much at home working with similar client groups. And the clients find themselves equally at home working with the people at Becket.

Welton Becket found very early that he could move easily among the top executives of great corporations. He became the close friend of many, and they introduced him to many others. He had the unusual quality of being able to relax with these people and to talk their language but at the same time to remain an architect and talk architecture in a manner they could understand. This led the firm into great numbers of projects for corporations and into recommendations by the executives who were satisfied clients, and often friends, to other executives with architectural problems to solve and commissions to hand out.

As time went on, Becket attracted into the firm other people who had innate abilities or aptitudes for contact with clients or potential clients on the highest level. First Jack Beardwood was brought in to head the firm's business development work, and then MacDonald Becket was thrown more and more into this work as he went through the steps of his thorough apprenticeship that led to the presidency of the firm. Very early, Welton Becket recognized the growing importance of public relations functions and was one of the first architects to equip himself with a complete department, staffed by highly competent people.

Another unusual circumstance has made great contributions to the almost uncanny ability of the firm to work smoothly with corporate clients, and even before that to acquire their work in quantity. This is the considerable amount of opportunity employees, particularly designers and project architects, have for close contact with clients. It is rare indeed to find an architectural firm in which designers and project architects are so well equipped on all levels for client contact and even for presentations designed to produce new business.

It should be mentioned here, although the subject will be examined thoroughly later, that one of the attractions WB&A has for clients lies in its ability to control the costs of construction. Over the years, the firm's record in this area has been very good indeed. And in the past few years, Becket jobs have come in an average of some 3 percent under their budgets.

Of the importance of this aspect of the practice, Welton Becket said, "Having started in architecture during the depression, the concern for costs and for accuracy of estimates was burned into my consciousness."

From the first, the firm has been deeply interested in good design. Certainly, the people here might define that word somewhat differently from the way architectural critics define it. Here, the term means close attention to all the aspects of architecture to bring about a solution that hangs together well functionally, structurally, systematically, economically, and aesthetically. For the most part, the word *design* would not be used simply to describe appearance or aesthetics. Some architects have described the work of WB&A as "good to competent." In the broadest sense, such criticism might often be justified, at least to an extent. But on the other hand, this pat way of putting down that with which one does not agree or that which one might have wished for himself but could not obtain, does not really prove much.

The fact of it is that a cool, impersonal look at the work of this firm will reveal a number of things. One is that the level of design has been continuously improving from the earliest days. There are times when a building ranks with the best being done anywhere. And there are times when a building leaves something to be desired, for some reason or combination of reasons. Such a look will reveal that this firm never erects monuments to itself. The buildings are for the clients. Viewed overall, the level of competence is very high indeed. Very few architects can match it—almost none who are anywhere near this size.

And if the definition of design as used in this firm and in some others, be accepted—that of integrating structure, function, aesthetics, economics, and all other aspects of architecture into a successful whole—the level of competence here is approached by almost no others.

Of course, it must be admitted that this is not what brings prizes to architects from their peers. WB&A has won its share of all kinds of awards (well over a hundred); it has won national AIA Merit Awards but not an Honor Award. But WB&A wins prizes enough of another kind, the kind that brings in an increasing amount of work each year and the kind that has caused great numbers of clients to come back every time they have a new building to do. And it produces the clients who recommend this firm to others. Pragmatically, what greater award can there be?

The philosophy in WB&A, first expounded by Welton Becket and now part of the folklore of his successors, included the deep and abiding conviction that architecture is indeed a profession and that an architect or an architectural firm owes its complete loyalty to the client, to the exclusion of all others. In a time when many view the architectural scene as chaotic, if not revolutionary, this conviction may seem to some very naïve, even reactionary.

But Welton Becket and those who succeeded him were, and are, convinced that they are right and that clients need and will seek the strictly professional services the firm provides. So far, they have been very right.

Again, pragmatically, as someone has said, what greater test can there be of a business than that it stay in business? And grow? And it might be added today, how better to resist the takeover plans many think the aerospace industry has for architecture, or the conglomerates who already have taken over

1967: Music Center for the Performing Arts, Los Angeles, California.

1967: Gulf Life Tower, Jacksonville, Florida.

23

1969: Xerox Square, Rochester, New York.

1969: Manila Hilton Hotel, Manila, Philippines.

some firms, or the construction firms that have taken over others?

The convictions of those in the firm about what things are proper and right for architects and what are not has led to another aspect of the WB&A practice that must be mentioned here.

This is the dedication of the firm to its clients. Welton Becket used to say, quite often, words to the effect that the role of an architect as he saw it was to understand the client and his problems and find the solution to the problems; and out of this a design would evolve. Once when a reporter asked why his architectural approach was so different from that of Frank Lloyd Wright, Becket quickly replied, "An architect who takes the position that he is a great creator and clients should seek his services is headed for failure." In a quieter moment, he expressed his feelings more accurately, "A building should reflect the client, not the architect. I see no reason why I should express Welton Becket."

Just as Becket himself always seemed to bring a discussion around to the importance of the client, so does much of the conversation of the architects and other professionals in the firm today. Something like, "Our primary job is to serve the client." And it soon becomes very apparent to anyone who spends any time around WB&A people that this is a matter not of slogans but of deep conviction. The people in the firm feel and believe in it, and clients, upon experiencing it, are overjoyed.

This is not to say that there is smug, self-satisfaction among staff members in placing so much emphasis on client service. For a long time, there has been some soul-searching going on about what really constitutes the best possible service. This hinges on the question of whether serving a client should involve more of giving him what he needs and maybe less of giving him what he wants. One of the tenets of the firm, from its inception, was the education in architecture of clients who were well schooled otherwise. Some staff members believe that the firm has drifted somewhat away from this principle and should make positive steps back toward it. Some would go as far as to say that those in the firm who have the closest relationships with clients should struggle with them more, argue with them more, when the cause at hand is concerned with the possibility of a better building for the clients than they are able to understand or accept at the moment. There is considerable evidence that those who think like this are increasingly having their way on an increasing number of occasions.

One strong piece of evidence is indicated by an examination of the work of the firm. Over the past years, there appears in much of the work an increasing amount of experimentation, a new inventiveness of form, structure, and function. And it would appear that the result has been better buildings—and more exciting architecture.

One most important result of the architectural services rendered clients has been the phenomenal history of repeat clients achieved by this firm. While many other architects are forced into beating the bushes pretty thoroughly and continuously to keep work in their offices, WB&A could have a very productive practice which only served its long-term clients. Of course, the firm would not be satisfied with such a practice; however, an examination of some clients tells much about the firm's success.

There may be no way to judge the total effect of repeat clients on the practice of WB&A, owing to mergers and other factors that cloud the issue. But it is safe to say that some seventy-five clients have come back to WB&A for one or more projects after the first. Some of these clients have each given the firm over twenty major projects to do over the years. And some are still giving the firm work twenty-five years after it did the first job for them.

Bullock's, now part of Federated Department Stores, for example: twenty-five major projects stretching from the early forties to the present. Hilton Hotels and Hilton International: six hotels, ten additions or smaller jobs, and feasibility studies for another fifteen hotels. May Department Stores: thirty major jobs. Emporium: twenty-two projects. Del E. Webb Corporation: fifteen major jobs.

And so it goes through a long list of blue-ribbon U.S. corporations and many governmental and institutional clients. And it goes almost without saying how much a record of this kind means to an architectural firm, in prestige, in continuing relationships with clients, in continuity of the firm itself. It might be added, although it should be perfectly obvious, that such a record of repeat clients is a highly salable characteristic to new clients.

Another characteristic of Welton Becket and Associates, and one that has been instrumental in producing repeat clients, is the penchant of the firm for big and complex work. WB&A is geared to work of great magnitude; the staff members are good at it; and they enjoy it.

The big complex work started coming in early, the first major example being the master planning of UCLA, on which work began in the late forties. The master planning led to more than forty major projects on the campus, including the University's Center for the Health Sciences. Starting in 1950, the firm has had Health Center work on its boards almost continuously ever since. Virtually completed now, the Center houses every imaginable kind of medical and dental treatment and research facility, and encompasses some 2 million square feet, at a total cost of approximately $100 million.

The trend toward big, complex work that began with the UCLA Health Center has continued ever since. Other important examples include the master plan, site improvements, and design coordination of Century City, and a number of buildings there. Another was the Los Angeles Music Center master plan and three theaters.

Through the years, there have been a number of other examples of master planning and the handling of large work. And the WB&A offices are usually filled with work of this sort these days. For example, in 1970, projects of this type included redevelopment of downtown Worcester, Massachusetts; Walt Disney World; the John F. Kennedy Educational, Civic and Cultural Center; a large development on Staten Island; the Kennedy Expressway Center in Chicago; Park Plaza in Oshkosh, Wisconsin; Cullen Center in

1970: Olive View Hospital's Medical Treatment and Care Facility, Los Angeles County, California.

1970: Aetna Life & Casualty Insurance Co., San Francisco, California.

25

Houston; the continuing work at UCLA; and about twenty-five other master planning, multibuilding projects, ranging in cost from some $6 million to over $500 million apiece.

It is, of course, axiomatic that an architectural firm that does work of this magnitude for corporate and other group clients must be organized very differently from a firm that works mostly for individuals on smaller projects. Thus it will come as no surprise that WB&A is highly organized, the major departments of each office being those most common in architectural firms: Design, Production, Administration and Business Development, with a number of subdepartments operative in each. It might come as somewhat of a surprise to find production divided into four main parts: Architectural, M&E, Structural, to be sure, but also *Production Administration*. And it might be surprising to some to find services during construction under Production or to find a function of store planning in design, or furnishing and decorating in addition to interior design.

And it certainly is out of the ordinary to find a complete corporate headquarters structure under which the five offices operate.

This is not the place to discuss these organizational factors in detail, as that will come in later chapters. They are mentioned here simply to make the point that, as a large diversified architectural firm, WB&A has quite a complex organizational structure. On a chart, as will be seen, it seems simple. In practice, it is anything but. The intricacies of the relationships between departments and between people, between function and among all of these factors can be demonstrated only by careful dissection, and this will be accomplished in later chapters.

One point which should be touched upon here is that while there may be no surprises in the complexity of the organization, and few in its details, it is very surprising to learn how little red tape exists, how often people cut across organizational patterns, how few the reports and memos required to keep this practice ticking. In other words, the organizational chart seems simple but is not. The organizational patterns seem complex but are not. Somehow, in spite of all, the forms and format that seem necessary to big architecture have been simplified here. And in turn, the formalities so often seen elsewhere are here reduced to extreme informality.

Here no one wears a jacket in the office, except by tradition when lunching in the Executive Dining Room. And the informality of attire is reflected in the relationships between staff members.

The organizational patterns of the firm are reflected in each of the offices, with some notable exceptions. For example, only the Los Angeles and Chicago offices have engineering, the other offices mostly using outside engineers for this work. In other respects, the offices are organized along similar lines, yet each has some attributes and attitudes all its own.

Maybe this stems from the personalities of the office directors, or the essential differences between a town like New York and one like Los Angeles. Both factors probably contribute to the differences. The Houston office seems quieter somehow, more low-keyed than the others; the San Francisco office is livelier, more colorful perhaps; the New York office is big (more than a hundred employees), more metropolitan; the Chicago office seems more conservative; the Los Angeles office seems more organized, more controlled, more self-sufficient.

Some think the varied qualities of the offices are reflected in the architecture each produces. And a case might be made for this in the buildings done by the offices. Yet strong ties exist between them, and in the things that count most, all subscribe to the overall philosophy of the firm.

The offices themselves demonstrate another aspect of that philosophy: from the first, this was destined to be a firm doing work all over the U.S. and in many foreign countries. Only in this way could it have a crack at the best work, wherever it was located. Only in this way could the future growth of the firm be assured and the rate of that growth maintained.

So what has happened is that over the years, WB&A has done work in almost every state in the Union and in some twenty-five countries abroad, on every continent except Antarctica.

Through the foreign work, the organization has become known around the world. Some of this work has been among its most exciting and productive. Because of it, Welton Becket and many of his people became world travelers, some remaining in foreign countries on projects for years at a time.

The foreign work also produced some of the now almost apocryphal stories still told and some of the worst headaches the firm ever had.

Welton Becket liked to tell about the time he was summoned by the president of Mexico, Miguel Alemán Valdés, to fly immediately to Mexico City with plans for a Hilton project there. With no time to obtain a tourist permit, he took the plane anyway, only to be arrested immediately upon landing. After eight hours, he was released after paying a fine of $700. Becket always added that soon afterward, Conrad Hilton got a bill of $700, but the hotel was never built.

The headaches were many, some of them also part of the fun of foreign work. The endless delays, the red tape, the necessity for translation of documents into other languages or into metric measure. Not the least of the problems was the difficulty of collecting fees at all, and then the further problem of getting the funds out of another country and in U.S. dollars. On several jobs done many years ago the firm has never been able to collect all its fees.

As a consequence, the firm's policy now embraces working abroad only for U.S. companies or others who are able to pay in dollars in this country. Notable among the foreign jobs now are the chain of hotels being done all over the world for Intercontinental in such places as Kinshasa, Republic of the Congo, Melbourne, and Auckland.

All in all, the principles of operation and the policies and organization that make them work actually are only facets of what Welton Becket and Associates calls total design.

In Part Two the organization will be dissected and examined, and in subsequent parts the methods—the how—of the organization, and some of the results—and hopefully the why of them—will be apparent.

Hartford National Bank &
Trust Company, Hartford,
Connecticut.

Part Two

THE FRAMEWORK FOR TOTAL DESIGN

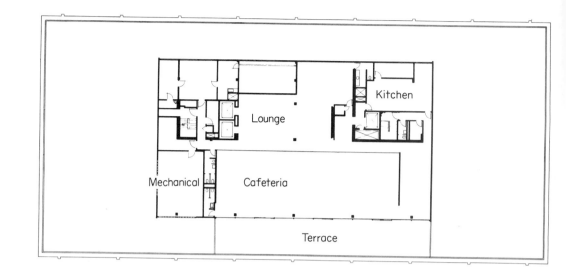

Fifth Floor

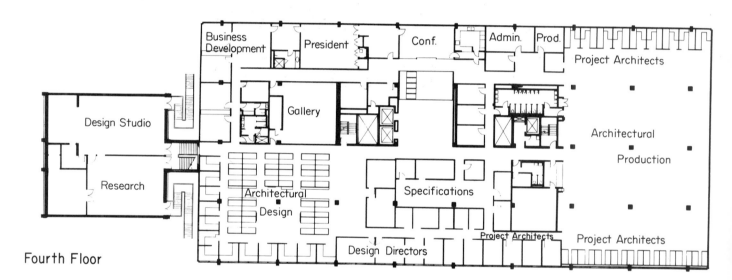

Fourth Floor

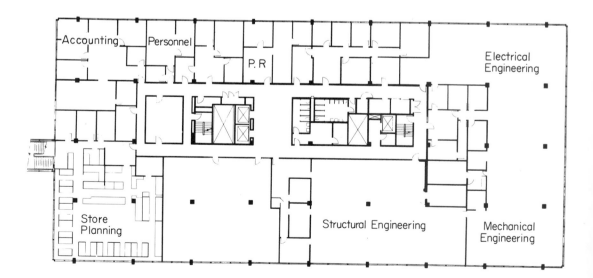

Third Floor

30

4
CORPORATE ORGANIZATION

The floor plans of the Welton Becket and Associates Los Angeles offices, shown opposite, are worth more than a passing glance because they show more than the size of the firm, the size and layout of its largest office, and the spaciousness of its quarters.

The plans also tell quite a bit about the organization of this firm. For example, it might be noted that design and architectural production are on the same floor, the fourth, with designers representing the one department in close proximity to project architects representing the other. And both are on the same floor with top administration. Also with business development, which is quite a switch compared to some firms, where designers and those in sales never quite meet, physically or intellectually. And how many architectural firms actually have a research center? On the third floor are grouped engineering and other departments, while the first and second floors are leased to other companies.

With the plans as an introduction, a detailed look at the overall organization can begin. In the first place, the firm is a corporation, chartered in the State of California. The corporate office is in Los Angeles,

in its own building, the one shown in the plans. Also housed in this building is a complete architectural office, one of the five operated by the firm. The four other offices are in San Francisco, New York, Chicago, and Houston. Each of the first three named occupies an entire floor of an office building in a central location in its own city. The Houston office is quartered in a remodeled house, to which a drafting room was added, in the residential fringe of the central city.

In all states where allowed, the firm practices as a corporation. In other states, MacDonald Becket, AIA, a single proprietorship (MacDonald Becket is registered in 35 states) contracts with clients and, with the approval of the clients, hires the corporation to perform the actual work. This partnership was set up long before Welton Becket died, with him as its third member. It remained completely dormant while he was alive, its role being played by a sole proprietorship, Welton Becket, FAIA, Architect.

The partnership—and the proprietorship before it—has no employees and performs no work. Its only reason for being is compliance with laws of the states

PROJECT PROCEDURE

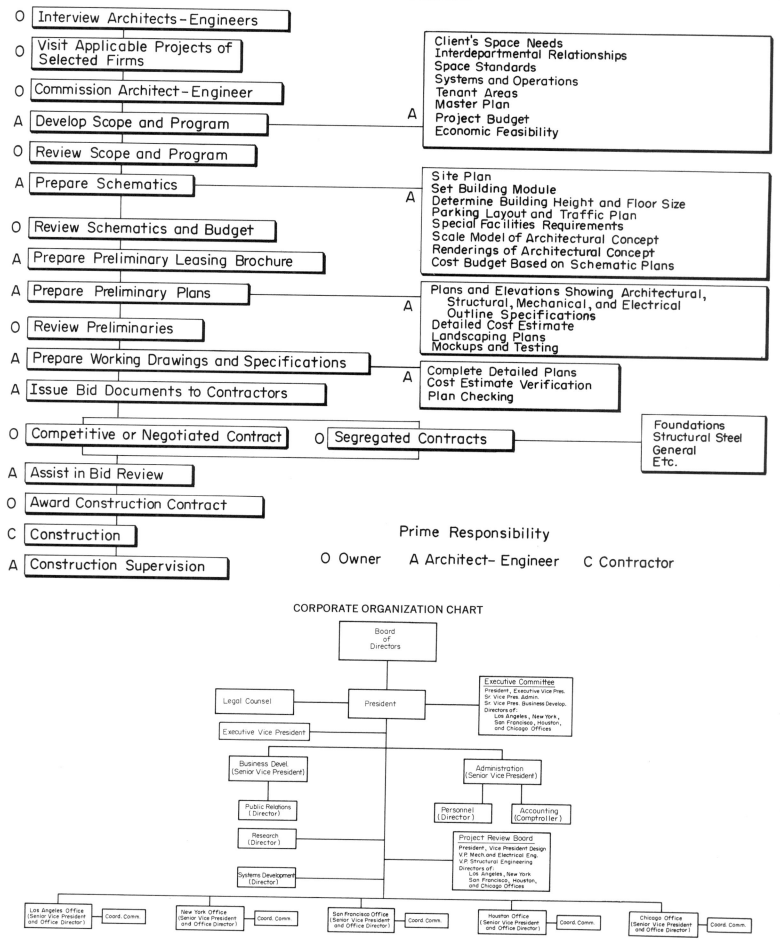

O Interview Architects–Engineers

O Visit Applicable Projects of Selected Firms

O Commission Architect–Engineer

A Develop Scope and Program

A — Client's Space Needs
Interdepartmental Relationships
Space Standards
Systems and Operations
Tenant Areas
Master Plan
Project Budget
Economic Feasibility

O Review Scope and Program

A Prepare Schematics

A — Site Plan
Set Building Module
Determine Building Height and Floor Size
Parking Layout and Traffic Plan
Special Facilities Requirements
Scale Model of Architectural Concept
Renderings of Architectural Concept
Cost Budget Based on Schematic Plans

O Review Schematics and Budget

A Prepare Preliminary Leasing Brochure

A Prepare Preliminary Plans

A — Plans and Elevations Showing Architectural,
Structural, Mechanical, and Electrical
Outline Specifications
Detailed Cost Estimate
Landscaping Plans
Mockups and Testing

O Review Preliminaries

A Prepare Working Drawings and Specifications

A — Complete Detailed Plans
Cost Estimate Verification
Plan Checking

A Issue Bid Documents to Contractors

O Competitive or Negotiated Contract   O Segregated Contracts — Foundations
Structural Steel
General
Etc.

A Assist in Bid Review

O Award Construction Contract

C Construction

A Construction Supervision

Prime Responsibility

O Owner   A Architect–Engineer   C Contractor

CORPORATE ORGANIZATION CHART

Board of Directors

Legal Counsel — President

Executive Committee
President, Executive Vice Pres.
Sr. Vice Pres. Admin.
Sr. Vice Pres. Business Develop.
Directors of:
Los Angeles, New York,
San Francisco, Houston,
and Chicago Offices

Executive Vice President

Business Devel.
(Senior Vice President)

Administration
(Senior Vice President)

Public Relations
(Director)

Personnel
(Director)

Accounting
(Comptroller)

Research
(Director)

Project Review Board
President, Vice President Design
V.P. Mech. and Electrical Eng.
V.P. Structural Engineering
Directors of:
Los Angeles, New York
San Francisco, Houston,
and Chicago Offices

Systems Development
(Director)

Los Angeles Office
(Senior Vice President
and Office Director) — Coord. Comm.

New York Office
(Senior Vice President
and Office Director) — Coord. Comm.

San Francisco Office
(Senior Vice President
and Office Director) — Coord. Comm.

Houston Office
(Senior Vice President
and Office Director) — Coord. Comm.

Chicago Office
(Senior Vice President
and Office Director) — Coord. Comm.

32

which do not allow architects to practice as corporations.

On page 32 is shown an organization chart of the corporate structure of WB&A. On it may be followed the lines of authority and relationships among officers, committees, and departments. Also on the same page is a project procedure diagram that demonstrates the major actions taken in the five offices on representative jobs.

Corporation top policy stems from the actions of its Board of Directors. Involved only in the most comprehensive, far-reaching decisions, the board consists of five members: MacDonald Becket, Chairman; and Bruce Becket, Furman Myers, Jack Beardwood, and Albert Grossman, the firm's attorney.

Executive functions begin with overall management delegated by the board to the president of WB&A. Reporting directly to him are the directors of the five offices and the major corporate departments in Los Angeles.

To start at the peak of the management pyramid, the president acts as the chief executive and operating officer of the firm, and, as has been pointed out, the directors of the offices and the major corporate departments all report to him. In addition, the president, as noted before, is chairman of the Board of Directors, which establishes overall policy on the highest level. He also wears another hat, that of chairman of the Executive Committee, which acts as an advisory group to the president and to provide effective liaison between top executives of the firm rather than as an arm of active management as is often true in other organizations.

Needless to say, the president of a nationwide architectural firm of this size has plenty to do. As the chief executive officer, his is the overall responsibility for all that takes place, not only in the corporate office but in the others as well. He is the top administrator, and his is the final word on all aspects of the practice.

It has been said that any position of such tremendous authority and responsibility will shape the man who fills it if he does not shape the position. In the case of Welton Becket, president for so many years, the man shaped the position, all right, but the position also had much to do with shaping the man. Of course, admittedly this was a highly unusual situation in that Welton Becket was the sole owner of the firm, as well as its president.

The fact that MacDonald Becket, as president, is not the sole owner but one who must share ownership with fourteen others, and probably more than that later, is bound to affect things. And of course, these two Beckets, Welton and MacDonald, though related by blood and by close association for many years, were anything but carbon copies of each other, each being an individual with his own characteristics and his own style.

Welton Becket played his role in a very understated manner. Quiet ordinarily, cool, design-oriented, a man who knew and understood the world of big business and finance but who had little patience with the details of office management. A man who would be called anything but aggressive, a superb salesman of the services of the firm, but it was all so soft-sell

President MacDonald Becket.

A meeting of the corporate executive committee in the Los Angeles offices.

Furman Myers, Senior Vice-President, Administration.

John McCartan, Director of Personnel, Los Angeles corporate offices.

Directors of Design, Arthur Love and Robert Tyler, of Chicago and Los Angeles respectively, recently retired Corporate Director of Design Maynard Woodard, Designer Neal Scribner.

Woodard and Director of Research Louis Naidorf.

Top executives during a coffee break in the Los Angeles office cafeteria.

The President and the directors of mechanical-electrical engineering, design, structural engineering, research.

that many clients had bought before they knew they were being sold. A persistent man, a man who seemingly knew where he was going at all times and how to get there. A man who had direct orientation toward two things in his professional life: architecture and people. And the latter orientation not inferior to the former. He was a man who personally sat down each year and wrote down the figures for annual bonuses next to each staff member's name. And one who would see that each got a bonus even in years—it only happened a couple of times—when the firm lost money.

Welton Becket was a man who hated the fact that he could not keep up with all of the vital details about every man in the office—it had grown too big for that. But he tried very hard to do so. And he hated the idea that he personally could not be involved in every detail decision on every job. It had grown too big for that too. But he did keep his hand in the biggest decisions of this sort, mostly by indirection but sometimes very, very forcefully.

This kind of man made one kind of president. MacDonald Becket, sharing many of the attributes of his uncle, but not all, is bound to make a different kind.

To begin with, MacDonald Becket seems to have more of an orientation toward organization. His manner is quiet, too, but his demeanor hides more aggressive attitudes especially toward the development of new business, an area in which he has spent much of his professional life. Somehow, he always seems to be going places. He hops on an airplane to cross the country for a client interview or other business reasons with the same nonchalance that another man might cross a street. And he maintains apartments in Chicago and New York as well as his home in Los Angeles. He is energetic, young (early forties), and on the go. His presidency has already seen things speeded up considerably. And he will no doubt have to forgo some of the personal involvement with details of design and people, in favor of putting even more reliance on the other key staff members than did his predecessor in this job.

In the organization itself, and particularly in the Executive Committee as now constituted, MacDonald Becket finds himself with strong advisors and equally strong leaders of the firm. The Executive Committee brings together, on a regular basis, the top executives of the corporation and the directors of the five offices. In addition to the president, as chairman, the Executive Committee consists of corporate officers Jack Beardwood, Executive Vice President; Donnell Grimes, of Business Development; Furman Myers, of Administration; and office directors Charles B. McReynolds, of Los Angeles; Charles R. Kuglin, of Chicago; Dominick Primiani, of San Francisco; Charles W. Stanton, of New York; and Gilbert Thweatt, of Houston.

As may be gathered from the composition of the Executive Committee, its duties and work are concerned mainly with executive and administrative problems that are corporate in nature and those which affect more than one office.

In addition to this committee, the corporate structure also includes a second important committee, the

Project Review Board. This board is composed of the same members as the Executive Committee, with the exception of the directors of Administration and Business Development and with the addition of Paul Sessinghaus, Director of Mechanical and Electrical Engineering, and Jack Meadville, Director of Structural Engineering. The Project Review Board also meets regularly, taking as its province the solving of architectural, engineering, and other technical and design problems as opposed to the executive and administrative problems handled by the Executive Committee. For example, the board regularly reviews the work of all of the offices to solve any problems of magnitude and to ensure a high standard of quality throughout the work of all offices. On the other hand, the board makes no attempt to make the various offices or individuals in the offices conform to anything resembling a standardized WB&A style or rely on standardized solutions in their architectural designs.

The president's corporate staff includes Executive Vice President Jack Beardwood, who acts as a special assistant to the president; the directors of Administration, Business Development, and Research; and the head of the Systems Development Group.

A major factor in the success of Welton Becket and Associates and one that has a continuing effect on all of the outlying offices as well as on the Los Angeles office and the overall operation is the strong Corporate Department of Administration. Directed by Furman Myers, Senior Vice President for many years, this department has complete charge of the general administrative functions of the firm not only for Los Angeles but for the other offices. In each of the other offices, there is at least one person who, though primarily a staff member of the office in which he works, also has a direct relationship with the department of Administration in Los Angeles and with its director and other personnel. The Director of Corporate Administration has two departments reporting to him—Personnel and Accounting.

John McCartan, the Personnel Director, establishes and administers companywide personnel and benefit programs. In addition, he handles almost all the preliminary interviews of prospective Los Angeles employees, no matter what their level. Working with one secretary, McCartan's role is to take the criteria set up by the Architectural Production Departments for draftsman or whatever, or those set up by another department looking for people, find people to be interviewed by whatever means he can, and interview them, weeding out the obviously unfit. Then he will call in the department head concerned for final interviewing.

In another important area, keeping personnel records, including those for vacations and sick leave, the Personnel Department handles the work for all the offices. Records are kept in Los Angeles, thus providing, in addition to complete histories on each employee, a very effective way of making comparisons in salaries, longevity with the firm, promotions, and so on throughout the country. An important part of the personnel function is the administration of the various employee insurance programs in the areas of health, life, and salary continuance.

Designer Cabrol, Director of Research Naidorf, Chicago Director of Design, Love, and designers Thomas Mathew, Jack Irvine.

Naidorf and designer Irvine flank Project Chief Bruce Becket.

Bruce Becket and Naidorf.

Model builders Jack Rogers and Richard Matthews.

Executive Vice President Jack Beardwood, MacDonald Becket.

Corporate Director of Business Development, Donnell Grimes.

William Feathers of Corporate Business Development, and Beardwood.

Martin Brower, Corporate Director of Public Relations.

In addition to its other duties, for the Los Angeles office, the Personnel Department oversees the work of the switchboard operators and mailroom employees. And finally, the Personnel Department head, John McCartan, is acknowledged by one and all to be the unofficial "chaplain" of the organization—he gets all the gripes and personal problems from all over the shop and attempts to be of help when he can.

Another department of the administration division which functions for the overall corporation and all five other offices is Accounting, headed by Carl Andrews, Vice President and Comptroller. This department functions in two major ways: it handles the general accounting for the entire firm in all of its aspects, and it acts as the center of control of the costs of performing services for clients. This department does not get involved in the control of costs of construction, which is handled by the architectural production departments.

All billing of clients is handled here, based on reports from the production and other divisions on the status of projects. Records are kept of the financial history of all projects and analyses made of the costs of producing them as compared to the budgets prepared by the production departments. In this way, comparisons can be made of budgets for services against actual performance, between projects of a similar type and scope, between projects handled by the various offices, and in many other ways of importance to the firm.

Because of the necessity for the firm to practice as a partnership in some states and a corporation in others, two sets of books are kept, which are consolidated at the end of each month to present the overall picture of financial performance.

Of course, accounting handles the usual functions of such a department in payrolls, other disbursements, and record keeping. But a major role is that of controlling the costs of producing architectural projects, further complicated by the fact that much of the work is done not on a percentage fee basis but on a multiple of payroll fee basis. And another large factor of the complexity of cost control lies in the ever mounting size of reimbursables or extras to be found in every architectural commission these days, the costs that must be billed to the client over and above the fees specified in the owner-architect agreement.

The other major corporate department is Business Development, Donnell Grimes, Senior Vice President and Director, who has a corporate staff working for him, including Public Relations, in Los Angeles. In addition, Grimes and his group work closely with the business development men in the other offices, with the various office directors, and with others in the firm who become involved in these functions.

A newer department in corporate headquarters is Research, headed by Louis Naidorf, Vice President and Director. Naidorf was formerly Assistant Director of Design for the Los Angeles office. Another new department is Systems Development, headed by Robert Dillon.

Business Development and the major new departments named are discussed in later chapters.

The Century City building of
Welton Becket and Associates
houses the corporate staff
and the Los Angeles offices.

Olive View Hospital's
Medical Treatment and Care Facility
Los Angeles County, California.

Elaine Stevely Hoffman Medical
Research Center, USC-County
Medical Center, Los Angeles,
California

5
ORGANIZATION
OF OFFICES

Under the umbrella of its corporate structure, located in Los Angeles, Welton Becket and Associates has five operating offices located in Los Angeles, Chicago, New York, San Francisco, and Houston. Each is an autonomous architectural office, performing complete services for its clients. On the other hand, each has close ties with the others and with the corporate organization. In this way, it is possible for each to operate independently but at the same time derive great benefits from the other offices and from the overall organization.

Each of the offices is headed by a director, who is a member of the firm's Corporate Executive Committee and Project Review Board. Thus each of the office directors practices, in a sense, as if he were the sole principal of an individual architectural office. At the same time, each of the office directors participates heavily in an architectural organization that is much larger in every sense than a single office operating from a single location.

As may be seen in the organization charts for the

five offices shown in the pages following, there are a considerable number of differences between offices. For example, only Los Angeles and Chicago have engineering departments, while the other offices use outside consultants for the most part. In several offices, specialized competence has been built up in areas of practice such as interiors, store planning, and the like to meet demands made by the clients in a given geographic area or for some other special purpose.

On the other hand, there are some strong similarities between the organizations of the various offices, a few of which may not be obvious from the charts. In each of the offices, design of all kinds, including interiors, graphics, and decorating, as well as architectural, is in the design departments, each of which is headed by a director. In all offices, architectural production has been organized under a director, to whom project architects, chief draftsmen, job captains, draftsmen, and specification people report.

In each of the offices, there is the counterpart of

*Los Angeles Office Director
Charles McReynolds, right,
with Designer Pierre Cabrol.*

Albert Peterson, Furman Myers.

the Production Administration Department shown in the organization charts for Los Angeles, New York, and Chicago. However, in the other offices, the function of production administration has not so far been developed into a full-scale department.

It will be noted that in Los Angeles and Chicago, in addition to the Architectural Production Department, there are departments for production of mechanical-electrical engineering and structural engineering. In both offices, these departments are headed by directors. In every case, except Chicago which has a separate department with its own director for services during construction, these functions are performed by people assigned to the production departments. In practice, this means that the architectural, mechanical-electrical, and structural production departments perform services during construction for projects, each in its own area of competence, for all projects.

In each of the offices, the director receives help in administration and related matters from a Coordinating Committee. As may be seen in the charts, these committees consist of the top people in administrative, production, design, and business development positions. Because of the varied sizes and needs of the offices, these committees vary in their membership and size, from the largest, eight people in Chicago, to the smallest, three people in San Francisco. For each of the committees, the office director serves as chairman, and all include in their membership the directors of all major departments within the offices.

As may be gathered from the composition of these committees, interdepartmental problems can be solved within the groups for the most part. Thus, the weekly meetings are chiefly concerned with subjects that are related to the handling of projects in the office at the time or ones coming up. Of course, purely administrative problems of broad scope can also be handled in this committee. But the main

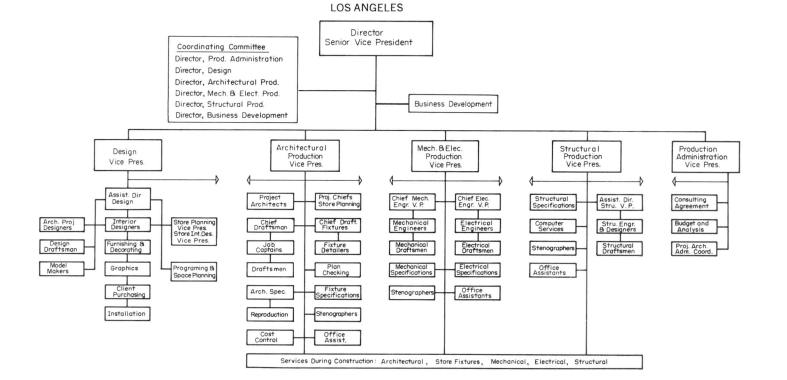

LOS ANGELES

Director
Senior Vice President

Coordinating Committee
Director, Prod. Administration
Director, Design
Director, Architectural Prod.
Director, Mech. & Elect. Prod.
Director, Structural Prod.
Director, Business Development

Business Development

Design Vice Pres.
- Assist. Dir Design
- Arch. Proj Designers
- Design Draftsman
- Model Makers
- Interior Designers
- Furnishing & Decorating
- Graphics
- Client Purchasing
- Installation
- Store Planning Vice Pres. Store Int. Des. Vice Pres.
- Programing & Space Planning

Architectural Production Vice Pres.
- Project Architects
- Chief Draftsman
- Job Captains
- Draftsmen
- Arch. Spec.
- Reproduction
- Cost Control
- Proj. Chiefs Store Planning
- Chief Draft. Fixtures
- Fixture Detailers
- Plan Checking
- Fixture Specifications
- Stenographers
- Office Assist.

Mech. & Elec. Production Vice Pres.
- Chief Mech. Engr. V. P.
- Mechanical Engineers
- Mechanical Draftsmen
- Mechanical Specifications
- Stenographers
- Chief Elec. Engr. V. P.
- Electrical Engineers
- Electrical Draftsmen
- Electrical Specifications
- Office Assistants

Structural Production Vice Pres.
- Structural Specifications
- Computer Services
- Stenographers
- Office Assistants
- Assist. Dir. Stru. V. P.
- Stru. Engr. & Designers
- Structural Draftsmen

Production Administration Vice Pres.
- Consulting Agreement
- Budget and Analysis
- Proj. Arch. Adm. Coord.

Services During Construction: Architectural, Store Fixtures, Mechanical, Electrical, Structural

subjects for discussion at the meeting are projects.

Without ever having really been organized, in words or memoranda, members of the committee work closely with one another outside of the weekly meetings. And problems between departments are more often solved in that manner than at the meetings themselves. This procedure is, in effect, indicative of the working relationships between departments and individuals throughout the firm.

While the office organizational charts shown here and in the pages following may look as if hard-and-fast lines of demarcation between functions had been set and as if the chain of command were extremely definite and rigid, the practice is quite another thing. Almost never must a person go up or down through organizational stairsteps to accomplish his purpose. Thus, if a project architect has a difference of opinion with a designer, ordinarily they simply get together and thrash it out between them.

Most of the time, this informality works very well. When it does not, the department directors may become involved, or maybe even the office director, or in extreme cases even the president.

As has been pointed out previously, each of the offices has divisions of design, architectural production, and so on that duplicate each other to an extent. Of course, the great differences in the sizes of the offices—about 300 people in Los Angeles, 125 in New York, 80 in Chicago, 40 in San Francisco, and 35 in Houston—affect their organization. The smaller offices are organized less formally than the larger ones, and people in the former tend to overlap in function more than the latter.

The directors of these offices, Charles McReynolds in Los Angeles, Dominick Primiani in San Francisco, Charles Stanton in New York, Gilbert Thweatt in Houston, and Charles Kuglin in Chicago, are in complete charge of their respective offices and report directly to the president of the firm.

Of course, all the offices have other less definable ties to the corporate office—for advice, consultation,

Chicago consultant O. H. Breidert and Office Director Charles R. Kuglin.

Chicago Office Assistant Director Joseph F. Ringhofer.

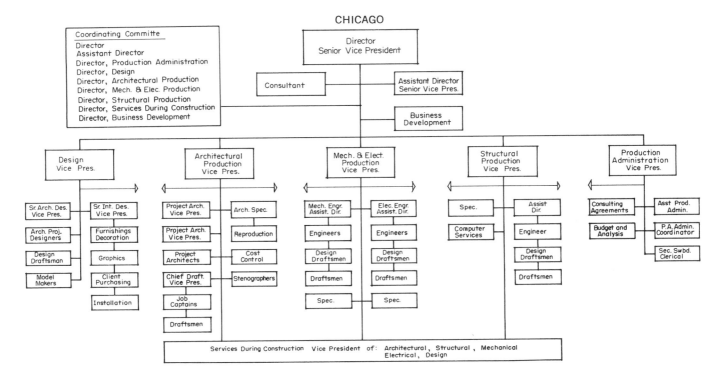

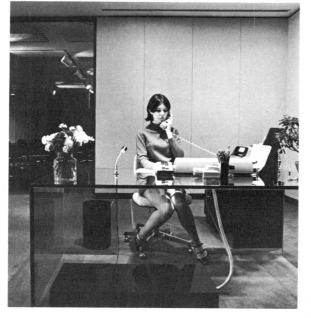

Receptionist in the San Francisco office.

San Francisco Office Director Nick Primiani.

backup, and in other ways. In brief, it might be said that each of the offices offers complete architectural services to its clients, but part of the services in any given case might be acquired from another of the offices. And certain more specialized functions such as store planning would most probably be handled in Los Angeles rather than in the other offices.

In addition, the corporate offices perform certain services for the other offices, such as a large part of business development, overall accounting and record keeping, public relations, and so on. In some cases, the corporate office would handle some aspect of these functions in its entirety; in another case it would be a cooperative effort between two offices. The prime principle is to handle matters between offices in the way that works best, or makes for the highest efficiency, without a plethora of formal directives or overorganized procedures if they can be avoided.

It should be remembered that in spite of the fact that the various offices act independently of each other, all act together when necessary. And the full weight of the entire firm can be brought to bear when circumstances warrant it.

In the corporate offices are located two major departments of the administration division which have no counterparts in the other offices: Personnel and Accounting. In functions of this sort, the corporate office handles much of the work for the five offices.

Although the other offices do not have personnel offices as such, they do handle almost all their own hiring and firing. On the other hand, a considerable amount of shuffling around of personnel takes place among the offices, particularly of people on management-executive levels. And many of these people originally go to work for the firm in the Los Angeles office. So the Los Angeles personnel operation does have some considerable effect on people in the other offices even though it does not hire a great percentage of them.

Although the organization and functions of the Production Administration Department will be discussed in detail in later chapters, a quick look is in

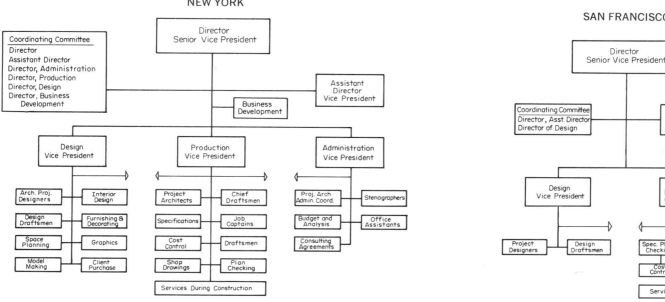

order here, because of its importance and to complete the picture of overall administration of the offices of Welton Becket and Associates.

In Los Angeles, for example, under Vice President Albert Peterson, Production Administration performs a number of functions that in another firm might be performed by project architects or partners-in-charge or others—serving as a center of operations for the administration of projects. The major principle behind administration of production as handled in WB&A offices is the conviction within the firm that, for the most part, the architects in charge of projects should spend their time on architecture in all of its phases, rather than on administrative detail. The belief here is that architects do architecture better than administration, they were trained that way for the most part, and they prefer it that way.

In general, and sketchily, project administration works like this: the Business Development Department makes an agreement with a client for a project; the agreement is then analyzed by Production Administration, with the help of other departments involved, and prepares a budget of man-hours and other costs of doing the work. During the course of the project, Accounting receives reports on expenditures, time and otherwise, and keeps records for continuing analysis by Production Administration and others concerned with the work.

In addition, Production Administration coordinates the work of the project architects from an administrative standpoint, even to the degree of helping them keep their own records and reports straight and writing letters for them.

Each office has either a department or individuals who handle this sort of work in a similar manner.

Individual differences and similarities between the offices may be seen in the charts. Perhaps a few of those not already mentioned should be pointed out. All offices but San Francisco have departments for model making, interiors, furnishing and decorating, graphics, and purchasing for clients. All but San Francisco and Chicago have departments for programming and space planning.

New York Office Director Charles W. Stanton, right, with Assistant Director Henry Brennan.

Houston Office Director Gilbert Thweatt.

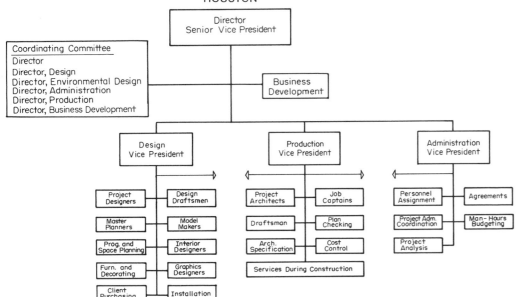

HOUSTON

First State Bank, Clear Lake City, Texas.

Automobile Club of Southern California, Los Angeles, California.

6
ORGANIZATION
OF DESIGN

With architecture in a state of change, with so much soul-searching going on among architects and among all those related to architecture in any way, the area of design would seem at first glance to be a haven from the storm. After all, just about everyone in architecture seems convinced that design is the central theme, the heart of the matter. Of course, there are those who define design as function, or appearance, or beauty, or in some other restrictive way. And there are those who think of design as the overall creative input a building gets from talented people who solve problems and make the solutions practical as well as aesthetic. And there are even those who think that everything an architect does in creating a building is design.

There are those who believe that architects, architectural firms, should perform every service necessary to create a building, from earliest problem solving through construction. And there are those who believe architects should do nothing but create the scheme, leaving the production, construction, and everything else to others. In the view of the latter, the highest calling is that of the architect as designer, while the detailers, cost estimators, draftsmen, inspectors, and workmen operate on some much lower plane—necessary, but uncreative and unexciting. In the view of the former, the architect sometimes appears as if he were a deity, creating everything out of nothing, master of all things.

In many ways, each of these attitudes has contributed mightily to the chaotic state of architecture today and to the widely separated ideas held by many architects of their role, their profession, and their relationships to other design professionals.

Designer Richard Magee, Maynard Woodard.

Los Angeles Director of Design Robert Tyler with designers Thomas Mathew and Karl Schwerdtfeger.

Designer James Meares and interior designer Henry Blair, Los Angeles.

Graphic designer Noel Davis in Los Angeles office library.

On the broadest base, such controversies, raging throughout architectural circles and among the conglomerates and builders who aspire to succeed to the role of the professional architects, are disruptive in the extreme within the profession and dismaying beyond belief to clients. A client may interview one large architectural firm, whose principal claims he makes all of the major design decisions or even that he designs all of his own buildings; then he may interview another of equal size in which the principal admits he is the executive officer only, delegating design to others. He may interview a third that proclaims that its design effort is made by "the team." A fourth declares that because it is small, the client receives all of the attention of the principal to design and everything else. A fifth may claim that because it is larger, the client gets specialist attention to every phase of his job. A sixth may give the potential client still another version. And so on ad infinitum.

Confused by all this, the potential client may find himself even more baffled by builders with architects and engineers on their staffs, who claim that the client gets a package from them complete in every way from inception to lock and key, or he may hear from these people that by using their services the client gets design that is really free or almost so since it is part of the package.

Clients say that it is like a breath of pure, mountain air to come into a conversation with the WB&A people, and particularly with designers, after having escaped an atmosphere elsewhere that may be either rarefied or unreal.

Here design is defined in its broadest sense—exterior, interior, furniture and furnishings, all of the things that make up a building. Here design is function; it is aesthetics; it is problem solving; it is process. In this firm, the talk centers around the facts of design, insofar as that is possible, not around the abstractions of design. Even among themselves, the designers and other key people here avoid, by choice, the rather esoteric jargon that many architects employ, by choice, when discussing design. And it goes almost without saying, that clients are never subjected to this jargon, often used by many to obscure facts rather than to explain them.

Not only do the designers at WB&A avoid the architectural jargon employed by many of their counterparts elsewhere, but surprisingly the word that crops up most in their conversation is *client*. The orientation toward the client found throughout the firm, in top administration, in business development, and in other departments is to be found among the designers too. This is so ingrained that one designer talking one day about his job used the word *client* some fifty times in an hour. And this is not an isolated example.

Perhaps some architects might think the client orientation here overdone, that bending in that direction to the degree that occurs here would tend to leave little running room for the designers to operate as designers in the most esoteric sense. And there would be some truth in that thought. Of course, this state of affairs would vary considerably between individual designers; would even vary in a single individual designer working on two different buildings for two divergent types of client groups.

It should be remembered that there exists no real WB&A style, in the sense of the Frank Lloyd Wright or Mies or Corbusier "styles." Style here starts with the absolute insistence that every project become a good, competent, technologically, and aesthetically acceptable building. It should be completed on time; it should come in within its budget; it should function; it should fulfill the requirements of its owner, the client. Now when these are the first criteria for projects being handled by an architectural firm, it is probably inevitable that the overall quality of all of the projects will be good but not great. Very seldom if ever will a tour de force be produced. Never will the prejudices, conceits, or arrogances of the architect be forced upon the client, to produce a building for the architect rather than for the client.

On the other hand, it must be quickly added that when the general level of competence in all phases of the creation of buildings is uncommonly high, opportunities for greatness occur with some regularity. An examination of a number of WB&A buildings of varying types and budgets and geographical spread will reveal what happens in this respect.

Generally, all the WB&A buildings do their jobs competently and probably would be rated above average in most or all respects when compared to all the buildings produced by architects in any given time. And among the WB&A buildings, a creditable number would be standouts when measured in the same manner.

This is not to say these standout buildings would be considered smashingly newsworthy, controversial, or as shrines to be visited by the aficionados of high art in architecture. This is not to say that WB&A produces buildings that affect such aficionados like Wright's Guggenheim or the Boston City Hall. Many such buildings, though newsworthy when built, turn out to be imperfect in the extreme when viewed as complete architecture, though they may be exciting in the extreme when viewed as exercises in aesthetics alone or as tours de force.

WB&A produces complete buildings—the firm calls the process "total design." From the viewpoint of the designers in the firm, and from that of the organization of the design departments, this means attention to all of the aspects of design, not only to aesthetics and function. To costs, to structure, to systems, to construction methods, to programming, to feasibility. But it also means that in WB&A, the design departments have been organized in a manner that differs considerably from the way design in most architectural firms is organized. And it also means that the staff of the design departments includes some talents and specialties not often found in other firms.

The design departments here seem very disorganized at first glance. Yet parts are highly organized; for example, this is one of the very few architectural firms in the country with a complete store planning function, equipped to handle all aspects of this specialty from programming and space planning through design and fixture detailing to overseeing the installation and purchase for the clients of furniture, fixtures, and furnishings.

Interior designers Arthur Posner, Randy Myers, Los Angeles.

Interior designer William Chappell, Los Angeles.

San Francisco design offices.

San Francisco Office Director Nick Primiani with Office Assistant Director Conley Weaver (R) and Assistant Director of Design Walter Hunt.

Chicago Design Director Arthur Love meets with designer.

Love and designer.

Chicago design offices.

Chicago interior designer Jack Bela.

The remainder of the design departments seem underorganized, mostly because they include all kinds of designers (architectural, interior, graphics, and so on), but many of these people double as space planners, master planners, or in other areas of design.

In WB&A, design in all its aspects has been under the overall direction of Maynard Woodard, Senior Vice President and Corporate Director of Design. Woody, as he is universally called, was with Welton Becket and Associates from 1945 to 1971, coming from MGM during the studio strikes. Trained as an architect, he had spent ten years in illustration work for MGM before returning to his real calling, architecture. Woody is a designer's designer; although much of his later work became administrative, he continued to act as consultant, critic, and adviser to the design departments of the various offices. Somehow, he managed to keep the paperwork and other red tape of his position to a minimum, spending most of his time with the designers and others who reported to him on the design problems rather than the administrative ones.

The directors of design in all of the offices theoretically reported to Woodard for matters of design, though they report to the directors of their offices in fact. In practice, the offices have complete design departments themselves, including all specialties required to perform total design, and are in fact autonomous in design as they are in other aspects of practice. However, only the Los Angeles office has a store planning function, and work of this sort out of another office would be performed here.

It should be pointed out that though Woodard did not directly control design in the other offices, by virtue of his long service, his position, and his reputation he was often called upon by one or the other of the regional offices for advice and counsel. And too, there were times when an office would bring its work to Los Angeles for critiques by Woodard and the other top people.

Thus Woodard functioned in the ex officio role of chief designer for all design, whether architectural, interior, decorating, store planning, or whatever, for all the offices. And in his positions on the Corporate Executive Committee and Project Review Board, he was in a position to make design policy for the entire firm.

The office design directors function in two major ways. Each of them takes on a number of projects on which he functions as the designer in fact. In this role, the office design directors act in a manner similar to that of any other architectural designer on the staff in any of the offices. They have the prime, direct responsibility for the complete design of the projects assigned to them. On larger projects, they might also assign other designers from their departments to assist with the work.

The design directors also have the administrative design responsibility for the work of the other designers in their departments. In this role, the office design directors perform in a manner similar to that of Woodard in the overall design operations, acting as advisors, critics, consultants, and administrators for the projects they are assigned to oversee. Of course, they report to the directors of their offices, and to an extent to the corporate Director of Design, and through them to the president of the firm.

For each project in an office, a designer is assigned by the director, in consultation with the director of architectural production, to whom the project architects report. Production is brought into the picture in the selection of the designers, mainly because the project designer and the project architect share the responsibility for projects assigned to them and must therefore work very closely throughout the life of the projects.

In addition to the project designers, one or more of whom is assigned to each job, WB&A also has a number of interior designers in its design departments. Leaving the store planning department out of the discussion for the moment, the interior designers here fall into two broad classifications, one the more usual specialty involved with furniture and furnishings and the like. In this firm, these operations are called furnishing and decorating. Less usual are the interior designers who actually function more like the interior architects of some European countries. These people are concerned with the interior *architecture* of buildings to which they are assigned. That is to say they function in the design of interiors in a manner similar to the way the usual type of architectural designer functions in the design of the entire building.

There are times when an architectural designer will handle the interior architecture as well as the overall design. In other cases, particularly for larger or more complex projects, an interior designer will be assigned to work with the architectural designer.

When the firm is handling the complete design job on buildings, including interiors, furniture and decorating, and the like (total design), designers who specialize in furnishings and decorating will also be assigned to the jobs. This function extends all the way from early analysis and programming, through design and selection, to purchasing items for the clients.

It should be remembered throughout this discussion that all of these design functions are handled within the design departments, not as separate functions, but as parts of the overall service. And all these people report to the office of Director of Design.

In some cases, the firm gets involved in the design of graphics of various kinds, signs, and similar things, and also in industrial design of furniture, tableware, and many other items. Several graphic designers on the staff handle work of this sort when necessary. Some of the graphics people are industrial designers by profession or training, and many of the interior people are also industrial designers; within these groups, a wide variety of talents are available for work in this area. They are further examples, prevalent in the firm, of people who can handle a variety of types of projects.

A similar thing is true in areas such as master planning and space analysis and planning. WB&A over the years has been deeply involved in master planning for many large projects and continues to attract this sort of work in considerable quantity. Contrary to what would be the case in many firms, WB&A has no master planners who spend all of their

New York office receptionist.

New York Design Director David Beer with Charles McReynolds.

New York designer Otto Taskovich.

Interior designer Robert Craig of New York Office.

49

John Rust, Director of Administration, Gil Thweatt, Office Director and Pleas Doyle, Director of Design, Houston.

Director of Design Doyle.

Doyle, Thweatt.

Thweatt confers with staff.

time in this type of work. Here, master planning becomes part of the work of the designers who handle buildings. At a given time, one designer might, for example, be assigned to the master planning of an urban redevelopment job and at the same time be handling a building or two. Since the temperament and talents of people are varied, certain designers are naturally more drawn toward this kind of work and are better equipped to handle it than others. But it is entirely possible that any designer might be handed such an assignment.

The same sort of thing happens in space analysis and planning, a type of service in which the firm becomes more involved in as time goes on. Here, too, designers ordinarily handle this work, and over a period of time some of the designers have become very experienced and competent in these functions.

Over the years, the volume of work in department stores and shopping centers has grown in the office to the point where a separate department of store planning was established a few years back, in the Los Angeles office, within the Design Department.

Store planning is no longer a separate department. Now it is a group within the design department that includes interior designers, merchandising specialists, fixture detailers, draftsmen, and people who write store specifications and inspect the work in the field.

This group has as its primary function the handling of the details of merchandising studies, interiors, furnishing, and decorating of department stores for which WB&A has the prime architectural commission. Thus it forms an extension of the principles of total design in retail trade building types. However, the group also does store planning for projects for which architects other than WB&A have the commissions and on remodeling and renovation projects where store planning forms the entire commission.

A corporate staff function which is quite new but is expected to be of growing importance is the Welton Becket Research Center. Although many people scattered in departments throughout the firm will eventually become involved in the activities of the Research Center, the prime purposes of the Center come closest to being design functions.

The details of the operation and functions of the Design Department are covered in later chapters, but it should be pointed out here that the overall result of the work of design results in schematics. Of course, schematics in this firm are very complete indeed, and in another firm might resemble preliminaries. The principle in this begins with the conviction that complete and thorough design and complete and thorough disclosure to the client of progress during design are the major milestones to be passed on the road to a successful building.

The result of this, in almost all cases, is a set of schematic drawings along with outline specs and cost analyses that explain almost everything of greatest importance about the building to the client. And these documents, when handed over to production for preparation of preliminaries and the final documents, are so complete and detailed that production can proceed in an orderly, efficient, and speedy manner.

50

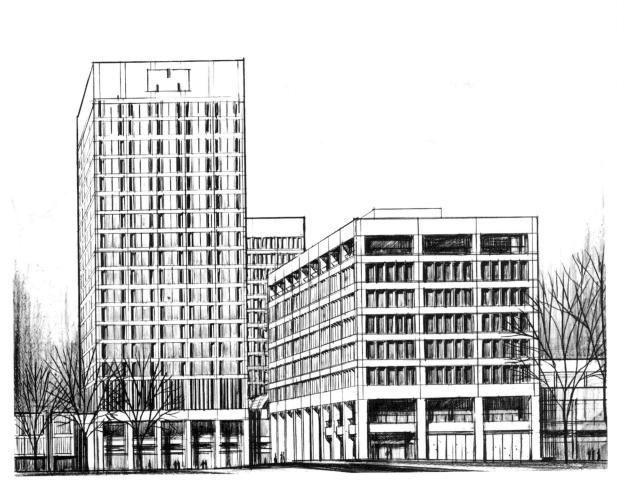

In order to give some insight
into the design process and
the presentation of its
results to clients, this page
and the next four following
contain sketches of various
types, renderings, and photos
of models of a single project,
Worcester Center, located
in the city of Worcester,
Massachusetts. The illustrations
represent some of the phases
through which this $100 million
urban redevelopment project
passed. Shown here are three
early study sketches and a
study model.

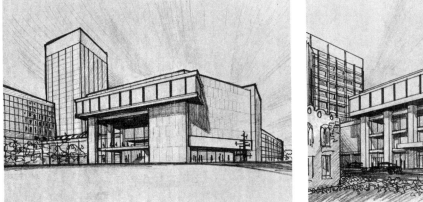

51

The sketches and models shown here further illustrate the steps in the design development of this major project. On a 34-acre site in downtown Worcester, the complex includes a 20-story office building and a second smaller one, two large department stores, more than 100 shops and stores and two parking structures for 4,300 automobiles, all tied together by a two-level, 60-foot high, 475-foot-long galleria.

The first phase of the Worcester Center construction was completed late in 1971. Later, a third office building will be added, along with a 325-room hotel, a civic theater, and additional parking. The Center is a testament to the faith of the townspeople and merchants in the future of their downtown.

Fashion Island,
Newport Beach, California.

Northgate Shopping Center,
San Rafael, California.

7

ORGANIZATION
OF PRODUCTION

In some ways the production departments (there are three—architectural, structural, and mechanical-electrical—that actually perform the production) of Welton Becket and Associates seem quite similar to those of any large architectural firm which has its own engineering. In other ways, the situation here is quite dissimilar.

As has been stated, the Los Angeles and Chicago offices have engineering and the other offices which do not go to the Los Angeles office or outside consultants for these services.

There is nothing very different about an architectural firm that offers engineering services or one that divides production into three departments in the manner of the Los Angeles and Chicago offices. In the other offices, there is nothing unique about the production departments (only architectural) with engineering provided by outside consultants.

And in any case, the production functions of architectural firms in general are certainly relatively noncontroversial, a state of affairs that is not always true in the case of design or sales. About the only controversy that still arises these days is that between the so-called architectural-engineering firms and those which are strictly architectural. The argument seems to center around the opportunity to provide virtually complete services under one roof. Opposed to this is the argument that architecture is architecture and engineering is engineering; and it is sometimes added that in-house engineering tends to become overorganized and stultified, while the use of outside consultants allows for the choice of the best engineer for the job at hand.

There is probably something to be said in favor of each of these cases, but those who try to blow such small controversies up into hurricanes are at best misguided or uninformed about the facts of life in architecture today.

The real facts probably come closer to this: the firms that are large enough have their own basic engineering—structural, mechanical, and electrical—going outside for the more exotic specialties such as soils engineering; those which are not large enough go outside for some or all of their basic engineering as well as the specialties.

And it follows that when the work becomes large enough and the volume great enough in a specialty such as traffic engineering or acoustics, the large firm will put such people on its staff, assuming it can keep them busy and make their work pay for itself and even produce a modicum of profit.

Thus in the WB&A firm, with over 300 people in Los Angeles, the three major engineering specialties are provided in the house, as they are in Chicago. In the other offices, considerably smaller, there are no engineers on the staff, although New York, with over a hundred people, may soon have to come to grips with this problem.

Possibly there are some other reasons why one architectural firm will have engineers on its staff while another will go outside. For example, some differences exist between the manner in which

architecture is practiced in different sections of the country. And the types of clients an office will attract vary in various sections of the country. In WB&A, these and other factors may be at work to some extent, but the factor that actually determines whether its offices have their own engineering or not seems to be the size of the office.

A glance at the overall WB&A organization chart for Los Angeles, on page 40, reveals how production functions are broken down in this firm. No surprises of major importance here in the fact that architectural production forms a separate department, maybe a minor surprise in the fact that structural is in a separate department from mechanical-electrical. But such an arrangement is not really unusual in architectural firms, some of which have their own people for only one of these specialties, some have two, others all three. The inclusion in the organization of a Production Administration Department probably will be surprising to many.

Engineering will be discussed in the next chapter, but production administration, which has relationships with both architectural and engineering production, belongs in this chapter for reasons of convenience and because it is perhaps more closely related to architecture.

To illustrate how architectural production is organized in the WB&A offices, the situation in Los Angeles will be used as a case in point. Architectural Production in Los Angeles is headed by a vice president, with the title of Director, Alan Rosen. Another veteran, with more than twenty years' service to the firm in every job from office boy up to his present position, Rosen directs the largest department of this office.

As was noted previously, in WB&A, the Design Department handles the services on a project from the beginning stages through the preparation of very complete schematics. For the architectural aspects of projects, architectural production then takes over all phases of the work through preliminaries, working drawings, specifications, and field inspection of construction to the finished building.

Generally, architectural production has five major departments: project architects, drafting, specifications, cost control, and field inspection.

In this firm, the practice on individual projects is to assign a designer to handle that aspect of the work for the design department, reporting to its director, and at the same time or shortly afterward to assign a project architect, from the Architectural Production Department, reporting to its director. A job captain is then assigned to the project architect.

In other words, each project will be headed by a two-man directorate, the designer having jurisdiction over design decisions and factors, the project architect over almost everything else, administration of the project, production, field inspection, and so on. In theory, the project architect has the prime responsibility for contact with the client during the job; in practice, both designer and project architect usually participate with the clients in varying degrees according to what is required at a given time.

The practice of naming a designer and a project architect for each building, with neither really in charge, may seem to be loaded for problems. Certainly it seems to break all the rules of good management; and many architects would shudder at the possibilities for misunderstandings. In some architectural offices, this problem is handled by the appointment of a partner in charge, an executive architect, or by making the project architect the nominal head of the team. In other offices, the functions of project architect and designer are combined in one person.

The WB&A system seems to work out very well in practice in most cases. One reason seems to be that so many of the designers and project architects have been here so long that they have, over the years, worked out real mutual understanding by virtue of long experience with each other. In cases where some important misunderstanding does occur, the arbitors are the directors of architectural production and design, who have worked together for years. They know what to expect from each other and from the people under them and can therefore usually settle a dispute without too much bloodshed.

The Los Angeles office of Production Administration, headed by Vice President Albert Peterson, also has an important role not only in keeping the administration of projects rolling but in avoiding problems with the projects, with clients, and between designers and project architects. Peterson is a veteran of thirty-four years' experience in all phases of architectural services, over twenty of them with the WB&A firm.

His current job involves the overall administration of projects, starting with the owner-architect agreement which would have been handled by the business development people, based on principles worked out over the years and now codified into a system based on the facts of the WB&A practice.

From that point, Production Administration will be deeply involved in each individual project, starting with an analysis of the owner-architect agreement, a delineation of what it means in terms of services to be performed, and the preparation of a detailed budget of man-hours and other costs required to do the work. Working with the project architects, the production administrator sets up procedures for handling reports on the progress of projects and generally performs as the overall administrative contact of the project architects as the various architectural and other functions are being performed.

The Production Administration office takes care of the preparation of consulting agreements required for projects—such things as landscape architecture, acoustics, and the many other specialties not actually performed by WB&A but necessary in specific jobs.

The relationships are a bit complicated, in that project architects report to the Director of Architectural Production and engineering personnel report to the directors of the engineering departments, and all of the technical details of production are handled within those departments. At the same time, there is a lateral relationship between these people and Production Administration, where coordination of all the paperwork takes place and the records are kept. As can be readily imagined, a considerable amount of coordination and cooperation between the heads

Chicago Director of Production David Tamminga and draftman in Chicago drafting room.

New York Office Assistant Director Henry Brennan and Project Architect Frank La Susa.

New York drafting room.

Project Architect Creighton Jones, and James Turner, New York.

of the various production departments is necessary to make this system work.

Production Administration also has a very close relationship with the Corporate Administration Department, under Senior Vice President Furman Myers, Director. In one way the Director of Production Administration reports directly to the director of his office; in another way he reports to Myers, who actually is the top man in all corporate administrative matters. In still another way, the Director of Production Administration also has a close relationship with the Director of Architectural Production. So again, the need for close coordination and cooperation can readily be seen.

After a project architect has been assigned a project, a job captain and draftsmen are assigned from the Drafting Department, headed by Jack Tropiano, chief draftsman, a man who has been with WB&A fifteen years. Specifications are handled in the house by the Specifications Department, under James Zerbe. Reproduction of specs is also handled by a subdepartment under Zerbe.

Cost control is a separate subdepartment in the Architectural Production Department, as are services during construction. It should be noted that a considerable amount of work in the field is done by the project architects, who are expected to get out to their jobs frequently for personal inspection of construction progress. And the designers get out there too as often as they can.

The situation in architectural production in the other offices parallels that of the Los Angeles office in most respects. Each has an Architectural Production Department with its own head, and each is autonomous in that it does not have to go back to the Los Angeles office for direction. Each office has a counterpart of the Los Angeles office Production Administrator, whose job it is to coordinate the reports and other paperwork and perform other functions as in Los Angeles. On the other hand, the offices also feed paper work and reports back to the corporate office for correlation of the entire effort. These go to Furman Myers, the Director of Administration. And he also functions, for the benefit of these offices, in matters of administration much as the design director functions in matter of design—as adviser, consultant, and any other role required for smooth and efficient administration and coordination.

In the Welton Becket and Associates offices other than Los Angeles, architectural production is handled in a similar manner, with some variations between offices mainly because of their size.

All of the offices have similar arrangements for the assignment of project architects to jobs; all assign job captains and draftsmen; in all, specifications are handled by departments within production.

In the methods of assignment of project architects and how they report, all offices are very much alike. These people are assigned early and together with the project designers perform a two-pronged executive and design function for each job.

But there are some dissimilarities between offices. In Los Angeles, for example, it would be rare indeed to find a designer performing any drafting services that would more properly belong under architectural production. In San Francisco and Houston, considerably smaller in size, such functions tend to overlap. In Los Angeles, the designers prepare somewhat elaborate schematics, almost the equivalent of preliminaries in other firms, and the production people translate these into what WB&A calls preliminaries, which are almost partial working drawings in some firms. In the smaller offices, Houston and San Francisco, it is very hard to tell where schematics leave off and preliminaries begin. In fact, many of the designers carry schematics into the preliminary and even the working-drawing stages.

Again, here is an example of the extreme flexibility worked out in this firm between the offices, because of the disparity in size, the personalities of their directors, and the clientele they serve.

But it should be remembered that all of the architectural production departments of all of the WB&A offices are modeled along similar lines. Here there is a division between the work of the designers, who are essentially wed to the more creative specialty of architecture, and of the project architects and others, who are at least affianced to the total world of architecture in all of its aspects.

As in other aspects of the practice carried on by WB&A, the relationships between the offices and between each of them and the corporate office are anything but rigid. While each director of an office runs his own show and offers complete architectural services within his own office or with the help of outside consultants, there exists a considerable amount of overlapping activity between the offices, a considerable amount of interplay between them, exchanges of personnel back and forth, even assignment of a commission obtained by one office to another.

Essentially the offices stand in a cooperative attitude one to the other, free of the competition sometimes found between offices of some other large architectural firms. Yet there is just enough competition in design, production, profitability, and other aspects to make each office unique in its own way, although closely tied to the large Los Angeles office and resembling it to some extent. There are checks and balances the corporate headquarters applies to the offices. The most important of these in the present discussion is the position of the Corporate Director of Administration to the administrative people in the other offices.

Taken all in all, the architectural production department of WB&A is organized much like its counterparts in other large architectural firms across the country. The role of the project architect may be a little different here from that in some firms, and the fact that he is assigned to production is somewhat unusual. Also the division of authority between designers and project architects may seem somewhat strange; however, it seems to work out very well.

The office of Production Administration is an innovation here without a counterpart in most other firms and plays a strong role in steering projects in the right direction.

How all of these things come together in the actual handling of the services for projects is examined in detail in later chapters.

Houston Director of Administration John Rust.

LEFT AND BELOW: *Director of Architectural Production David Morris of Houston, with Gil Thweatt.*

Morris with Pleas Doyle.

61

Pauley Pavilion, University of
California at Los Angeles.

Memorial Sports Arena,
Los Angeles, California.

62

8
ORGANIZATION
OF ENGINEERING

The provisions within the Los Angeles office for mechanical and electrical engineering have existed for years, but for several reasons structural services were always provided by outside consultants even in this office until 1969.

This is a bit out of the ordinary among architectural firms who perform any part of the engineering services themselves. Many firms, when the time comes to add engineers to their staffs, ordinarily start with the structural functions since they always seem to be so closely related to the architectural functions.

In the case of WB&A, it didn't work out that way. Perhaps the main reason was Welton Becket's early realization that the systems involved in mechanical and electrical engineering were growing in size, complexity, and cost to the point where they were rapidly becoming a major consideration in most of the building types being handled by the firm. And, importantly, he also recognized that these systems could be extremely important factors in the success or failure of a building design. Anyhow, a number of years ago, the M&E Department was founded, and Paul Sessinghaus, now Senior Vice President and Director of Mechanical and Electrical Engineering, came into the firm in 1945.

Another factor in operation during the years before 1969 obviated the necessity of on-staff structural engineers. This was one of those out-of-the-ordinary happenings that seemed part of the style of Welton Becket. For years, some one-half to two-thirds of all of the structural work of WB&A was handled by an outside firm of consultants, Stacy and Meadville, and its predecessor firms going all the way back to the end of World War II. Some years ago, Stacy and Meadville moved in as tenants of WB&A. They have been there ever since, working closely with the Becket organization, doing most of its structural work, readily available right in the building. Thus, for many years, there seemed to be no good reason for WB&A to start its own structural department, capitalize it, and support it; after all, it had the equivalent of a built-in department without doing these things.

Early in 1969, the climate seemed right to all concerned for the acquisition of Stacy and Meadville by WB&A, and the long-time outside structural consultants became a department of the architectural firm. At the present time, then, the Los Angeles office of WB&A provides complete engineering services in the major specialties while the other offices, with the exception of Chicago, do not.

Organizationally this means that the Los Angeles and Chicago offices production setups differ somewhat from those in the other offices. In Los Angeles and Chicago, there are three major production departments—architectural, mechanical-electrical, and structural. In the other offices there are only architectural production departments.

As is true in architectural production, the engineering production department directors report directly to the office directors but have a lateral relationship with the administration department and with production administration, as was explained in Chapter 7.

The structure of the mechanical-electrical department and that of structural are similar in many respects but in the interest of completeness each is described separately here. Again the organization in Los Angeles will be utilized for this discussion, since that in Chicago is similar.

The Los Angeles Mechanical-Electrical Department, directed by Paul Sessinghaus, is subdivided into two major departments, one for each of the engineering specialties involved. The Mechanical Department is headed by Vice President and Chief Mechanical Engineer Ivan Garet; the Electrical Department by Vice President and Chief Electrical Engineer G. Bradley Karr.

The two departments are very similar in almost every respect. Each includes engineers and draftsmen trained and experienced in the specialty of the department. Each has specification writers who handle the mechanical or electrical sections of the specs. And each has field men who oversee work of the subcontractors who construct and equip the mechanical or electrical components of the buildings.

The benefits to WB&A of having mechanical and electrical handled by its own people in Los Angeles have been many. Perhaps the greatest benefit has come from the opportunity for these people, who are often responsible for 30 to 50 percent of the cost of buildings, to be deeply involved in the design and decision-making processes very early in the game. Instead of calling in the mechanical and electrical engineers after many of the major design decisions have already been made and the design has started to become frozen, in WB&A the engineers get into the act from the beginning.

This has had a very healthy effect on the work of everyone in the firm. In this way, these engineers play a more creative role than might be true otherwise. And buildings come together in all their parts, the mechanical and electrical, as well as the architectural, much more smoothly and efficiently than might otherwise be the case. Clients get fewer surprises. There is less reworking of drawings. Time is saved during the entire process. And the systems are better integrated into the buildings. All of which, of course, makes for better buildings and for total design rather than architectural solutions into which the heating, air-conditioning, lighting, power, and other systems have somehow been made to fit.

Having mechanical and electrical engineers and other engineering personnel continuously available and involved in the work pays big dividends for the firm in other ways. With the engineers—essentially doers, usually practical—continuously exposed to the architects, particularly to the designers—essentially dreamers, often impractical—a very important relationship between points of view has been established and maintained. And the clients and their buildings are the beneficiaries of the times when the points of view clash as well as when they coincide.

Another advantage, of almost incalculable value to WB&A, derived from having its own mechanical and electrical people, stems from the fact that in E&M, as in other departments, people tend to stay on for very long periods of time. In this way, a continuity of effort is achieved here which benefits the entire firm and which is almost without parallel among architectural firms.

WB&A has over the years been able to attract and hold engineers in spite of the great opportunities available, particularly to electrical and mechanical engineers, in industry. Quite a large number of these professionals have been with WB&A ten to fifteen years. Many stay here because they feel work on buildings to be more satisfying than other types of engineering available to them and they find the working conditions, benefits, and salaries equal or superior to those to be found working for another architectural firm or for a consulting engineering firm. And importantly, in this firm, engineers are accepted as professionals who are very necessary to the success of total design.

It should be pointed out at this juncture that while only the Los Angeles and Chicago offices have their own mechanical and electrical people, a considerable amount of this type of work is handled by Los Angeles for the other offices. The amount varies somewhat between offices, very little being done for New York, some for Houston, quite a bit for San Francisco. On the other hand, there are times when the mechanical-electrical department becomes so overloaded that some of its work must be farmed out to consultants even in Los Angeles.

The Director of Mechanical-Electrical also performs another important service for the other offices, one that his counterparts in other divisions also perform. This is the role of adviser and consultant to the regional offices on matters within his field of work. The director makes a number of trips each year to the other offices, as do some of his staff members, to take a look at the engineering there. And people from the other offices come back to the Los Angeles office with drawings and other information for review when necessary or for counseling.

In addition, the director and his chief mechanical and electrical engineers spend some time with consulting engineers working with the other offices, in order to assure that outside work will be in line with principles and criteria that have been established for the firm as a whole. In this way, the work of all engineers working WB&A projects can be kept up to the standards that have been set for such work.

As has been noted, the firm has had mechanical and electrical people on the staff almost from its inception back in the days of Wurdeman and Becket.

The addition of structural people to the staff took place in 1969. Before that another alternative solved the problem in what must be a somewhat unusual manner. A structural engineer, Murray Erick, who had been in private practice since 1923, started working closely with the Becket organization in the forties. As time went on, this engineering firm became more and more closely identified with WB&A and, as the years went by, came to do the majority of its structural work.

Los Angeles Director of Structural Engineering Jack Meadville.

Structural engineers, Los Angeles office.

Assistant Director of Structural Engineering Richard Troy.

Meadville with Arthur Stacy.

Chicago Director of Structural Engineering Walter Goebert, right.

Chicago Director of Mechanical and Electrical Engineering Rudolph Houkal.

Engineering offices, Chicago.

Typical regional office drafting room.

Over the years, Clarence Stacy and James Skinner became principals in the firm; when Erick died, its name changed to Stacy and Skinner in the late fifties. Jack Meadville became a principal, after the death of Skinner in the sixties, and the firm became Stacy and Meadville, in 1965. During these years, the engineering firm continued to do most of the Becket structural work.

Early in 1969, the timing and the idea seemed right, and Stacy and Meadville was merged into WB&A to form a forty-man structural division under the directorship of Clarence Stacy with Jack Meadville as Assistant Director. In mid-1969, Stacy died, after a short illness, and Meadville assumed the position of Director of Structural Engineering in the Becket Los Angeles organization. Stacy's son, Arthur Stacy, became an Assistant Director, as did Richard Troy. All three are Vice Presidents.

A structural division within the firm's organization seems to make a great deal of sense. The concept of total design certainly must, by its nature, include this phase of architectural services. Looking back on it now, the only reason that seems plausible for not including such a department before this seems to have been the close and unique relationships that had held WB&A and the outside structural firm together for so many years. The new arrangement shows every possibility of being even better than the old and does much to round out the philosophy of total design.

As to organization, the Structural Department is pretty much modeled after that of the Mechanical-Electrical Division. With Meadville, as director, reporting to the office director, the department has on staff structural engineers and designers, structural draftsmen, specification writers, and field inspection people. In addition, the engineers here ordinarily handle quantities of structural items on the jobs to which they are assigned, instead of going outside for services of this type.

All in all, the addition of the Structural Department to WB&A rounds out the engineering services that can be handled for clients in the Los Angeles office. While structural for the other offices was almost always handled by engineers in their own localities in the past, there is now the distinct possibility that some of this work may eventually be handled in the house.

The organization of the engineering production departments in the Chicago office follows along the lines of their counterparts in Los Angeles. In Chicago, the Mechanical and Electrical Production Department is headed by Rudolph Houkal, Jr., Vice President and Director, and the Structural Production Department by Walter Goebert, also a Vice President and Director of the Department. Each has a complete operation in the specialty named, very similar to that in Los Angeles with the exception that in Chicago there is a complete department for field services, while in Los Angeles these functions are handled by people in the engineering production departments.

The organization then of the engineering divisions is quite straightforward; the details of how they perform their work and mesh it with that of the other WB&A divisions are discussed in later chapters.

Beach Facilities and Life Guard Station, Santa Monica, California.

Canyon Village, Yellowstone National Park, Wyoming.

9
ORGANIZATION
OF SPECIAL FUNCTIONS

As with so many aspects of the Welton Becket organization, it is not easy to describe the interests of the firm in endeavors that would be considered special functions by most architectural firms.

In a manner of speaking, there exists no real organization here for projects like specialized design of hospitals or other buildings types, foreign work, or other unusual endeavors. On the other hand, there have been times in the firm's history when the attempt has been made, and abandoned, to set up specialized departments of one kind or another. A few of these attempts have been long-lasting like the recently abolished department for store planning. But most experiments of this kind (such as the attempt to departmentalize the practice by building type, tried some ten or so years ago) were indulged in for only a short period of time and then abandoned.

In Welton Becket and Associates, the era of departments of medical planning, hotel and apartment house planning, and commercial planning, each with its own director, has come and gone. Yet something of value was retained from these experiments—the specialized knowledge acquired by the firm during the time and the competence gained in the various building types. Another factor of considerable mo-

ment that has lasted has been the people who were deeply involved in the building-type departmental organization of the fifties. For example, medical-building expert Harry Widman, and Bob Haller, expert on hotel buildings.

Over the years, since the specialized-building-type organization was tried and given up, a very large number of people now in the firm have been so deeply engrossed in various other specialized subjects and have worked on so many buildings of one type or more, that many other specialists abound in the firm. For the most part, though, these people have not become so completely involved with one specialty that they have lost their effectiveness in dealing with other areas or with other building types.

On the contrary, what happens is that a project architect like Clyde Whitlow will be placed by circumstances, by the work in the office, and even by choice or temperament, in a position to become deeply involved in work with building codes. This does not mean that he spends all of his time with this work or that he will not be assigned as a project architect to buildings of various types. What it does mean is that, in addition to his regular work, Whitlow has also become a specialist able to take on the task of participating in the rewriting of entire codes, or writing portions of them, when the occasion demands it. And it means that he can take on the task of masterminding an entirely new code such as the one he handled for the Walt Disney World area near Orlando, Florida.

In a similar way, Chicago Design Director Art Love has become an expert in airport analysis and design, especially airports for the hypersonic and jumbo jets of the future, without relinquishing his role in the design of projects of other types.

And so on, throughout the firm. The huge amount of work accomplished here, the great number of projects, the enormous size and complexity of some of them, the large number of people on staff and their varied backgrounds, training, and capabilities—all contribute to the making of experts in many unusual, even rare, phases of architectural work. Yet, in this firm these experts do not ordinarily retreat into a corner to practice their acquired specialties to the exclusion of being architects in the largest meaning of the word.

Just as having the opportunity to participate deeply in aspects of architecture that are out of the ordinary develops experts in these areas within the firm, so does the knowledge thus developed help the firm acquire unusual commissions and perform services for them.

Some projects of this sort are shown and discussed in other chapters. For example, Walt Disney World has been mentioned here as an example of how specialized knowledge in code writing can be applied. The same project might also be cited for various other reasons; master planning of an unusual sort, design of prefabricated bathrooms, design of five hotels each tied to a culture—contemporary, Persian, Polynesian, Venetian, and Asian.

Also shown and discussed elsewhere are such activities of the firm as the analysis and design of a hypersonic airport accomplished as a research project, sans client, because the firm felt it had the know-how and there was a need for the study. Another example is the Welton Becket Research Center, discussed in another chapter; another, the hung stadium, also shown elsewhere. Many other examples might be cited, but perhaps these are sufficient to demonstrate the work on special projects.

WB&A actually does not have an organization neatly plugged into a chart for projects of the unusual sort; almost everyone here participates in them at one time or another, in one capacity or another. Because of this, perhaps the easiest way to get a view of how these things happen would be to describe, in some detail, one such project and one man's experience with it.

Interior designer Scollard Maas was assigned to work on the Manila Hilton Hotel for a number of reasons—experience, temperament, interest, and so on—but the reason of importance here is that Maas had been deeply involved in other jobs similar to Manila and had become an expert of sorts in an unusual type of work, handling the interiors of foreign hotels, designed for a U.S. international hotel chain but owned by nationals of the country in which they are built.

And to demonstrate further the degree of this specialization, these hotels were to have every modern convenience world travelers have come to expect, yet they were also expected to be indigenous in design to the countries in which located, to utilize native materials to the largest extent possible, to be built, furnished, and decorated by native workmen, craftsmen, artisans or artists as might be required for the accomplishment of the work.

Scollard Maas came into the Manila Hilton job early in its design stages and handled the interiors from that point right through to the actual manufacture or purchase of the items and their installation in the hotel. The reason for his assignment (now the point of view of this chapter) was experience that led to specialized knowledge in an unusual field. He had spent five years working on the Nile Hilton, in Cairo, at the site. And he had repeated his role there on other hotels in foreign countries.

In all, Maas was to spend some three years in Manila, less than he had in Cairo, but then the Suez War had held things up in Egypt for quite a while.

But to start at the beginning, the Manila Hilton project was handled out of the New York office of WB&A, and there the major portions of the design were accomplished. This was to be total design in the ultimate sense of that phrase: architecture, engineering, landscaping, interiors, right down to the smallest details of uniforms for personnel, china, ashtrays, the logotype. Associated with the Becket organization in the work was architect Carlos Arguelles of the Philippines, who had been a WB&A project architect during the fifties. The hotel operator was to be Hilton International in New York and the owners the Delgado family of Manila.

The hotel was to be constructed, as completely as possible, of native materials, using local contractors, labor, and suppliers. The charge from the owners and the operators was to make the hotel sophisticated, complete, and indigenous. WB&A had done projects of this sort before, in Cairo, in Havana—total design abroad with native materials and workmen. As in the previous cases, the decision was to complete the architectural and engineering design to the extent possible in the United States, make the overall, prime decisions about interiors and other details there, and then send a top designer to complete the work on the spot.

Thus Maas got the assignment and went to Manila to live with the project for many long months. He had some surprises waiting for him. First, the beauty of Manila—the tropical atmosphere, the harbor. Most of all, the sunsets; he agrees with others who have seen the sunsets that they are indescribable. Then there was the heat.

The Filipinos themselves held a great number of surprises in store for him. Worldly, educated, cultured, wealthy—these were his impressions of great numbers of the Filipinos he met. Most spoke English, and many French or other European languages. Many had been educated in Europe.

But perhaps the greatest surprise of all was when Maas quickly discovered, as he puts it, "All of these people are hep." No problems here like those of Cairo, when thousands of workmen were required

These six views of the interior of the Manila Hilton give some indication of the rich and varied treatment made possible through the very close attention to each detail of the furniture and furnishings and to their design and production.

to handle the simplest construction. Manila had up-to-date contractors, equipped with modern machinery, and trained workmen in all of the usual building trades. He had some inkling of what was in store for him, from reading, from hearsay, but the impact of Manila and the Philippines was considerably different from what he had expected.

He had one further major surprise yet to come—from what he had heard, the Filipinos were very good artisans and artists. And he knew that many people in the country collected fine china and other art objects—in fact some had amassed the best collections of their sort in the world, in Chinese porcelains, for example. What came as a great shock was that the artists and artisans only did certain limited things and the collectors were most taken with the pursuit of art other than that which had deep roots in the Philippines.

The artisans made beautiful linen, of course, as everyone knows, but only of light materials, no upholstery or curtain fabrics. No one used the fine natural fibers available everywhere here. No one cared very much about the Spanish colonial furniture to be found almost everywhere. No one was excited about the beautiful shells that abound in the area.

As Maas puts it, "These people are educated and sophisticated, and they like good things. But at that time, if it was local, it just couldn't be good or exciting." Maas himself was dismayed, but very excited about the prospects for the interiors and other details of the hotel.

He then proceeded to stir things up a bit. Starting with Spanish colonial antique furniture: he began to buy every piece he could get his hands on. Of course, it did not take too long for the word to get around about what he was up to. And the prices started to skyrocket. Everyone wanted to get in the act, and soon there had been established a whole new Manila market in Spanish colonial antiques. But not before Maas had been successful in gathering together quite a collection for the new hotel. As a result, it is now possible to reserve a room in the Manila Hilton furnished with furniture that is the real thing, the best of its era.

Another by-product of the pursuit of Spanish antiques has been an increased awareness of the possibilities in the manufacture of indigenous Philippine furniture. As it happened, this was an idea that had found its time, and Filipinos jumped at the chance to establish furniture factories to handle the demand generated by the Manila Hilton and by the other major hotels that were built at approximately the same time in Manila. Thus another new industry was born in the country.

Maas was taken from the first with the beauty and variety of seashells available in the country. Many of these were to be used in the hotel in various forms, in lamps, in frames, for pictures and mirrors, and in other ways. He was surprised at first to find such an important and beautiful natural resource overlooked by the Filipinos. But this is often the case everywhere—when a thing is readily available and costs little, it is often reckoned to be cheap and undesirable, which are not the same things at all. Naturally, this triggered a new interest, among Fili-pinos, in the natural beauty and other attributes of their native shells to be found on all their many great beaches.

In need of fabrics of various kinds for the hotel, Maas sought out the native weavers and artisans in this field. Again he was surprised to find how talented the people doing this work were—and he was even more surprised to find an American woman working with the Filipinos to further develop the art.

The weavers here worked with light fibers of flax and wove wonderful linens for handkerchiefs, blouses, and similar things. No upholstery fabrics; no curtain fabrics. Only woven patterns, no silk screening or other methods of developing patterns. No use of the native fibers in fabrics. Wallpaper in small quantities, yes, but nothing like the quantity needed for a major hotel. Maas found the quality of all of this work very good indeed, but the artisans did the same designs over and over, out of the same materials. They felt no calling to be either experimental or inventive.

The challenge was too exciting to ignore, and Maas went to work to see what could be made out of the situation. Eventually, he found an American woman who had been working with the Filipino weavers and other artisans, helping them to adapt their native ability and the wide array of materials available to new designs and methods. She had found a Chinese who was teaching the Filipinos silk-screen printing on fabrics and wallpaper, something they had no experience with. And she had started some of the artisans on experimental work in various materials. Maas teamed up with these people to produce various things for the hotel, including woven fabrics for upholstery and curtains using heavy linens together with natural fibers and silk-screened prints for fabrics and wallpaper.

As time went on, Maas was to spend many hours working with the Filipino craftsmen and artisans, teaching them, experimenting with them, searching for native materials of value, cajoling and directing the workmen.

During his time in the Philippines, Maas of course reported back regularly to the Becket office in New York which had the overall responsibility for the project. In addition, he kept in close touch with the Director of Design, Maynard Woodard, in Los Angeles. By working closely with the associated architect, Carlos Arguelles, the interior detailing was handled in Manila to elevations that had previously been prepared in New York.

Several times Maas had to go back to New York to keep the work going properly and to review the progress and problems of the Manila Hilton with the director of the office and with other WB&A people. And on several occasions WB&A people, including Welton Becket, came to Manila to observe progress at the site.

The result was a hotel, sophisticated, modern in every way, luxurious to a degree, in which almost every item of furniture or furnishings was made of beautiful native materials by Filipino workmen in designs done specifically for the hotel. A very revealing example of the lengths to which the WB&A firm will go to achieve total design.

Mutual Benefit Life Insurance Company, San Francisco, California.

OPPOSITE: *Xerox Square, Rochester, New York.*

Part Three

THE BUSINESS OF TOTAL DESIGN

*California Teachers Association,
Burlingame, California.*

76

10
MANAGEMENT
FOR ARCHITECTURE

Management of an architectural firm as large as Welton Becket and Associates entails many of the problems and details that management of any large, complex corporation would include. However, in architectural practice, the service aspects of the work and its somewhat intangible nature combine to make management even more difficult than might be the case, say, in a company manufacturing furniture. Perhaps a large share of the management problems that arise in architecture come from the fact that design must be transposed into contract documents,

which are then translated into actual buildings by contractors.

In the case of the furniture manufacturer, the entire process can be carried out by one organization, often under one roof. This makes possible close cooperation between those who research the product, those who design it, and those who actually produce it. Long experience, one department with the other, and the many opportunities for comparison of the actual production results of one design against another can effectively improve the work not

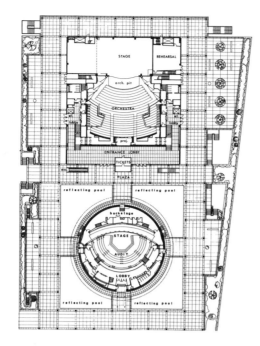

MARK TAPER FORUM & AHMANSON THEATRE

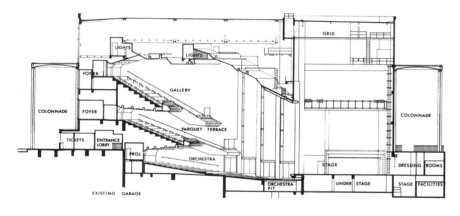

AHMANSON THEATRE

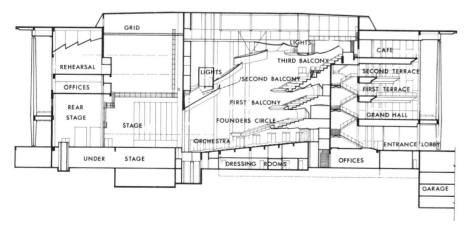

DOROTHY CHANDLER PAVILION

only of the designers but of the producers. And mutual respect between departments can be nurtured and improved as time goes on.

In an architectural firm, there is not enough opportunity for the growth of mutual respect between those who design and those who actually produce the final product—the contractors and workmen (rather than those called "production" people in architectural firms but who are not actually the producers of the final product).

In Welton Becket and Associates, considerable effort is expended to overcome the difficulties in managing a large service organization offering the intangibles that are architecture. Because of this, a great many aspects of this organization are reminiscent of those to be found in nonarchitectural organizations.

First of all, Welton Becket and Associates has a corporate structure, very much like that of other corporations in other fields. Here, there is a board of directors acting in the area of top policy decision making, a president, charged with running the actual operations of the company, a corporate headquarters with top staff, and what might be termed, in another business, operating subsidiaries in five cities spread across the United States.

Also very much like corporations in other fields is the Welton Becket and Associates executive committee composed of top corporate officers plus the directors of the five operating offices. And though the corporate project review board here may not have an exact counterpart in other industries, it could be likened to a quality control board at a high corporate level in a manufacturing concern. In a similar manner, the coordinating committees in the five operating offices could be compared in many ways to committees of a similar sort in subsidiaries of a manufacturing company.

The five offices are autonomous to an extent, in the way that subsidiaries of a manufacturing firm might be. The five offices receive certain overall services from the corporate office and report to the top officers, again rather like a manufacturer with subsidiaries. And the five offices cooperate with each other in certain ways, in this too maintaining the parallel with a manufacturing firm with subsidiaries. Then it should be said that Welton Becket and Associates resembles a manufacturing firm in that it runs its business as a business under the same kinds of controls, restraints, checks and balances as any well-run corporation. And Welton Becket and Associates brings to its business operations the same sort of executive abilities, attention to detail, and growth-oriented philosophies as a well-run corporation, one that is progressive and growth-minded, in another field.

Many other similarities between the organizational patterns and management methods of Welton Becket and Associates and firms in other fields might be cited. On the other hand, since the Becket firm is engaged in architecture, there are a considerable number of differences too. It should be borne in mind that an architectural firm, by the nature of the services it provides, can never really be entirely organized and managed like a product manufacturer.

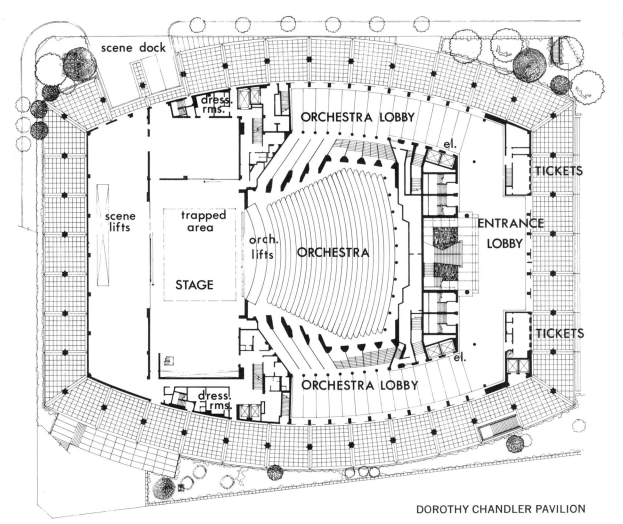

In the plans shown on these pages may be seen two fundamentals of the scheme developed for the Los Angeles Music Center. As may be seen, the most basic decision was to develop three completely separate theaters, each tailored to its purpose, and to relate each to the others with arcades, a great plaza and similarities in exterior treatment.

scene dock

dress. rms.

ORCHESTRA LOBBY

TICKETS

scene lifts

trapped area

orch. lifts

ORCHESTRA

ENTRANCE LOBBY

STAGE

el.

el.

TICKETS

dress. rms.

ORCHESTRA LOBBY

DOROTHY CHANDLER PAVILION

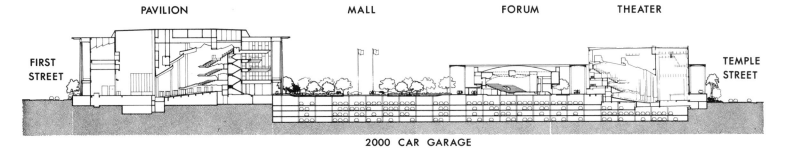

PAVILION MALL FORUM THEATER

FIRST STREET

TEMPLE STREET

2000 CAR GARAGE

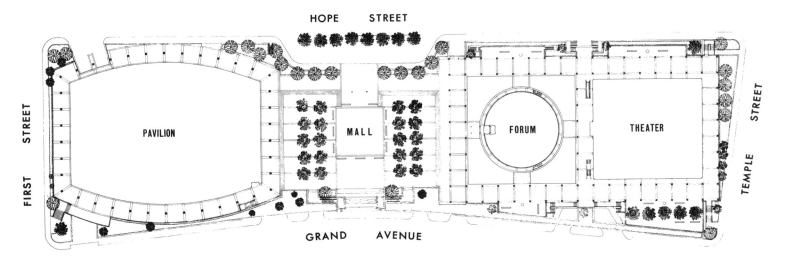

HOPE STREET

FIRST STREET

PAVILION MALL FORUM THEATER

TEMPLE STREET

GRAND AVENUE

79

Here and on the next two pages may be seen some of the aspects of total design in action, the architecture of the exterior and of the interior having been handled by Welton Becket and Associates, along with the complete interior design including selection or design of all of the furniture and other furnishings.

80

The major aspects of the organization for management of Welton Becket and Associates at the corporate and individual office levels have been pointed out in previous chapters, as well as the prime tenets of management at those high levels. Perhaps, it would be appropriate and helpful to examine some of the details of management at this point.

First, since architectural services are mainly effected by the people who perform them, a look at the policies in the personnel area is in order. It will be seen that the policies here are similar to those in industry or other businesses. On a comparative basis, some of the benefits available to employees are much better than those elsewhere in architecture, while other benefits are about the same as those in most other medium to large firms. Still others are really not quite up to the level of benefits in some of the better architectural offices.

One thing that should be said, though, is that in Welton Becket and Associates the whole area of benefits has been worked out to constitute a total package that very few architects can match.

The situation here in salaries can be very simply stated: salaries are competitive with those in other architectural offices in the geographical areas served by the five offices. In other words, one man here might make a little more than he would in some other architectural office or a little less. But the average comes out about the same. This leaves out the situation on bonus and profit-sharing arrangements, but more about these later.

Vacation and sick leave policies are rather strict and are probably on a par with those in other architectural offices, though they certainly linger behind the more liberal policies of many companies and organizations in other fields. Here, an employee accrues five-sixths of a day a month vacation time after six months' employment; or ten days a year. When he has been on the job for five years or more, he gets fifteen days a year; after fifteen years, he gets four weeks. That is it. And vacations must be taken within the twelve months after they are earned. No accumulation after the twelve months is allowed, except when demands of the work make a vacation impossible.

Sick leave, after six months' employment, is accumulated at one day per month of work for salaried people and at half that rate for those paid by the hour. Sick leave can be accumulated indefinitely.

Welton Becket and Associates has quite a complete insurance program for its employees. The basic coverage in life insurance amounts to $3,000 on each employee completely paid for by Welton Becket and Associates with additional amounts available, based on earnings, paid for by the employees themselves at low group rates. This policy also covers accidental death and dismemberment. In addition, employees may apply for amounts of life insurance through the group plan of AIA at low rates. The first coverage mentioned is available after sixty days' employment; the second after ninety days'.

Accident insurance is taken out on each employee in the amount of $10,000, paid for by Welton Becket and Associates, with additional amounts available and paid for by the employees. A salary continuance

plan is available to all employees, at low rates paid by them. In addition, disability insurance under the laws of the states where the offices are located is carried providing an additional weekly benefit during periods of disablement.

The hospitalization and surgical policy of Welton Becket and Associates covers all employees, after sixty days, for expenses of this sort and includes a major medical feature. Paid for by the firm for its employees, similar coverage may also be obtained for dependents at minimal cost to employees. Of course, the legal requirements of the various states in which Welton Becket and Associates practices and of the federal government are met in the areas of unemployment insurance, workmen's compensation, social security, and the like.

In 1956, Welton Becket and Associates initiated one of the first complete profit-sharing and retirement plans in the architectural profession. This is a funded and qualified plan. All employees are eligible after $4\frac{1}{2}$ years of continuous employment, providing they are below the age of sixty when they reach the eligibility stage.

All the money deposited in the plan comes from Welton Becket and Associates; no employee contributions are required. The amounts placed in the fund each year are related to the financial performance of the firm for the year but are limited by the charter of the plan to no more than 15 percent of the salary of each individual.

The funds in the plan are invested under the direction of the firm's Profit Sharing Administration Committee, with the aid of investment and legal advisers.

The benefits from this plan to an employee include, in addition to the retirement payments, amounts payable to him if he leaves the firm for any reason other than being fired for a criminal act and amounts payable to him if he is disabled or to his estate or heirs if he dies. An employee's vested interest in the amount in the plan in his name at any given time is based on the years he has been in the plan. After the first year, he holds a 10 percent vested interest, and each year following up to ten he receives another 10 percent until he owns the entire amount at the end of the tenth year and thereafter.

One method of payout under this plan once an employee is eligible for payments because of retirement, disability, or otherwise is to pay off his interest in quarterly installments over five years. However, the usual method is payment in a lump sum.

How much retirement pay then can an employee expect under this plan? As is usual in such cases, it is very difficult to say, there being so many variables in the amount put into the plan in given years, the salary differences between people, the changes in salary over the years, the number of years in the plan, the degree of success in investments of the funds in the plan.

In order to demonstrate how the plan works, a hypothetical case might be discussed. Let's say that a draftsman comes to work in the firm six months after his thirty-fifth birthday. He becomes eligible for participation when he turns forty. He is then making $10,000 a year, but promotions and salary increases

Another aspect of the total design performed by Welton Becket and Associates for the Music Center is in the area of industrial design. All of the items of dinnerware, china, tapestries, rugs, chandeliers and so on were either selected by the Welton Becket and Associates people or designed by them for production on special order by artisans.

THE MUSIC CENTER
OF LOS ANGELES COUNTY
DEDICATION WEEK
APRIL 9 THROUGH APRIL 15, 1967

DOROTHY CHANDLER PAVILION | MARK TAPER FORUM | AHMANSON THEATRE

The Music Center Building Fund,
Suite 300, Union Bank,
325 West 8th Street,
Los Angeles 14, California.

at a regular rate over the next twenty years mean he is making $20,000 at age sixty. In every year, assume that the maximum of 15 percent of his salary was credited to his account. At age sixty, he would have approximately $45,000 vested for the principal credited alone. In addition, because of money forfeited by those employees who left the firm before complete vesting and because of the growth of the funds through wise and prudent investment, he would actually have considerably more than $45,000. Assuming that growth added $15,000 to the account, the employee would have $60,000 fully vested.

It should be noted that what has been discussed here would not exactly fit any specific case, but it does give some indication of the retirement benefits available to employees through the Welton Becket and Associates plan. If this employee had died at any time, the entire amount that had been credited to him at the time of his death would have been paid to his beneficiaries. If he had become disabled during that period, the entire credited amount at the time of disablement would have become his property.

It should be remembered, as is usual in such plans, that the money deposited to the account of employees is tax-free to them until they actually withdraw funds from the plan.

In addition to the profit-sharing and retirement plan, Welton Becket and Associates has a liberal cash bonus plan. Ordinarily paid at Christmastime of each year, bonuses are awarded to employees on the basis of merit, although longevity, position, and so on play some part. In the years when Welton Becket was the sole owner of the firm, awarding bonuses was a singularly personal sort of activity, accurately reflecting this man and his deep-rooted philosophies. In effect, he decided each year on a total percentage of the firm's profits which was to be distributed in bonuses to the employees who had contributed to the making of the profits. Then he would sit down with a list of these people and carefully allocate amounts of Christmas bonus to each. At times, he asked for the advice of other executives of the firm, but in the end the amounts reflected his own personal judgment as to the worth of each person's contribution to the success of the firm. Although the amounts were never made public inside or outside the firm, it can be said that trusted employees of long standing and in positions of trust and confidence might have received bonuses in amounts that approached or even exceeded their salaries.

The cash bonus arrangements have been continued, but now the judgments are made in a more organizational manner; but recommendations from department heads still come to the president, who makes the final decisions.

As has been pointed out, the benefits to employees in the Becket firm are considerable. And few architectural offices can match them. Because of this, people tend to stick here. But there are other important reasons for this also, reasons not so easy to ascertain or understand. The working conditions are good, the atmosphere informal—this is a shirt-sleeve working force. And there is considerable *esprit,* more of a sense of working toward common goals than might be the case in most other organizations.

Dorothy Chandler Pavilion Grand Hall, The Music Center for the Performing Arts, Los Angeles, California.

Eight slides, selected at random, from the Welton Becket and Associates Sound/Slide presentation to prospective clients. The complete show has eighty slides beginning with accomplishments of the firm in the past, each expressing some service of importance, and proceeds into the scope of the services available to clients and how they are performed.

11
BUSINESS DEVELOPMENT

There was a time when architects habitually assumed the attitude that the world—and clients—would eventually hear about their great works and beat a path to the door. But that was long ago. And it never did work very well even then.

The slightest attention to the history of architectural practice, even in its earliest eras, will reveal architects selling their services to pharaohs, kings, wealthy merchants, and others. Yet the myth that architects need not sell their services persists even down to the present.

It is not too difficult to find architects today who make grandiose claims about clients seeking them out, eager to hand them commissions, while the architects themselves make no effort at all to seek out the clients. Or architects who say they refuse to take any of the commissions offered unless they carry with them the highest fees, the largest budgets, and the promise of glory—for the architects.

Needless to say, this is not the way architects ordinarily obtain commissions today, although it must be admitted that a client will walk in cold once in a while into almost every architectural office.

On the contrary, architects today—most of them, nearly all the successful ones—are deeply engaged in what is commonly called in other quarters "sales." Of course, some architects also call the process sales

but many prefer to soften the connotations of that word into some phrase which to their ears sounds more professional, or less businesslike.

Call it what they will, the commonly accepted term for the process of obtaining a buyer for what you have to offer is *sales*. Or perhaps it really should be called "marketing," although that word implies considerably more talent, knowledge, and ability in this area than most architects have.

In any other field but architecture (and maybe a few others that must sell their services), a complete marketing plan would be composed of many things. Definition of the universe, preparation of prospect lists, product test marketing, preparation of a marketing plan and budgeting for its implementation, advertising, public relations, direct selling with presentations, personal contact, and by letter and telephone. And other items.

Architects in general find it quite difficult, if not impossible, to generate such an overall marketing plan and put it into action. In the first place, many architects somehow have the uneasy feeling, sometimes voiced but often not, that there is something unprofessional, even slightly dishonest, about sales and marketing. To them, such endeavors smack of hucksterism or worse. So if they approach the subject in any meaningful way, it is with distaste.

And then there are the prohibitions inherent in the code of ethics of architects preventing them from advertising their services. While the impact of this varies from time to time, the overall effect has usually been the prohibition of advertising in any form, even "compliments" in a high school yearbook, prohibition of boldface listings in the yellow pages, denial of the right to have the architect's picture or any hint of endorsement in product ads depicting his buildings, even a prohibition against sending a direct-mail piece to people who are potential clients but who are not personally known to the architect.

This is not the time or place to discuss these restrictions on architects, but it is important that they be mentioned here as they place almost insurmountable obstacles before an architect who attempts a complete marketing plan along the lines of those used in almost every other type of business.

And it is not only the restrictions on advertising that cause trouble. The prohibitions that apply to advertising and the widespread feeling among architects that sales and marketing are somehow degrading or unprofessional make for suspicion and soulsearching in any architectural firm which tries to develop an overall marketing plan. More times than not, the result falls far short of what would be most effective for the firm.

In addition to the problems inherent in architectural marketing caused by ethics and other aspects mentioned above, or maybe because of them, another important obstacle looms before the firm attempting a complete marketing plan. The shortage, almost complete lack, of architects who know marketing principles and can perform in this area.

Perhaps this could be overcome very well in most cases by going outside the profession, finding top marketing and sales people to bring into architectural firms. But even in this, there are quirks in the backgrounds and temperament of architects, and even in some of their ethics, written or understood, even in the registration, licensing, corporation, or other laws under which some of them operate.

For example, in many jurisdictions an architectural firm would be prevented by custom, by law, or by both from bringing in a top marketing executive as a partner or stockholder. Short of this, no firm can hope to attract such people from other endeavors where they can, theoretically at least, climb to the top of the ladder if they are good enough.

Thus the architectural profession, and the firms practicing architecture, find themselves on the horns of a dilemma—some observers think the position is almost schizophrenic.

On one side of the dilemma, the facts are plain: architecture has become big business (although some architects won't admit it is business at all); buildings have become bigger, more complex, more costly. Architectural services have broadened considerably, to the point where no one person can master them all. The biggest and best clients have tended to become groups, corporations, institutions, governmental agencies, rather than individuals. And for the most part, these are businessmen, comfortable among others of their kind, not quite so much at home among idealists, artists, intellectuals.

Most architects would probably agree that this is the way it is and they, the architects, must come to grips with the existing situation.

On the other side of the dilemma, the facts are equally plain: the old-time professional—the architect who did it all himself (with a little help from draftsmen and others, of course), the architect who felt his work spoke for him and that potential clients would hear what it said and come to him without being beckoned by any action on his part—this kind of architect is gone forever, if in fact he ever did exist.

Many architects find this state of affairs most distressing and spend considerable time and effort pretending that those good old days, whenever they were, are still here.

The upshot of all of this comes out in the sorry spectacle of architects selling their services like crazy, all the while pretending that they are not selling at all.

Maybe those who call this schizophrenia have chosen the right word after all.

In any case, Welton Becket and Associates is atypical of architectural firms in general, even of large firms. WB&A has developed over the years methods of dealing with the facts of architectural sales and marketing, if not with the philosophical principles of it.

In this case, the sales and marketing functions work impressively. The firm gets its share of work. And the record of clients who come back to the firm for additional work is impressive indeed. To explain how the firm achieves this record is another matter entirely.

In some ways, WB&A has found ways to overcome many of the obstacles that tend to prevent architectural firms from mounting effective marketing plans and systems. In other ways, this firm like many others finds itself constrained by the seeming impossibility of mounting a complete, total effort in marketing and sales.

Some things are organized very well, others not so well. WB&A does many things in a manner very similar to the methods used by other top firms; some things it handles very differently.

In any case, the sales effort of WB&A, and its marketing program, would no doubt seem quite rudimentary and incomplete, let's say to the marketing executives of an automobile company or a soap company or to one of the conglomerates or even to the newer types of professional service organizations such as management consultants or computer programmers. But it must be repeated: it works.

The first step in determining how the sales and marketing effort of Welton Becket and Associates works involves an examination of how these efforts are organized.

In the first place, the firm calls its sales and marketing efforts "business development", and the department that handles these efforts is the Business Development Department.

The official Welton Becket and Associates organization is quite simple and straightforward. The department, for many years directed by Jack Beardwood, has been headed by Donnell Grimes, Senior

Left and below:
Center Plaza, Boston,
Massachusetts.

Vice President, since late 1970. Public Relations is organized as a separate office, located in Los Angeles, with its head reporting directly to the director of Business Development. The director has a corporate staff in Los Angeles and also directs business development men in Houston, Chicago, and New York as well as in Los Angeles.

It should be quickly pointed out that Welton Becket, during all of the years he was developing and building the firm, was acknowledged by one and all to be the best salesman the firm had. And he was very active in this part of the practice.

Also it should be stated that many others in the firm who are not directly assigned to business development have been deeply involved in this area over the years and still are. Many of the designers get into the act on various occasions, as do project architects and many of the department heads.

In the third place, the directors of the five offices, without exception, are deeply concerned with business development and generally spend a good deal of their time in these endeavors in their regions. Others in these offices also take part in the process.

And lastly, but of utmost importance in the future, MacDonald Becket, the president who took over the reins in January 1969, spent much of his time before that in Business Development. He was involved in this aspect of practice on a national scale in all of the offices. With such a background, coupled with his inclination toward client contact, including business development, he can be expected to keep his hand in this aspect of the practice in the future.

From the above, it might be gathered that in the Welton Becket and Associates firm, business development, or sales and marketing, is the province of all and therefore subject to the sin of not being aptly handled by any. Nothing could be further from the truth.

The Director of Business Development of the firm runs his own show. Don Grimes was selected from among the project architects and was assigned to Business Development under Jack Beardwood in the middle sixties. In 1968, when the New York office needed an assistant director, Grimes was appointed to that position. In that role, he divided the responsibilities for business development with the office director. Grimes returned to Los Angeles in 1970 and was made Director in December of that year when Jack Beardwood was appointed Executive Vice President.

Grimes heads a department which could be characterized as very small or very large, according to the point of view. In terms of people actually assigned directly to it, the corporate department numbers only four, including the director, his assistant William Feathers, and two secretaries in direct sales in Los Angeles, plus four people and a secretary in Public Relations.

Looking at it another way, business development has a very large number of people working for it in addition to those assigned there—the president, the office directors, and the many others who sometimes get involved in sales.

In the first instance, this constitutes a very small amount of manpower for business development in a firm as large as Welton Becket and Associates. Many firms half this size have twice as many people in sales, or even more. Very few firms have as large a Public Relations Department, or one staffed as well or as well organized. The Director of Public Relations, Martin Brower, is a veteran of long service in architectural public relations and a trained journalist.

On the other hand, probably no architectural firm in the country can boast of the large number of people who can ably work with business development in the pursuit and capture of clients—and in keeping them—that are to be found in this firm.

In practice, the director of the department and the people directly assigned to it, take the lead in the sales efforts of the firm. Most information about potential projects is developed by them, and any information from others in the firm is ordinarily passed on to this division for follow-up.

The director and his assistants then contact the potential clients themselves, either singly or as a group, or they may call on the president of WB&A or others to make the contacts with them or separately. In some cases, the directors of the offices may make direct contacts without the presence of anyone from business development or may make at least an initial contact. In most cases, someone from Business Development will be called in early. This is necessary not only to ensure overall direction of the entire effort, but also because ordinarily the Business Development Department will be deeply involved in writing contracts with clients when they are obtained and the department makes a point of keeping contact with clients and with the work being done for them at all stages of their projects.

The Public Relations Department too is organized not only to obtain exposure for the work of the firm through magazines, newspapers, and other media but also to serve the overall sales effort of WB&A and needs of its clients in this area.

It should be mentioned here that public relations performs numerous functions that might more properly be called marketing or client service functions than public relations. The department is organized to prepare sales presentations such as the audio-visual presentation, part of which is shown on page 92. In addition, the department often assists clients in setting up public relations functions on their buildings, press conferences, brochures, and other needs, and in some cases handles the entire job for them.

To sum up the organization of business development functions in Welton Becket and Associates, it should be pointed out that the organization is anything but hard and fast. Rather it is a core composed of a small number of people directly assigned to this function, who are in a position to call upon the services of a great number of others throughout the firm for assistance in this area. In a way, it almost seems like everyone in the firm is a salesman in some fashion or another.

That this rather loose, relatively unstructured sales effort works is demonstrated by the large number of big and important jobs for which clients commission the firm each year and by the number of those clients who come back later.

97

Right and below:
Stern Brothers Department Store,
Willowbrook Shopping Center,
Wayne Township, New Jersey.

98

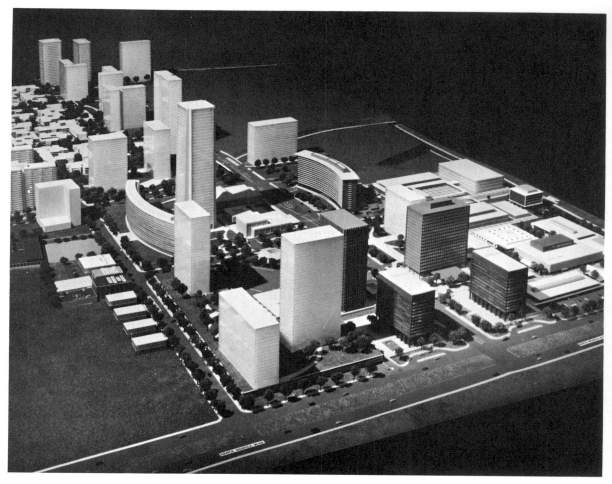

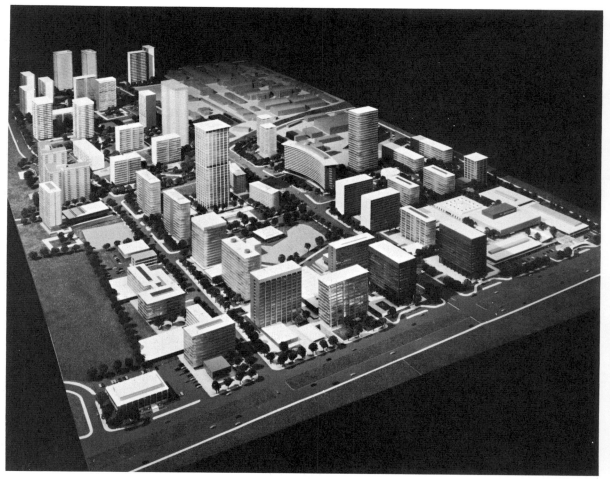

12
DIMENSIONS
OF THE PRACTICE

One of the most important aspects of the success of Welton Becket and Associates, perhaps even the most important, is the attitude of the firm toward its clients. *Dedication* is the word for this; and the dedication is evident in everything the firm does. No architecture for architecture's sake here—or almost none. The orientation is toward the desires of clients and, presumably, toward their needs.

Perhaps the best way to get at this situation is to start with clients themselves and their buildings. Who are these clients? What kinds of work is WB&A doing for them? And where?

Perhaps the dimensions of these factors might be grasped by taking a look at the work of the firm on a single day, about the middle of 1969.

On that day, the active work in the office amounted to some 170 projects, or about one project for each three employees. Obviously, not all of these projects were going full speed ahead in design, production, or construction. Some were stopped, awaiting action by clients or other people. Some were proceeding normally through the firm. Some were on a crash basis rather than on normal schedules. Yet, all in all, this is a very large number of active projects for a firm of this size to handle concurrently. And the dimensions of the situation become even

more evident when it is pointed out that many of these projects involve a number of buildings rather than a single structure. It should also be pointed out that quite a few of the projects involved master planning and that a good number of these would lead inevitably to additional building projects within the complexes being planned.

The types of projects being handled by the firm, in mid-1969, were varied. Of the total, the largest number were office buildings, forty-two of them, not including public buildings. Next in number came master planning, thirty-two projects. Shopping centers and stores, thirty of them, were in third place. Of the remaining sixty-six projects, five were auditoriums and other public assembly buildings, ten were educational facilities (elementary, secondary, technical schools, and university projects), eighteen were hospitals and other medical facilities, twenty-four were hotels and apartment buildings, and the remainder miscellaneous types including two airline terminals.

In some of the master planning projects, WB&A was handling one or more buildings which have been included in the totals given above. In others, the firm could be expected to handle additional buildings not included in the totals. In some of the projects, there actually were more than one building.

Adding up the totals again, in another manner, the firm in mid-1969 had thirty-two master planning projects in progress, in addition to some 150 buildings. Geographically, the work in the firm on that date was widespread, the domestic projects being located in twenty-one states and the District of Columbia. Also, the firm was handling jobs in ten foreign countries: Antigua, New Zealand, Portugal, Philippines, Republic of the Congo, Spain, Mexico, India, Singapore, and Argentina.

The domestic work was spread all over the continental U.S., but as might be surmised, the largest number of projects was in California, the home state of WB&A, some eighty of them, or about one-half of the total. Tied for second place were the states of New York and Texas, with some twelve projects each.

Such are the bare statistics of the work that was being handled by WB&A as of one day in mid-1969. Obviously, the work in this architectural firm as in any other ebbs and flows and may change radically from one period to another. There have been times when the number of projects was much smaller than the number cited here. For example, when WB&A was involved with the total design of the Los Angeles Music Center, an unusually high percentage of its local office people were assigned to that project, thus reducing the amount of other work that could be handled. On the other hand, at certain times in the life of the firm, a larger number of projects were in the house.

So it is impossible to generalize from the figures cited here for one specific year, but perhaps the figures do serve a useful purpose in establishing a benchmark from which to measure the dimensions of the work handled by the firm.

What of the dimensions of the clients served by the firm? And who are they? It would be just about impossible to quote a figure for the number of clients served by the firm from the beginning to the present. They would number several thousand, as a conservative estimate. Perhaps some intimation of the numbers and types of clients served might be gathered by looking again at that day in mid-1969 when some 150 buildings and 32 master planning projects were in progress in the firm.

Among the office buildings underway at that time in the offices were those for First and Merchants Bank of Richmond, Virginia; Dayton's headquarters, Minneapolis, Minnesota; Pittsburgh National Bank; the 33 Washington Building for Mutual Benefit Life Insurance Co., Newark, New Jersey; the First National–Southern National Building, Birmingham, Alabama; Citizens Fidelity Bank Building, Louisville, Kentucky; Colorado Interstate Corp. Building, Colorado Springs; Hirshmann Office Building, Chicago; Shell Data Service Center, Houston; Equitable Life Assurance Society Building, Los Angeles; Aetna Building, San Francisco; Mutual Benefit Life Insurance Co. Building, San Francisco; Garrett Corporation Headquarters, Torrance, California; North American Rockwell Corporation Building, El Segundo, California; Tishman Westwood Building, Westwood, California; Northrop Building, Los Angeles; and Jet Propulsion Laborato-

ries Administration Building, Pasadena, California. In addition, the firm was active on twenty-five other office buildings. The range of costs of these buildings stretched from a low of about $1 million to over $30 million, with most of the projects in the $6- to $10-million bracket.

Thus the office buildings underway in mid-1969 were being handled for a blue-ribbon list of U.S. merchandisers, financial institutions, and industries. A complete list of WB&A clients for office buildings over the years would be long, and no real purpose would be served by it. Perhaps it will suffice to say that such a list would indicate the involvement of the firm with many of the top companies in the country, including in addition to those cited above, such companies as Alcoa, Anaconda, Bendix, Bethlehem Steel, Capitol Records, DuPont, Ford, General Electric, General Petroleum, Gulf Oil, Hallmark, Humble, Kaiser, Lever, Lockheed, Packard Bell, Phillips Petroleum, Remington Rand, Scott Paper, Shell, Del E. Webb, Xerox, and a large number of others.

Among financial institutions, such a list would include California Federal Savings and Loan, Crocker-Citizens Bank, Fidelity Bank and Trust, North Carolina Mutual Life, Massachusetts Mutual Life, Prudential, Security Pacific National Bank, and many others.

The list of clients for other building types, companies, federal and municipal governments would also be long and impressive, but perhaps the office building information given here will serve to demonstrate the breadth and depth of the firm's client lists.

One further bit of information might be of interest, however, a sampling of the client list in the area of stores, which reads almost like a directory of national merchandising. Among these clients have been Abraham & Straus; Bamberger's; Broadway-Hale; Buffum's; Bullock's; Carson, Pirie and Scott; Crescent; B. Dalton; Emporium-Capwell; Gimbel; Goldwater's; Kaufmann; Lerner; McCrory; Macy; I. Magnin; J. Magnin; May, Meier and Frank; Montgomery Ward; Ohrbach's; Rexall; Saks; Sears Roebuck; Stern Brothers; Stix, Baer and Fuller; Strawbridge and Clothier; and F. W. Woolworth.

Another dimension of the practice of Welton Becket and Associates may be found in the volume of work done by the firm. As has been mentioned previously, the annual volume varies, as might be expected. But such variations have ordinarily been minor for some years now. The construction put in place during the late sixties averages about $150 million per year and would rise to some 25 to 35 percent more than that figure in a very busy year or decrease by about the same percentage in one that was slow. In 1969, for example, construction starts totaled $209 million for twenty-five projects for an average project cost of $8.4 million. In 1968, the twenty-six buildings put into construction totaled $157 million, or an average cost of $6 million each.

Even more revealing as a measure of the firm's size would be the dollar value of projects actually being handled by the firm at a given time. Again utilizing the mid-1969 timing as benchmark, the estimated amount of work in progress came to almost $1 billion in buildings alone, not including the thirty-two active

Century City Gateway Buildings and other work of Welton Becket and Associates.

master planning projects. How spectacular that $1 billion figure really is becomes quite apparent when it is remembered that the total amount of building construction in the U.S. over the past few years runs from about $40 to $50 billion construction in place. However, it should be remembered that for WB&A the $1 billion figure is for work in progress; the firm's record for work started in a year being the previously mentioned approximately $209 million in 1969.

In any case, and by any measure, the amount of work being accomplished by this firm is impressive. Using the $50 billion figure for total building construction along with the $209 million for WB&A projects started in 1969, the firm is currently handling more than $\frac{1}{250}$th of the total. A more useful measure would be obtained by eliminating from the total figure the approximately $17 billion devoted each year to one- and two-family houses, a type not handled by the firm. Figured this way, WB&A is handling almost $\frac{1}{160}$th of the construction total. Judged against the share of the market acquired by any of the big three automobile manufacturers or the share IBM has of the computer market or against the situation that exists in almost any industry, the WB&A share of its potential market seems small indeed. However, it should be remembered that only slightly more than 1 percent of the architectural firms in the country average as much as $50 million in volume per year, that the average volume among architectural offices is only about $5 million, that over 90 percent of firms average less than $10 million. By these standards, the true size of the work of WB&A can be measured.

To clarify the picture, it should be pointed out by way of contrast that only about 1 percent of the architectural firms in the country have as many as 100 employees, that the average is about 9 per firm, and that over 90 percent have fewer than 20 employees. As indicated previously, WB&A to handle its annual volume employs more than 500 people.

These then are some of the bare statistics of the clients of Welton Becket and Associates and the dimensions of the work generated by the clients. Further insight into the client picture can be had throughout the chapters preceding and following, in which the work accomplished for the clients mentioned here and many others is shown and discussed. To this point, the concern has been with the bare bones of the subject. Perhaps the most useful way to flesh out, clothe, and bring to life the subject would be to give attention to some of those in Welton Becket and Associates who are continually working with clients in one capacity or another.

First are the words of Welton Becket: "I don't think there is an architectural firm in the country, or in the world, that operates more efficiently and smoothly than we do. Out of some 200 jobs in progress at any one time about one-quarter are jobs for repeat clients. Our average number of jobs for each of the fifty repeat clients is more than seven. You don't get repeat clients by doing a bad job. You get them by holding to the budget, solving the client's problems, handling the work efficiently and on time, and giving him a good building. These are the prime reasons for our success in getting work into the office—satisfied clients who come back with repeat jobs and who recommend us to their friends and associates."

So far so good, but what about new clients for whom WB&A has never worked, to whom the firm may not have been recommended by a former client? In the words of Houston office director, Gilbert Thweatt, here is how it went with one job: "We keep a file of potential clients and dig through it periodically for leads. Of course, we also try in every way possible to keep the file up to date. As an example of how we work, let's take a building for which we were recently commissioned by a client for whom we had never worked directly. We had done some work for people with whom the client was associated. As a potential client, this one had great possibilities—doing quite a few buildings, but none by us. First of all, I found out everything possible about the work being done and began a series of visits to the people in charge of commissioning architects. Every two or three months, I was in their office talking, showing them things we were doing.

"After a couple of years the client decided to build an $8 million building and invited us to be interviewed for it. All of the long years of legwork now held promise of paying off. At the time, we did several other things. We let the associates of this client, those for whom we had done work, know we were being considered and this resulted in some good recommendations. Also, the then Business Development Director in Los Angeles, Jack Beardwood, as usual, had some contacts with people who could put in a good word for us, which they did.

"All right then, this is all well and good, the continuing calls on a potential client, the recommendations and so on, but not enough to sell the client, of course. What finally sold him was our presentation of our past work of the type he was contemplating. And even more importantly the client was very impressed with the fact that our firm had an office in his area to serve him locally but was part of a complete, integrated national architectural firm. He knew the Houston office could get all of the help, all of the backup needed from the Los Angeles office and that we had the knowhow, the manpower, and the experts needed to handle his project correctly."

These then are some of the important dimensions of Welton Becket and Associates and the clientele served by the firm. Of course, the mere quantitative look taken here can only partially describe the firm as it exists and operates. The qualitative dimensions are not so easily described. However, two aspects of the quality can be discerned very easily—the planning and other architectural aspects of the work of WB&A in the illustrations throughout the present book give some indication of the quality achieved. And the high incidence of repeat clients serves as an indicator of the quality of the services furnished by the firm.

In the chapters immediately following, the services offered by WB&A are described in some detail. In these descriptions may be found some measure of understanding of the process utilized here, a process which leads to the large amount of work handled, the completeness of that work, the quality achieved, and the satisfied clients.

Repeat client: Tishman Airport Center and other examples of the fifteen major projects handled for this client.

Repeat client: Eight of the projects of Inter-Continental Hotels Corporation; those shown are located in Oberoi, Lisbon, Phnom Penh, Saigon, Antigua, Kinshasa, Singapore, Buenos Aires.

106

107

Repeat client: University of California at Los Angeles. From left to right, top row: Center for Health Sciences; Neuropsychiatric Institute. Second row: Marion Davies Childrens Clinic. Third row: Jules Stein Eye Institute; Reed Neurological Research Center. Fourth row: School of Public Health; Institute for Chronic Diseases.

Repeat client: Bullock's. Some
twenty-five jobs have been handled
starting in the early forties; the stores
at Westwood, Lakewood, La Habra,
Sherman Oaks, and
Pasadena, California are shown here.

Part Four

THE PRACTICE
OF TOTAL DESIGN

Public Library, Civic Center,
Pomona, California.

City Hall, Civic Center,
Pomona, California.

112

13
ADMINISTRATION OF PROJECTS

A unique, and very effective, aspect of the offices of Welton Becket and Associates is the way projects are handled administratively. There are actually three major levels of administration of projects: the overall executive administration at the top level of each office and of the corporation, the production level at which project architects are assigned, and the production administration level.

Overall administration has been previously discussed, and production is handled in a succeeding chapter. At this point, the functions of production administration—one of the important factors in the handling of projects—will be outlined in some detail, and the relationships between these functions and those of the architectural and engineering departments will be clarified.

In the first place, in each of the WB&A offices, there is a department or individual with specific responsibility for the performance of the major details of administration for all projects. These production administrators work very closely with the project architects, to whom is assigned the administrative responsibility for individual projects.

The relationships between project architects and production administrators is a lateral one since the project architects report to the director of architectural production, who in turn reports to the director of his office. The production administrators also report to the office director. Therefore, it should be pointed out that all the relationships between production administration and project architects are founded on a division of the work of administration between them. In the simplest sense, this division

of work entails assignment of the details of administration that are architectural in nature to the project architects and those which are of a business nature to the production administrator. Thus the project architect would have the responsibilities for the buildings themselves, production of drawings and specifications, services during construction, and the like, while the production administrator would have the responsibilities for handling the administration of the owner-architect contract, the contracts with consultants, proper billing procedures in the correct amounts, the general paperwork affecting projects, and things of a similar nature.

The production administrators play another important role, that of acting as advisers to the project architects on the details of businesslike handling of projects. Thus a production administrator very often will find himself working with job orders, change orders, and field instructions, attempting to interpret the intent of the owner-architect contract and the construction contract as an aid to the project architect. This sort of thing frequently extends even to such details as to how a letter to an owner, contractor, or consultant should be worded.

Perhaps one way of putting it would be to say that the production administrators handle the horrendous amount of detailed paperwork to the extent possible, thus freeing the project architects to spend the major portion of their time on the projects themselves.

Another way to get at the role of the production administrator, or at least to put it into perspective, might be to study the project flow chart shown on page 114. This flow may vary between projects and between offices of WB&A, but for the most part is standard procedure in the firm.

As may be seen, after an agreement has been reached with a client, a project enters the architectural process through production administration, where the first step consists of a thorough analysis of the owner-architect contract and any related information. From here, after a project designer and project architect have been assigned to it, the project proceeds through programming and scope study and definition. In this process, both production and design take part. The design department then proceeds with studies and schematics and program refinement. After approvals have been obtained on the schematics and related studies, the project goes into production—architectural with WB&A and engineering within the firm or by outside consultants. The production departments handle preliminaries, working drawings, specifications, and services during construction. During the entire process, production administration is playing its role somewhat as staff to the other departments in handling the business details and other administration.

As the first step in the architectural process, it was mentioned that production administration makes a first-contract analysis. While this process often entails a considerable amount of detailed study, the results are easily ascertained by an examination of the contract-analysis forms shown across-page.

After the actual contract with an owner has been prepared by the business development department, with the aid of other departments as required, and signed by the owner, the contract comes to production administration for analysis. With the help of others if necessary, the production administrator then analyzes the contract in detail and prepares the contract analysis.

As may be seen in the forms shown, this analysis goes into considerable detail covering every conceivable aspect of the contract as it relates to work to be accomplished, which departments will handle the work, consultants if any, information for accounting and billing, and so on. A very important part of the analysis is that of reimbursables and nonreimbursables, which in architecture today account for larger portions of the total cost of architectural services each year.

Copies of this analysis are furnished to all in the office handling the project who are in any way affected and to those in others of the WB&A offices who might play some role in the services for the project. Copies are furnished to design, project architects, production, and so on, but it should be pointed out that also receiving the analyses are the cost control department, top corporate management, business development, and public relations. Thus the departments who must produce the work, of course, receive their copies along with accounting, who must handle the books, billings and so on, but also those who are concerned with the executive functions of

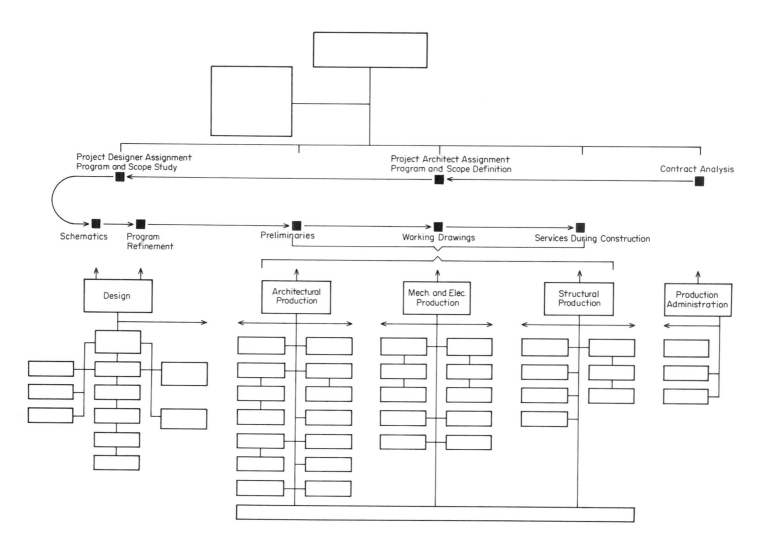

the firm, its new business development, and public relations are also kept completely informed.

Many other types of reports and forms are utilized within the firm to guide, analyze, and control projects. Some of these that are more directly related to the work of the production departments are discussed and shown elsewhere. However, it should be pointed out that the largest single cost item in the performance of architectural services, the cost of people, gets particularly close attention in this firm. To illustrate some of the aspects of the control of time in WB&A, a copy of the time card employed, front and back, and of the employee earnings record form are shown on the two pages following.

The time card is self-explanatory, for the most part, but perhaps a few things should be pointed out. It will be noted that the reverse side outlines a very complete list of services an individual might perform in the firm. Thus, the code, consisting of two-digit numbers from the first group, say 20 "architectural drafting," and a third digit describing more exactly what kind of drafting, say 5 "work on preliminaries," is inserted on the proper line on the obverse side. These codes define very exactly what functions a man actually performed in the time spent. Also it will be seen that unlike some time cards used in other architectural offices, this one has extra columns for overtime performed during the regular work week.

One further thing should be mentioned, the dash number column. Here are inserted numbers assigned to a project when some extra service or an extraordinary function is to be performed. For the most part, time against dash-numbered functions is billed as extra services.

The other form shown is actually from the accounting department. Time from the time cards goes onto the computer, which prints out forms for each employee like that shown. In addition to the bookkeeping, accounting, and payroll purposes of this form and the computer which prepares it, this information also performs a major function in production administration by distributing the payroll costs against individual projects for cost accounting purposes and on times-payroll jobs for billing owners. These costs are accumulated by the computer for each job and combined with other costs, and a printout is produced every two weeks showing the total costs to date for each job.

These reports are then analyzed at the end of each two weeks and again at the end of each major phase of projects. In this way, the actual output and progress of the various departments can be analyzed and, if necessary, steps taken to improve a lagging performance. The ramifications of this analysis have already been discussed. But it should be pointed out here that the work of the accounting department in this area has been closely coordinated to mesh with the actual work of the other departments in the firm, as well as with production administration, to ensure a smooth and efficient operation.

WELTON BECKET AND ASSOCIATES

TIME CARD FOR TWO WEEKS ENDED _____

EMPLOYEE'S NAME _____

PLEASE FILL OUT IN PENCIL

[Time card table with columns: JOB NO., JOB NAME, Dash No., CODE (See Reverse), and days SUN MON TUE WED THU FRI SAT (R / OT) for two weeks, HOURS (REG. / OT), AMOUNT (REGULAR / OVERTIME), ✓]

ABSENT (EXPLAIN BELOW)

TOTALS

REMARKS

HOURS OK _____

ABSENCES OK _____

| | REGULAR RATE | |
| OVERTIME RATE | |

DEDUCTIONS

| INC. TAX | F.I.C.A. | S.D.I. |
| PRUD. | HOSP. | A.I.A. |

REGULAR _____
GROSS PAY _____
TOTAL DEDUCS. _____
NET PAY _____

MAN-HOUR CODE

PART I — (FIRST AND SECOND DIGITS)

CODE	DEPARTMENT	FUNCTION
07	FIXTURE	DETAILING AND DRAFTING
08	FIXTURE	SPECIFICATIONS
09	FIXTURE	SHOP DRAWINGS
14	FIXTURE	FIELD INSPECTION (INSTALLATION)
15	FIXTURE	DESIGN
16	FIXTURE	PROJECT COORDINATION
17	FIXTURE	STUDY MODELS, RENDERINGS, MOCK-UPS, BROCHURES, PRESENTATION MATERIALS
10	DESIGN	EXTERIOR ARCHITECTURAL
11	DESIGN	INTERIOR ARCHITECTURAL
12	DESIGN	GRAPHICS AND ART WORK
13	DESIGN	FURNISHING AND DECORATING
18	DESIGN	SPACE PLANNING AND/OR PROGRAMMING
19	DESIGN	MASTER PLANNING
20	ARCH.	DRAFTING
21	ARCH.	SPECIFICATIONS (WRITING, EDITING)
22	ARCH.	SPECIFICATIONS (TYPING, REPRODUCTION, COLLATING, BINDI
23	ARCH.	SHOP DRAWINGS
24	ARCH.	FIELD INSPECTION
25	ARCH.	PLAN CHECKING
26	ARCH.	PROJECT COORDINATION
27	ARCH.	COST ESTIMATES
28	ARCH.	SPACE PLANNING AND/OR PROGRAMMING
29	ARCH.	MASTER PLANNING
30	ENGR-MECH	SPRINKLERS (DESIGN, DRAFTING, LAYOUTS, CALCULATIONS, ESTIMATES)
31	ENGR-MECH	SPECIFICATIONS (WRITING AND EDITING)
32	ENGR-MECH	SPECIFICATIONS (TYPING, REPRODUCTION, COLLATING, BINDI
33	ENGR-MECH	SHOP DRAWINGS
34	ENGR-MECH	FIELD INSPECTION
35	ENGR-MECH	PLAN CHECKING
36	ENGR-MECH	PROJECT COORDINATION
37	ENGR-MECH	PLUMBING (DESIGN, DRAFTING, LAYOUTS, CALCULATIONS, ESTIMATES)
38	ENGR-MECH	HEATING, VENT., AIR COND. (DESIGN, DRAFTING, LAYOUTS, CALCULATIONS, ESTIMATES)
39	ENGR-MECH	MASTER PLANNING
40	ENGR-ELEC	DESIGN, DRAFTING, LAYOUTS, CALCULATIONS, ESTIMATES
41	ENGR-ELEC	SPECIFICATIONS (WRITING AND EDITING)
42	ENGR-ELEC	SPECIFICATIONS (TYPING, REPRODUCTION, COLLATING, BINDI
43	ENGR-ELEC	SHOP DRAWINGS
44	ENGR-ELEC	FIELD INSPECTION
45	ENGR-ELEC	PLAN CHECKING
46	ENGR-ELEC	PROJECT COORDINATION
49	ENGR-ELEC	MASTER PLANNING
50	ENGR-STR.	DRAFTING, LAYOUTS
51	ENGR-STR.	CALCULATIONS, DESIGN
52	ENGR-STR.	SPECIFICATIONS
53	ENGR-STR.	SHOP DRAWINGS
54	ENGR-STR.	FIELD INSPECTION
55	ENGR-STR.	PLAN CHECKING
56	ENGR-STR.	PROJECT COORDINATION
57	ENGR-STR.	COST ESTIMATES
58	ENGR-STR.	CIVIL ENGINEERING
59	ENGR-STR.	MASTER PLANNING
60	ENGR-BARS & KITCHENS	ALL WORK RELATED THERETO
70	TRAFFIC	ALL WORK RELATED THERETO
80	ECONOMIC ANALYSIS	ALL WORK RELATED THERETO

PART II — (THIRD DIGIT)

CODE	PHASE
1	MASTER PLANNING
2	ECONOMIC ANALYSIS
3	SPACE PLANNING AND/OR PROGRAMMING
4	SCHEMATICS
5	PRELIMINARIES
6	WORKING DRAWINGS
7	CONSTRUCTION, SHOP DRAWINGS, FIELD INSPECTION
8	DESIGN, SELECTION AND/OR PRESENTATION (F & D & GRAPHICS ONLY)
9	PURCHASING AND INSTALLATION (F & D & GRAPHICS WORK ON

NOTE: CODE ALL TIME CHARGES, INCLUDING DASH NUMBERS.

EMPLOYEE EARNINGS RECORD
WELTON BECKET AND ASSOCIATES

1

NUMBER

NAME

ADDRESS

S. S. NO.

M ☐ S ☐

M ☐ F ☐

PHONE NO.

DATE EMPLOYED

DATE LEFT

REASON

DEPT.

RATE CHANGES

DEPT.	DATE	AMOUNT	PER	DATE	RATE	AMOUNT	PER

NO. DEP.	RATE	HOURS		EARNINGS			DEDUCTIONS			OTHER		PERIOD ENDING	TO DATE BALANCES				VERIFICATION FACTOR
		REGULAR	OVERTIME PREMIUM	REGULAR	O.T. PREMIUM	GROSS	INCOME TAX	F.I.C.A.	S.D.I.	CODE	AMOUNT		EARNINGS	INCOME TAX	F.I.C.A.	S.D.I.	

NCR

Mall Building, Almaden Fashion Plaza, San Jose, California.

Almaden Fashion Plaza Mall, San Jose, California.

118

14
RESEARCH AND OTHER STUDIES

Among architects and others in the environmental design professions, the word *research* often becomes a catchall for any activities that are not design, production, or construction and which produce information of any sort. Thus, a designer who goes to the library and makes what might be called a literature search of architectural magazines and books is doing "research." And an architect who goes out to visit buildings may also be deemed to be performing "research."

Researchers themselves would probably not call either of these activities research in the real sense of the word. Or at best, they might admit them to be adjuncts of research or a low-level form of it.

For years, the Becket firm has endeavored to perform real research in its offices. For the most part, the activities in the firm could not be termed pure research, and often even the applied research attempted scarcely rose above the level of the literature searches or field trips in which most architects engage on a more or less regular basis. For years, many of the Welton Becket and Associates people felt that their activities in this area were less than satisfactory and that eventually they would have to equip themselves and their firm to attack research in a meaningful and fruitful manner if they were to keep abreast of the times.

Certain exploratory attempts toward a research capability were carried on in the firm over the years. In 1970, the early and ongoing attempts to develop research capabilities culminated in the opening of the Welton Becket Research Center in its own wing attached to the Welton Becket and Associates Los Angeles office. The center is concerned with all aspects of research related to architecture, planning, and environmental factors. Vice President Louis Naidorf, at the time serving as Assistant Director of Design for the Los Angeles office, was named as the Director of Research for the firm and the functions of the center assigned as corporate function. One of the first moves of the new director was to work out an agreement for cooperation with the Environmental Design Workshop of the School of Architecture and Urban Planning at the University of Cali-

Views of the prefabrication processes used in producing and erecting the hotel rooms in the Contemporary Resort Hotel at Walt Disney World, Orlando, Florida.

fornia at Los Angeles. Harvey Perloff, Dean of the school, will coordinate its participation in the work.

At the opening of the new research activity, Perloff said, "We will be providing access to university expertise in research methodologies as well as access to a broad range of both design and nondesign disciplines. There is an increasing concern over the interrelationships of the social sciences, such as economics, sociology, and psychology to urban planning and design."

In announcing the program of the research center, President MacDonald Becket said, "The five major goals of the center are to create a mechanism for testing alternatives to current professional methods and information handling techniques, to act as a forum for the exchange of ideas and for discussion, to evaluate the actual performance of completed projects as weighed against their design objectives, to study emerging architectural problems, and to establish an information center for correlation and dissemination of data resulting from research."

Projects to be taken on in the research center will range widely, from basic research to applied research, testing, and development work. Some idea of the range can be gathered from the activities already under way. These include a study of new directions for architecture as a profession, one on emerging building types and forms, and a third on the impact of societal and technological changes on the construction industry. Another project well under way is concerned with the development of a prototype regional airport. This study is discussed later in this chapter, and some of the drawings are shown.

In its new building, the research center has been provided with a variety of research tools including shops and audio-visual equipment for demonstrations of many kinds. Computer capability is available within the firm in the Los Angeles office. Through the use of its own facilities and those of UCLA at present and of other universities in the future, the center will be capable of most of the latest research techniques, including gaming and other computer techniques, graphic problem-solving methods, and many forms of systems analysis.

Of course, a complete rundown on the types of research to be handled in the center would be impossible. However, the areas of study under consideration include basic research in such subjects as environmental simulation studies, urban design, urban systems analysis, behavioral studies, and studies of the future. Applied research areas are expected to include prototype buildings and systems, computer applications in architecture, construction techniques, building materials, building systems, and equipment.

It might be expected that the Becket Research Center would operate with its own staff and carry on its activities independently of the rest of the operations of the firm. Actually, the converse is true. As time goes on, the staff assigned to the center may be expected to grow as the activities increase, but there is no intention of insulating the research functions from those of the workaday world. By cooperating in research with UCLA and other universities the center will broaden and extend its capabilities.

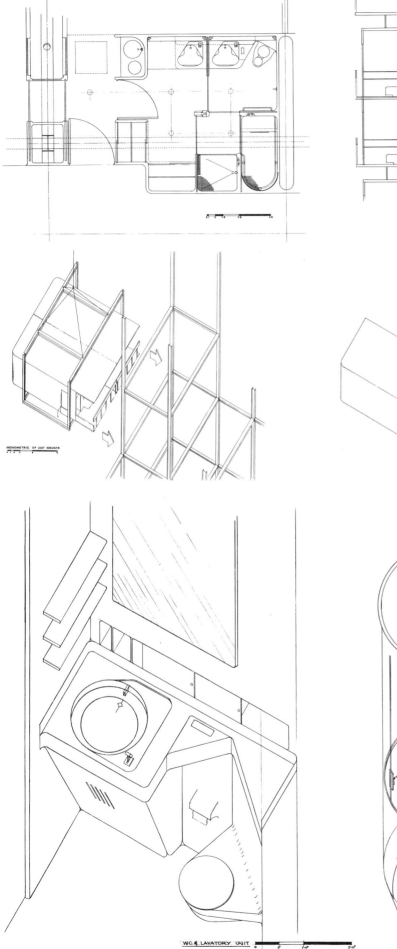

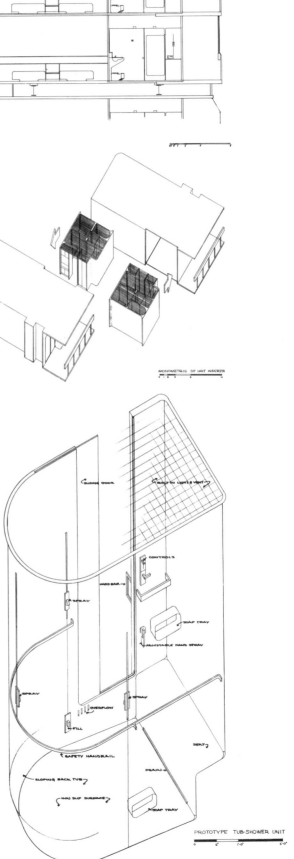

Early versions of drawings to demonstrate the principles of the prefabricated bathrooms developed for use in the hotels at Walt Disney World.

AXONOMETRIC OF UNIT INSERTS

AXONOMETRIC OF UNIT INSERTS

WC & LAVATORY UNIT

PROTOTYPE TUB-SHOWER UNIT

SLIDING DOOR

BUILT IN LIGHT & VENT

CONTROLS

HAND BAR

SPRAY

SOAP TRAY

ADJUSTABLE HAND SPRAY

SPRAY

OVERFLOW

SPRAY

FILL

SEAT

SAFETY HANDRAIL

DRAIN

SLOPING BACK TUB

NON SLIP SURFACE

SOAP TRAY

121

And it is certainly conceivable that the center will take on projects in conjunction with other institutional research facilities and, if the occasion arises, with commercial research firms. In this way, there will be no natural limits to the amount or type of research which may be taken on.

In another way too, the Welton Becket and Associates firm has acted to prevent proscribing the activities of the center or allowing it to become inbred. People from all over the firm will be brought into projects of the center. In this way, for example, a design team assigned to a project might find itself using the center's facilities to solve problems. Or designers, project architects, production people, and others might be assigned to a research project and find themselves working independently within the center or cooperating with center personnel on a project. Obviously, the activities of the research center will benefit greatly from this arrangement. And considerable benefit should accrue to the design and other personnel in that they will have an opportunity for thought and study outside their everyday work or collateral to it.

While the research emphasis at Welton Becket and Associates will now be concentrated in the research center, it should be pointed out that not all of the studies made by the firm will be handled there. For many years, Welton Becket and Associates has engaged in studies of various kinds. Some of these have been related to specific building projects, others to master planning or to space programming and planning and many other subjects. Over the years, the firm has taken on the task of special studies for which there seemed to be a need but no client.

Throughout this book may be seen many examples of various efforts made by the firm in these directions. All were done by regular personnel of the firm, sometimes working with outside consultants or specialists, sometimes not. It is interesting that, after several experiments, such activities as master planning studies have evolved, not into specialized departments for such work, but into functions carried on by design and production personnel who produce these studies along with their usual work in building design and production. For example, a designer who eventually works on a building within a complex may well have been the designer who produced the master plan. Thus, it can be seen that the tendency toward increasingly narrower specialization has been resisted here. And that is the way the firm can reasonably be expected to operate in the future.

An example of some of the aspects of one type of study handled by Welton Becket and Associates may be seen in the drawings of a unitized bathroom developed in conjunction with U.S. Steel Corporation for the Contemporary Resort Hotel in Walt Disney World near Orlando, Florida. The bathrooms were researched at the Welton Becket and Associates Los Angeles office along with the unitized hotel rooms of which they are part. What came out of these studies was a standardized steel-framed hotel room, approximately 15 by 30 feet in size, which could be completely prefabricated and lifted into place in the hotel. Self-supporting for three stories, the units were assembled in a plant at the site; plumbing, lighting,

and air conditioning were installed, the door was locked, and the unit was lifted into place. Once in place, the units were interlocked and the systems connected with plumbing and other utility lines.

The unitized hotel rooms described here are the result of considerable research and testing, which extended to many different kinds of systems and numerous materials including concrete and plastic. The steel system finally adopted allowed the weight of each room to be kept down to 6 tons rather than the 30 or so tons which have been usual in other developments. The fabrication and assembly was fast, as was the erection, and lighter handling equipment was needed.

Study projects involving activities such as master planning and the like and other activities not directly related to building design for a given client are illustrated in various chapters of the present book, including the Worcester, Massachusetts master plan (Chapter 6), the Los Angeles Airport terminal study and the prototype air-traffic control tower (Chapter 17), and a hypothetical hung stadium and other projects (Chapter 23).

Another kind of special study handled on a regular basis by the Becket firm is that of research into the requirements of clients and space planning of these needs. As in many other phases of architectural services, Welton Becket and Associates actually has no space-planning group as such. This work is handled by designers and other individuals who perform functions other than that of space planning. It is true, however, that not every designer or production person makes a good space planner. Consequently, only a limited number of these people find themselves with this sort of semispecialty in addition to the other functions they perform. The same is true of master planning.

Shown opposite and in the two pages that follow are a few representative pages and charts from a fairly typical space-planning project.

The charts shown in the pages following indicate the thoroughness of the space planning for this building. Interviews were held with people in all departments on all levels in the company. No detail was overlooked. For example, the wastepaper from a large computer department might completely tie up an average-sized freight elevator. Or the passenger elevator service might be properly designed for the number of people and areas served yet become a bottleneck if every secretary in the building had to take photocopying work to one central location.

Coffee breaks were studied as well as the flow of people and paper between departments. Some of the functions of the studies may be gathered from the sample pages shown. It will be noted that these pages mention small things as well as large and when combined with the information in the remainder of the study become a very detailed guide for the design of the building. In fact, in many cases such studies lead to a redesign of some of the functions and relationships within a company's organization.

Some of the drawings which illustrate a hypothetical research project of Welton Becket and Associates are shown here. This study of a prototype regional airport was undertaken by the firm not for a client

Building Description General Features

VALLEY NATIONAL BANK

Valley Center is the new headquarters facility for Valley National Bank.   Now in the design phase, the office tower and parking garage will be located on a two-block site bounded by Central Avenue, Second Street, Van Buren and Monroe.   The tower has been designed as a cluster of office spaces grouped around a service core which contains high speed passenger and service elevators, stairs, restrooms and communication and mechanical systems.   The building concept grew from the Bank's requirement for highly flexible space which could be planned either along conventional lines or using new open planning techniques.   The cluster concept also gives the office tower a distinctive form which is a sharp departure from the usual office "block".   The tower is surrounded by a landscaped garden which will provide a cool and shaded setting for the office building and the downtown branch bank pavilion.

A concourse level covering an entire city block will be located below the garden.   The concourse level will have a wide variety of facilities including the bank cafeteria and auditorium, a public restaurant, shops, brokerage and additional branch bank space.   All of these facilities open to a 40-ft. high atrium under the office tower.   The atrium forms an air-conditioned mall for pedestrian circulation. Escalators and elevators will connect the concourse level with the building lobby which bridges the open atrium.   An employee library-lounge and an art gallery adjoin the garden level lobby.   The large parking facility consists of twin structures separated by a landscaped court.

As the design phase progresses, many other facilities and building systems will be studied.   Your response to the questionnaires will assist the bank and the architects in this design development process.

Survey Objectives

In the proposed Valley Center project, space planning efforts will be directed toward developing space into a flexible, functional and creative environment in which to work.

In order to accomplish these goals we are making this survey of your headquarters and home office departments.

The survey objectives are:

1. To obtain the best possible understanding of your operations as they relate to your work environment.

2. To study the inter-department adjacencies, communications and work flow.

3. To establish office and open area arrangement locations which are reponsive to your organizational needs.

4. To determine 3 and 8 year space and personnel projections, using your present quota as a basis.

With your help we will be able to develop the proper amount and the best kind of space for your department or unit.

Survey Instructions, Phase I

.The Survey is divided into two phases.   The purpose of the Phase I survey is to help us determine where your department or unit will be located and how much space it will occupy in the new building.

Phase I deals with departments or units as a whole and their relationship with other departments or units of Valley National Bank.

Phase I does not deal with individual employees except to determine the total number of employees and the size of the area those employees will occupy.

The Phase II survey will be concerned with individuals and their space and equipment requirements.   Departmental equipment needs will also be considered.   This survey will be conducted at a time close to the move-in date in order to minimize changes.

SCHEDULE

This sheet indicates when the Phase I survey will be taken and on what date it should be completed.

DEPARTMENT AND UNIT LIST

This list of departments or units will enable all of us to use the same nomenclature in referring to the individual parts which make up Valley National Bank.

SURVEY FORMS: SHEETS #1 - #5

Please fill in the department and/or unit name in the upper right hand corner of each sheet.

At the bottom of each sheet, indicate who filled out the form and the date.

Make a copy of each of the filled out survey forms (Sheets #1-#5) for your files.   Return the originals at the end of the survey period.

When filling out the survey forms, please type the information whenever possible.

Survey Instructions, Phase I

SHEET # 1:   DEPARTMENT ADJACENCY

Refer to the directions at the top of the sheet.   They will assist you in completing the block diagram.

SHEET # 2:   TRAFFIC AND WORK FLOW

We are interested here in traffic and work flow among departments or units rather than among individuals.

SHEET # 3:   PERSONNEL REQUIREMENTS

This sheet was designed to assist you in arriving at total square foot requirements for the people in your department or unit.

Under "Position or Title" fill in a separate line for each person you anticipate will be added to your department or unit by the presumed MOVE-IN DATE (1973).

Do the same for your 1978 requirements.

The set of office and open area arrangements, which is attached to Sheet #3, is provided as a guide in determining individual area needs for 1973 and 1978.   No square footage figures are necessary for your current space.

SHEET # 4:   SPECIAL DEPARTMENT AREA REQUIREMENTS

These are the special areas within your department.   This sheet will help you arrive at the total square feet required for special areas.

SHEET # 5:   NOTES AND COMMENTS

Any additional information which you feel will be of value in developing our understanding of your space requirements and needs should be noted here.

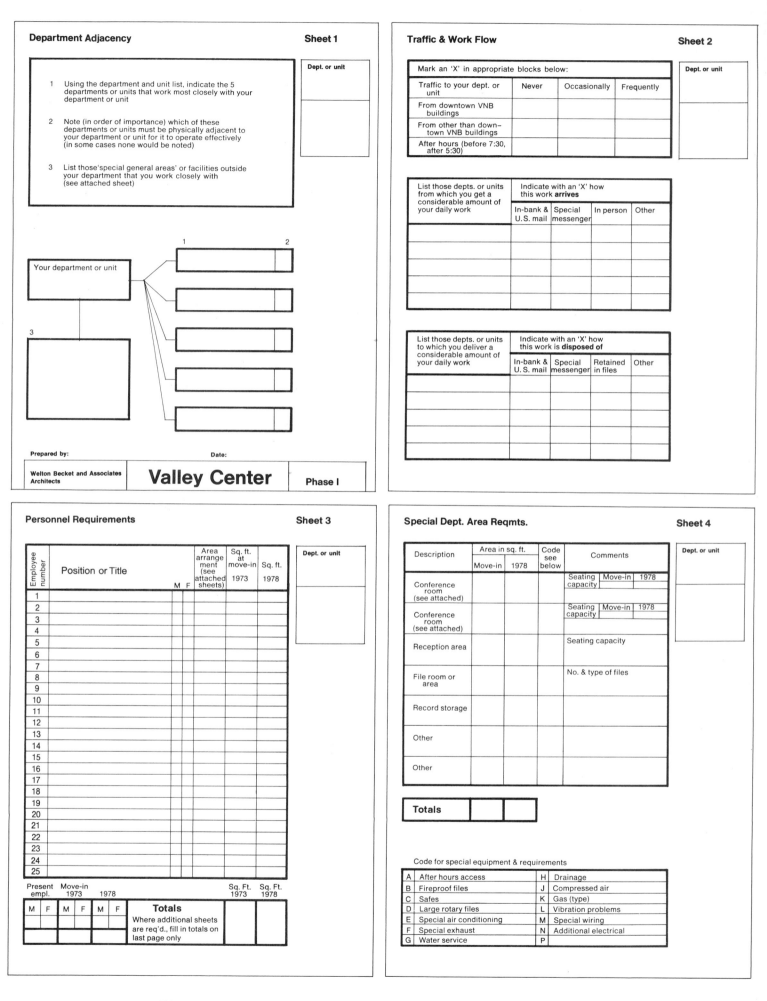

Department Adjacency — Sheet 1

	Dept. or unit

1. Using the department and unit list, indicate the 5 departments or units that work most closely with your department or unit

2. Note (in order of importance) which of these departments or units must be physically adjacent to your department or unit for it to operate effectively (in some cases none would be noted)

3. List those 'special general areas' or facilities outside your department that you work closely with (see attached sheet)

Your department or unit

1   2

3

Prepared by: Date:

Welton Becket and Associates
Architects

Valley Center   Phase I

Traffic & Work Flow — Sheet 2

	Dept. or unit

Mark an 'X' in appropriate blocks below:

Traffic to your dept. or unit	Never	Occasionally	Frequently
From downtown VNB buildings			
From other than down-town VNB buildings			
After hours (before 7:30, after 5:30)			

List those depts. or units from which you get a considerable amount of your daily work	Indicate with an 'X' how this work **arrives**			
	In-bank & U.S. mail	Special messenger	In person	Other

List those depts. or units to which you deliver a considerable amount of your daily work	Indicate with an 'X' how this work is **disposed of**			
	In-bank & U.S. mail	Special messenger	Retained in files	Other

Personnel Requirements — Sheet 3

	Dept. or unit

Employee number	Position or Title	M	F	Area arrangement (see attached sheets)	Sq. ft. at move-in 1973	Sq. ft. 1978
1						
2						
3						
4						
5						
6						
7						
8						
9						
10						
11						
12						
13						
14						
15						
16						
17						
18						
19						
20						
21						
22						
23						
24						
25						

Present empl.		Move-in 1973		1978			Totals	Sq. Ft. 1973	Sq. Ft. 1978
M	F	M	F	M	F		Where additional sheets are req'd., fill in totals on last page only		

Special Dept. Area Reqmts. — Sheet 4

	Dept. or unit

Description	Area in sq. ft.		Code see below	Comments		
	Move-in	1978				
Conference room (see attached)				Seating capacity	Move-in	1978
Conference room (see attached)				Seating capacity	Move-in	1978
Reception area				Seating capacity		
File room or area				No. & type of files		
Record storage						
Other						
Other						

Totals		

Code for special equipment & requirements

A	After hours access	H	Drainage
B	Fireproof files	J	Compressed air
C	Safes	K	Gas (type)
D	Large rotary files	L	Vibration problems
E	Special air conditioning	M	Special wiring
F	Special exhaust	N	Additional electrical
G	Water service	P	

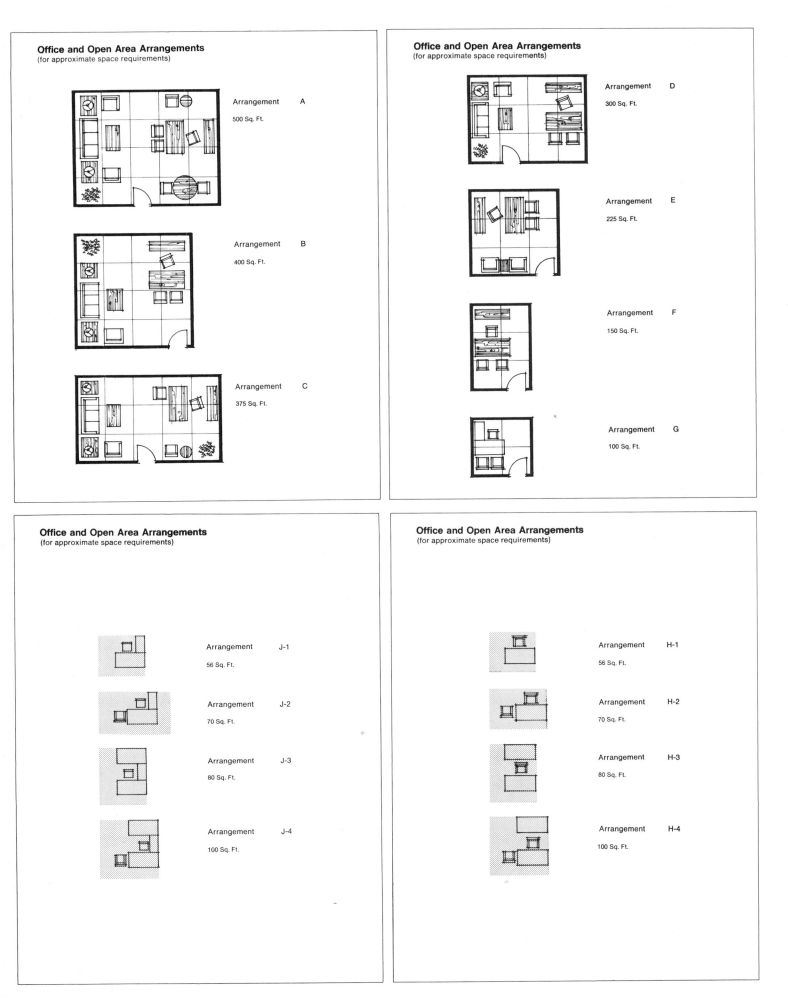

Office and Open Area Arrangements
(for approximate space requirements)

Arrangement   A

500 Sq. Ft.

Arrangement   B

400 Sq. Ft.

Arrangement   C

375 Sq. Ft.

Office and Open Area Arrangements
(for approximate space requirements)

Arrangement   D

300 Sq. Ft.

Arrangement   E

225 Sq. Ft.

Arrangement   F

150 Sq. Ft.

Arrangement   G

100 Sq. Ft.

Office and Open Area Arrangements
(for approximate space requirements)

Arrangement   J-1

56 Sq. Ft.

Arrangement   J-2

70 Sq. Ft.

Arrangement   J-3

80 Sq. Ft.

Arrangement   J-4

100 Sq. Ft.

Office and Open Area Arrangements
(for approximate space requirements)

Arrangement   H-1

56 Sq. Ft.

Arrangement   H-2

70 Sq. Ft.

Arrangement   H-3

80 Sq. Ft.

Arrangement   H-4

100 Sq. Ft.

125

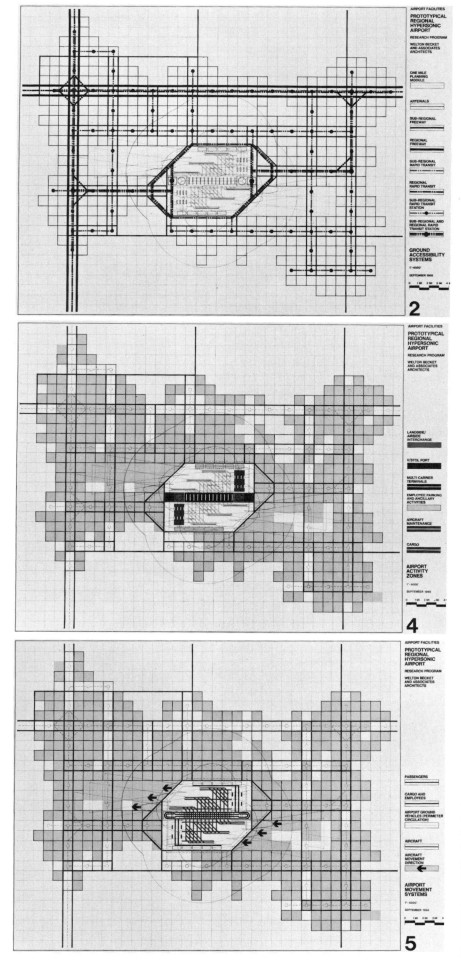

(they had none) but because it was felt that an attack on the air-travel problems of the future should be made. In this way, the firm could learn something of the problems and their solution and might then be better prepared to cope with the problems when the time came to serve a client for this kind of complex. Then, too, it was felt that airport design usually involves only the airport itself, not the larger scale of the environment in which the airport is placed. Here was an opportunity to attack the total problem, rather than a part of it.

Accordingly, Arthur Love, then a Los Angeles designer and vice president and now Director of Design of the Chicago office, embarked on a study of the overall problem together with a small team of assistants. The study has been proceeding for some months now, and the drawings shown indicate some of the intermediate-range results.

In the first place, an attempt was made immediately in the study to put the airport into context in relationship to its environment, to the urban system which it serves and of which it is part, and with the worldwide aspects of air travel. Land-use studies were made; research was directed toward the effects of noise; interrelationships between air travel and ground travel were probed. Some months of study were spent on all aspects of the impact of the airport on the communities it serves, on the area in which it is located, on the people who use it, service it, and are otherwise involved. The research on the airport proper did not proceed until some meaning had been found in larger problems of this sort.

These early studies led to a scheme for an airport that would be located far from highly populated areas, on virgin land, with a site large enough for any future expansion that could be imagined. And the studies led not to an airport that existed only in its own sense but one that would be an integrated factor of a regional development, its community, and the society in which it exists.

Thus, the results of this study envision a community which contains not only the airport and its service facilities but residential, commercial, and industrial areas with a considerable amount of open and recreational space. Restrictions on use are mainly based on noise levels, heights of structures, and ground accessibility. Thus, areas of highest noise concentration and lowest height restriction are to be used for industrial purposes and are surrounded by open green areas. Commercial development, institutions, and multifamily housing surround the green space, while single-family houses are placed on the periphery.

Ground transportation of various kinds is separated and divided into types according to actual distances and the mode. Thus, high-speed rapid transit, buses, automobiles—and even VTOL and STOL aircraft—connect at a landside terminal with an interterminal ground system which interconnects with the airside terminals.

The projected load on the airport is 100 million passengers a year—four to five times the load of large terminals of today, supported by 300,000 employees in a city that might grow to some 2.5 million in population.

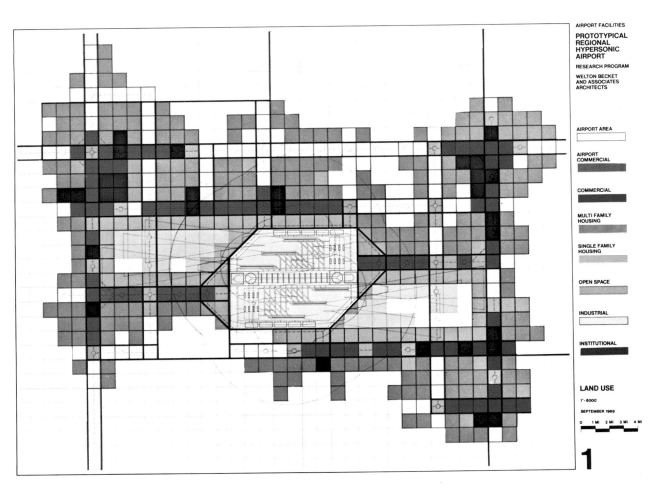

AIRPORT FACILITIES

**PROTOTYPICAL
REGIONAL
HYPERSONIC
AIRPORT**

RESEARCH PROGRAM

WELTON BECKET
AND ASSOCIATES
ARCHITECTS

AIRPORT AREA

AIRPORT
COMMERCIAL

COMMERCIAL

MULTI FAMILY
HOUSING

SINGLE FAMILY
HOUSING

OPEN SPACE

INDUSTRIAL

INSTITUTIONAL

LAND USE

1"-6000'

SEPTEMBER 1969

0   1 MI   2 MI   3 MI   4 MI

1

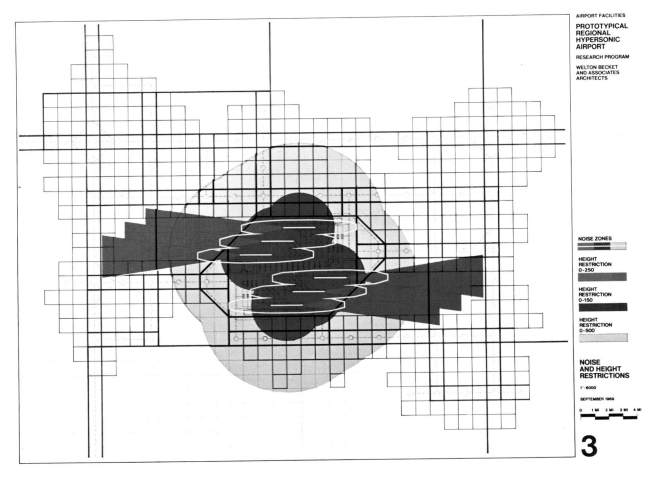

AIRPORT FACILITIES

**PROTOTYPICAL
REGIONAL
HYPERSONIC
AIRPORT**

RESEARCH PROGRAM

WELTON BECKET
AND ASSOCIATES
ARCHITECTS

NOISE ZONES

HEIGHT
RESTRICTION
0-250

HEIGHT
RESTRICTION
0-150

HEIGHT
RESTRICTION
0-500

**NOISE
AND HEIGHT
RESTRICTIONS**

1"-6000'

SEPTEMBER 1969

0   1 MI   2 MI   3 MI   4 MI

3

An example of the type of presentation made to clients; eight selected slides of scheme for a cultural, convention, and athletic complex accomplished for the city of Saginaw, Michigan, as a part of its downtown urban renewal program.

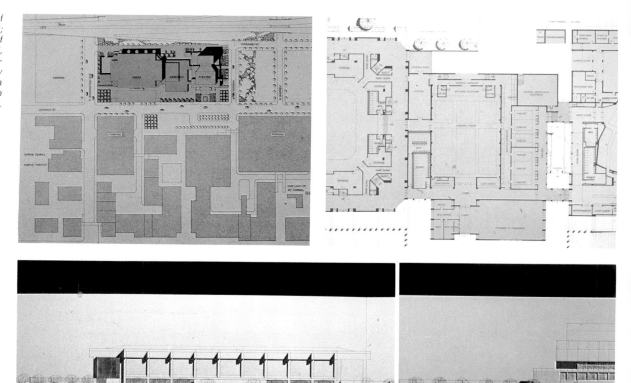

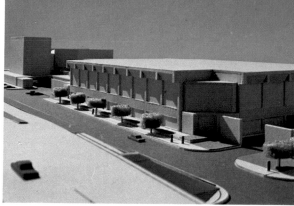

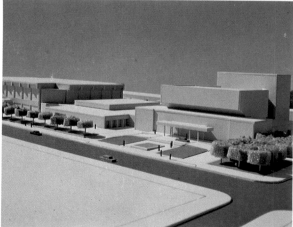

15
DESIGN AND
SCHEMATIC DEVELOPMENT

Design at Welton Becket and Associates constitutes a very broad discipline. For the most part, a designer here becomes not a specialist but a generalist first of all. Now everyone knows that architects have called themselves generalists from time immemorial.

Designers here find themselves assigned to buildings of all types. No one gets stuck in the rut of designing office building after office building for the remainder of his career. And all of the designers, to one extent or another, are involved in what is called here "total design." Thus, an architectural designer, almost always a registered architect, will most often find he gets an assignment to a project very early in its history. He finds himself operating on a par with the project architect, in sort of partnership. He finds himself very quickly concerned with all of the early studies and research. And he becomes increasingly concerned with the "total" aspects of the project, with the interiors, the landscaping, the

graphics, as well as with what in the past might have been called the "architectural" aspects.

Here, the all-encompassing word for all of these concerns and activities is *architecture*. And the designer works with them all. In that way, in a very real degree, the designer functions as a generalist.

On the other hand, the differences between individuals cannot be overlooked, the differences that cause one designer to find that he really is good at space planning, for example, and even more importantly likes doing it. Or in another case, a designer through accident or otherwise finds himself working on a series of airport projects and one day finds he has become an expert or specialist in airports. To take the idea a bit further, this metamorphosis of the generalist designer who comes to Welton Becket and Associates into the specialist designer happens all of the time here, in perhaps the majority of the cases. Therefore, the designers on the staff include people

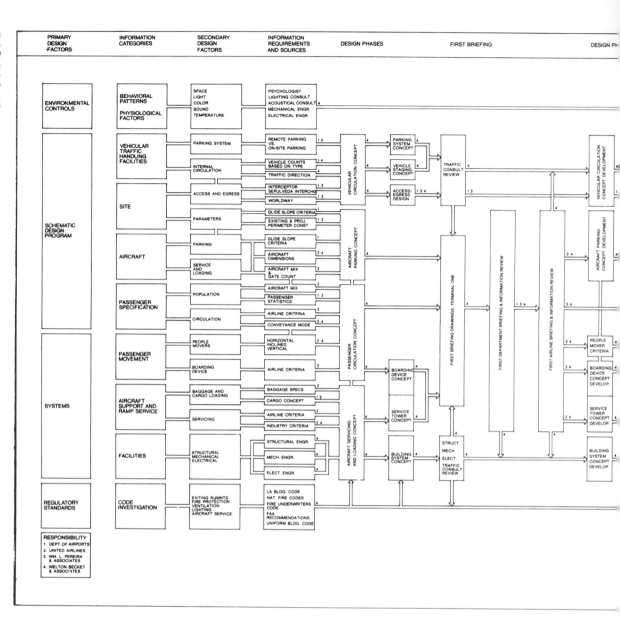

who have come to specialize to an extent in interiors, in graphics, in specific building types, in research, and so on. However, it is important to recognize that in this firm, these designers usually do not become stuck in their acquired specialties to the exclusion of all other work. Perhaps it would not be stretching the point too far to say that what happens is that they become specialists in one or more areas without losing their status as generalists.

At this juncture, it should be pointed out that there is no Becket "style" as such in the sense of that of Mies or TAC or SOM. The Becket style consists of what might be called a multifaceted style. This sounds somewhat puzzling, but it does approach the truth of the matter. The designs of this firm are all attempts to fit the solution to the problems, to produce a building that reflects the needs and desires of the client to the extent that is possible without

compromising the integrity of the firm as architects.

Thus the firm finds in itself no conflict—perhaps it would be more accurate to say little conflict—when faced with the prospects of doing five resort hotels in Walt Disney World. All utilize a very advanced solution in prefabrication and site assembly. One is strictly contemporary, but the others consciously styled to cater to the escapism of vacationers into Polynesian, Asian, Venetian, and Persian surroundings.

To return to the generalist-specialist theme for a bit, the drawings shown here and on the two following spreads demonstrate some of the results of the design work of Arthur Love, who directed the research work on a regional prototype airport shown in the preceding chapter.

Love has worked on numerous airport projects. He likes the field, is good at it, and has become one

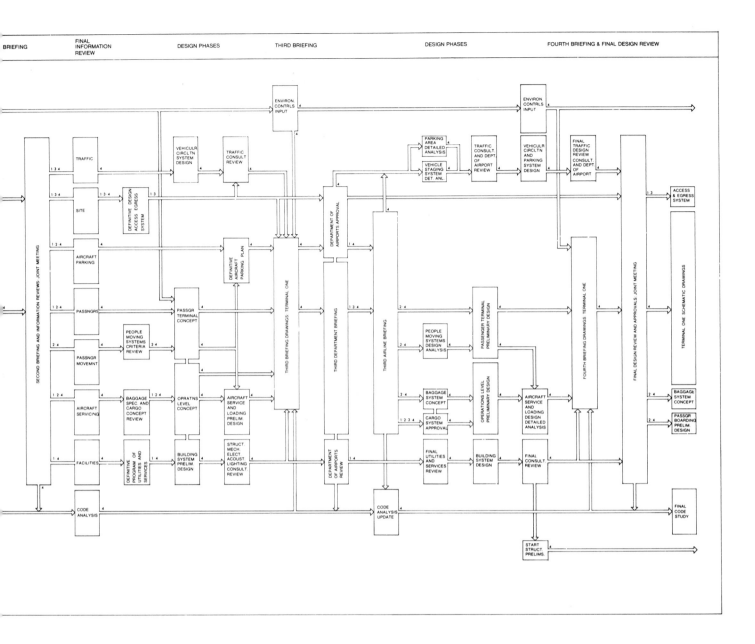

of the country's advanced thinkers on the subject. Accordingly, when United Air Lines commissioned the firm to study the impact of jumbo jets and SSTs on airports in general and on the United terminals in particular, it was natural for Love to be assigned the design job. His background was just what was needed for this project, and there were people in the firm upon whose knowledge he could draw.

Welton Becket and Associates was a natural for the job, too, since it had handled a number of airports in the past, including San Francisco International and a large part of the development of Los Angeles International, in association with two other firms, during the sixties. Thus the designer and the firm came to this project with considerable experience in and knowledge of airport design for jet traffic.

The development of Los Angeles International had been large and costly, some $70 million. It was a

complete airport in every sense, from the master planning to the administration building, control tower, and satellite terminals. And it included all of the facilities required to operate a jet-age airport. But it had been designed for the airplanes of the mid-sixties, at which point it was handling about 11 million passengers a day. By the late sixties, the traffic had grown to more than 21 million, and the jumbo jets were a reality. Coming were the SSTs. The Welton Becket and Associates design team decided to make a fresh start on the United terminal project. The criteria of the past were no longer valid. The great size of the airplanes, the increasing number of them to be handled, the rise in the numbers of passengers carried per plane, the growing difficulty of ground transportation called for a new approach.

At first, Love and his team studied only the functions and their relationships, proceeding from these

131

The drawings and photographs of models shown here and on pages 134 and 135 indicate the results in design of following the detailed study of the phases of design for a Los Angeles terminal building shown on pages 130 and 131.

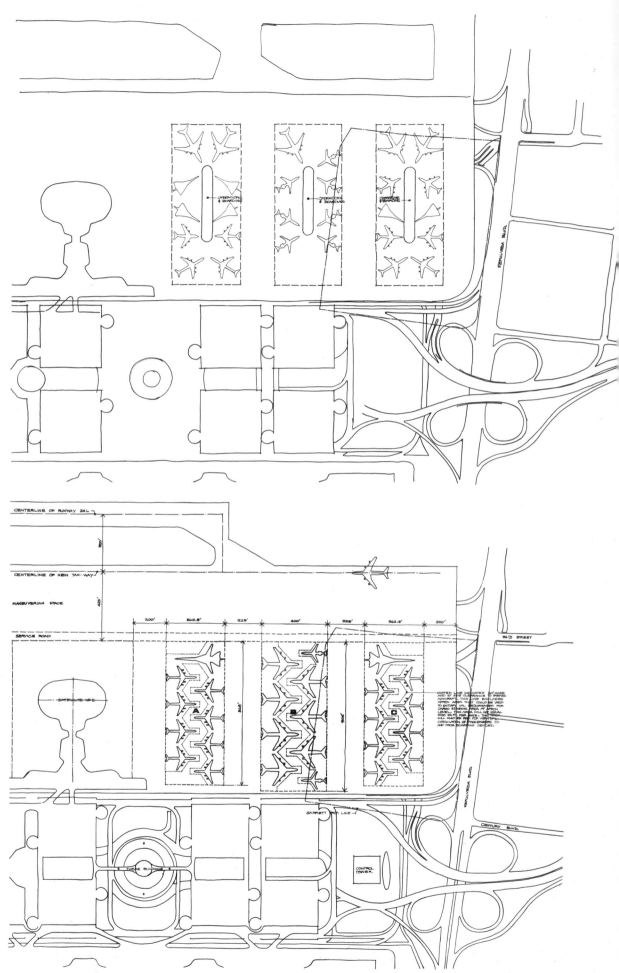

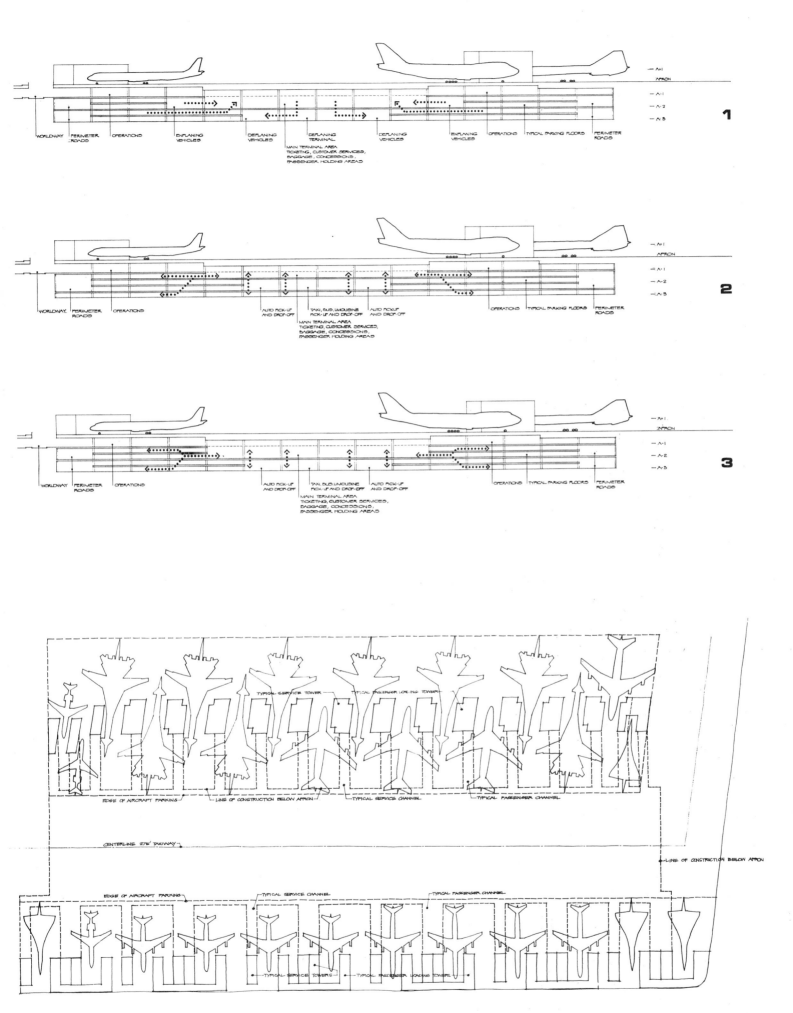

1

WORLDWAY | PERIMETER | OPERATIONS | ENPLANING | DEPLANING | DEPLANING | DEPLANING | ENPLANING | OPERATIONS | TYPICAL PARKING FLOORS | PERIMETER
ROADS | | | VEHICLES | VEHICLES | TERMINAL | VEHICLES | VEHICLES | | | ROADS

MAIN TERMINAL AREA
TICKETING, CUSTOMER SERVICES,
BAGGAGE, CONCESSIONS,
PASSENGER HOLDING AREA

2

WORLDWAY | PERIMETER | OPERATIONS | AUTO PICK-UP | TAXI, BUS, LIMOUSINE | AUTO PICK-UP | OPERATIONS | TYPICAL PARKING FLOORS | PERIMETER
| ROADS | | AND DROP-OFF | PICK-UP AND DROP-OFF | AND DROP-OFF | | | ROADS

MAIN TERMINAL AREA
TICKETING, CUSTOMER SERVICES,
BAGGAGE, CONCESSIONS,
PASSENGER HOLDING AREAS

3

WORLDWAY | PERIMETER | OPERATIONS | AUTO PICK-UP | TAXI, BUS, LIMOUSINE | AUTO PICK-UP | OPERATIONS | TYPICAL PARKING FLOORS | PERIMETER
| ROADS | | AND DROP-OFF | PICK-UP AND DROP-OFF | AND DROP-OFF | | | ROADS

MAIN TERMINAL AREA
TICKETING, CUSTOMER SERVICES,
BAGGAGE, CONCESSIONS,
PASSENGER HOLDING AREA

TYPICAL SERVICE TOWER — TYPICAL PASSENGER LOADING TOWER

EDGE OF AIRCRAFT PARKING — LINE OF CONSTRUCTION BELOW APRON — TYPICAL SERVICE CHANNEL — TYPICAL PASSENGER CHANNEL

CENTERLINE 275' TAXIWAY

LINE OF CONSTRUCTION BELOW APRON

EDGE OF AIRCRAFT PARKING — TYPICAL SERVICE CHANNEL — TYPICAL PASSENGER CHANNEL

TYPICAL SERVICE TOWERS — TYPICAL PASSENGER LOADING TOWERS

134

considerations to the flow between functions. As may be gathered from the schematic diagram shown on pages 130–131, these early studies led to a highly organized concept of the functions of an airline terminal.

As time went by, the conceptual studies became the basis for a large number of varied attempts to handle the functions and flow in the best possible manner. Some of these attempts are illustrated in the pages preceding, along with design models showing where they led.

The illustrations of the United terminal project give some indication of the kind of design that is accomplished in Welton Becket and Associates when a complex, intricately interwoven set of problems is attacked by a designer with an organized and orderly approach. A casual glance through the pages of this book will indicate the breadth and variety of design solutions produced for other projects. The reasons for this are quite simple. Each project design starts from the client and his needs. Each was assigned to a designer who, it was thought, could develop the project to meet those needs. And no effort was made on the part of anyone in the firm to cause the design or the designer to proceed along any narrowly defined lines or to adhere to any specific style or to end with any prescribed solution.

Design purists will no doubt decry this approach to architecture. And admittedly, the results are uneven. When the client and his problems, and the designer and his talents, and the adequacy of the budgets, and all of the other variables meshed together properly, the resulting designs are outstanding. When these things did not happen, as is apparent in some of the buildings shown in the pages of this book, the results do not achieve the highest standards.

But the average is high—Welton Becket and Associates does not do bad buildings. All of them are competent, well-planned, fitted to the clients. Schedules are met; budgets are adhered to; the buildings work; the clients are satisfied. And sometimes award-winning architecture is produced—over 100 high awards—sometimes not.

The design functions are handled in approximately the same manner in all five offices. The major differences between offices comes from the variation in their sizes. The larger offices, Los Angeles, New York, and Chicago, are more highly organized, and designers there tend to take on their assignments in individualistic ways and pursue them to the end. In the smaller offices, Houston and San Francisco, it sometimes seems like everyone gets into the act. The designer assigned to a project may find himself working with several of the other people in the office rather than pursuing his own work virtually alone.

Projects are assigned to designers by the design director in each office. The number taken on by an individual designer at any given point varies considerably. One person might have as many as five or more jobs in various stages of completion at one time. Another might only have one. The norm would probably be about three jobs. Of course, the number of projects being handled by one designer at any given point is to some extent dependent on the complexity of the projects and their current status. On a crash project, being handled on a tight timetable, a designer might devote almost all of his efforts over a period of time. And he might have another designer or even two assigned to assist him.

However, it would be rare indeed in this firm for a designer to spend all of his time on a single project. One reason for this is that designers are expected to get out into the field, to observe how their work is translated into actual construction, to ensure that their designs are properly built, and to solve design problems that arise during construction.

Increasingly, designers in this firm have come to work with models instead of relying strictly on drawings. For the most part, they are study models of form, mass, space, and texture. Most of the designers have become adept at the building of study models and the intensive use of them as design tools.

How do the designers themselves feel about the work of Welton Becket and Associates? There is no easy answer, in fact no single answer. The opinions of the designers are as varied as the designers themselves. Their opinions range from the delight of many of the younger designers at the prospect of participating in the design of big, important projects—even at having such projects assigned to them on occasion—to the comfortable feeling of some of the older designers in working in a stable atmosphere in which they can design at the uppermost level of their capabilities.

Perhaps it would be enlightening to hear what some of the designers say about their work.

Here is how Maynard Woodard put it: "I don't know exactly how it happened, but our office always had strong people. And this is particularly true of our designers. We have never attempted to mold them into people who work in a prescribed style. We just go out and find strong designers, talented designers, and give them the autonomy and backup they need to do the best jobs they can."

Robert Tyler, director of design in Los Angeles, says much the same thing: "Our design philosophy is as varied as the people in the department. We have a great variety of talent; but all are flexible in their interpretation of design philosophy."

These two views, perhaps with the addition of the Becket philosophy of total design and service to clients, describe the general attitude toward design of the designers to some extent. A sampling of the views of other designers in the firm produces a patchwork of opinion like this:

"It's a good place to work for a while to learn how to handle big buildings, but eventually I'd like to produce significant buildings of my own"—a very young designer speaking.

"This is the only office I could find, after several tries, where they don't try to force your work into some preconceived design theory"—a designer of some years' experience.

"It's sort of like having a patron who believes he can trust his money to a young designer"—another younger man.

Whatever their reasons, the designers here almost universally feel they can do their work well within the organization.

White Plains Mall,
White Plains, New York.

William Beaumont Hospital,
El Paso, Texas.

137

First & Merchants National Bank,
Richmond, Virginia.

New Queens High School,
Queens, New York.

138

North American Rockwell Corp.,
El Segundo, California.

Hampshire Plaza, Manchester,
New Hampshire.

*Northrop Building,
Los Angeles, California.*

*Shell Information Center,
Houston, Texas.*

*Medical Field Service School,
Brooke Army Medical Center,
Ft. Sam Houston, Texas.*

*State Street South, Quincy,
Massachusetts.*

141

*Esco Building,
Los Angeles, California.*

*Middlesex Bank,
Burlington, Massachusetts.*

142

Sheraton Hotel,
Tehran, Iran.

Com/Ed West,
Monterey, California.

*Downtown Office Building,
Los Angeles, California.*

144

*North Carolina Mutual Life
Insurance Company, Durham,
North Carolina.*

Wells Fargo Bank, San Rafael, California.

Center Plaza, Boston, Massachusetts.

16
PRELIMINARIES
AND PRODUCTION

In the Welton Becket and Associates firm, the design department works very closely with production, but the two are organized separately. A designer, upon being assigned to a project, finds that his counterpart in production, a project architect, has also been assigned. Each will follow the project all the way through from earliest conferences to the finished building. The designer will report to the director of design, the project architect to the director of production.

Thus what ensues as the work goes ahead might be likened to a partnership between the designer who has certain responsibilities and authority and the project architect who has others. Needless to say, there are times when these responsibilities overlap between the two. And as in any good partnership, the problems that inevitably arise out of the overlap must be resolved between the parties.

In a sense then it might be said that there also exists a partnership between the directors of design and of production to whom the designer and project architect report. Here too, problems of overlap and of disagreement between departments must be resolved. In extreme cases, when the designer and his opposite number, the project architect, cannot come to grips with their specific differences of philosophy or approach, then the department heads must step in to handle the case.

In the essentials, the setup works quite well in most cases. The major responsibility of the designer, of course, is to handle the early studies, programming, and the like and to come up with schematics that solve the big problems and are acceptable to the client. In this firm, schematics are very complete indeed. At this juncture, the major responsibility for the production of preliminaries or design development and, after that, working drawings and specifications, becomes that of the project architect.

The designer retains responsibility throughout the life of the job for all decisions of a primarily design nature. This responsibility extends through production and into the services during construction.

The project architect retains responsibility for the overall project, including its administration and working with the client throughout the entire life of the job. And his is the prime responsibility for the services performed during construction.

However, none of the foregoing should be construed to mean that the designer or the project architect can remain uninvolved in the work of the other. Actually, they become considerably involved, sometimes to the extent where it is almost impossible to tell where the work of one leaves off and that of the other begins. This fact should be kept in mind when examining how the production phases are handled in Welton Becket and Associates.

Perhaps a description of how a project goes through production will serve the purpose of dem-

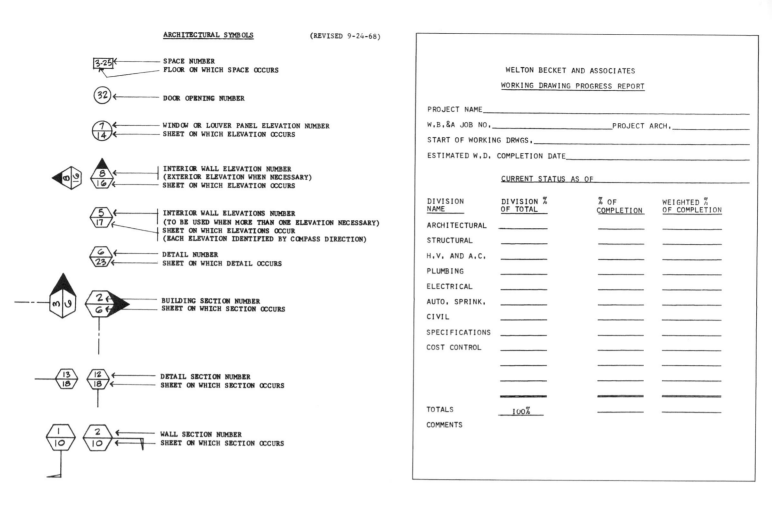

ARCHITECTURAL SYMBOLS   (REVISED 9-24-68)

3-25 — SPACE NUMBER / FLOOR ON WHICH SPACE OCCURS

32 — DOOR OPENING NUMBER

7/14 — WINDOW OR LOUVER PANEL ELEVATION NUMBER / SHEET ON WHICH ELEVATION OCCURS

8/16 — INTERIOR WALL ELEVATION NUMBER (EXTERIOR ELEVATION WHEN NECESSARY) / SHEET ON WHICH ELEVATION OCCURS

5/17 — INTERIOR WALL ELEVATIONS NUMBER (TO BE USED WHEN MORE THAN ONE ELEVATION NECESSARY) / SHEET ON WHICH ELEVATIONS OCCUR (EACH ELEVATION IDENTIFIED BY COMPASS DIRECTION)

6/23 — DETAIL NUMBER / SHEET ON WHICH DETAIL OCCURS

2/6 — BUILDING SECTION NUMBER / SHEET ON WHICH SECTION OCCURS

13/18   12/18 — DETAIL SECTION NUMBER / SHEET ON WHICH SECTION OCCURS

1/10   2/10 — WALL SECTION NUMBER / SHEET ON WHICH SECTION OCCURS

WORKING DRAWING PROGRESS REPORT

WELTON BECKET AND ASSOCIATES

WORKING DRAWING PROGRESS REPORT

PROJECT NAME_____

W.B.&A JOB NO._____   PROJECT ARCH._____

START OF WORKING DRWGS._____

ESTIMATED W.D. COMPLETION DATE_____

CURRENT STATUS AS OF _____

DIVISION NAME	DIVISION % OF TOTAL	% OF COMPLETION	WEIGHTED % OF COMPLETION
ARCHITECTURAL			
STRUCTURAL			
H.V. AND A.C.			
PLUMBING			
ELECTRICAL			
AUTO. SPRINK.			
CIVIL			
SPECIFICATIONS			
COST CONTROL			
TOTALS	100%		

COMMENTS

WELTON BECKET AND ASSOCIATES
ARCHITECTS AND ENGINEERS

COST CONTROL DEPARTMENT
LOS ANGELES, CALIFORNIA

PRELIMINARY PROJECT INFORMATION

JOB INFORMATION   DATE _____

Project Name _____   JOB NO. _____

Location _____

Client _____
Job Phase: Schematics _____ Preliminaries _____ Working Drawings _____
Completion Dates: Estimate _____ Drawings _____

PRODUCTION STAFF

Project Architect _____   Job Captain _____

Designer _____   Specifications _____

Structural Engineer _____   Mech.-Elect. _____

Additional Consultants _____

PROJECT DESCRIPTION AND SCOPE

Bldg. Type _____   Foundation _____   Frame _____
No. Stories _____   Story Heights: Bsmt. _____   1st Fl. _____   Typical _____
No. Basements _____   Penthouse _____
Ceiling Heights _____   Bsmt. _____   1st Fl. _____   Typical _____

SCOPE OF WORK _____

ALTERNATES (If Any) _____

ITEMS NOT INCLUDED IN CONTRACT _____

COMMENTS _____

WELTON BECKET AND ASSOCIATES - ARCHITECTS AND ENGINEERS
GENERAL CONSTRUCTION SUMMARY

Page 1 of _____

Estimate Phase_____   Estimated By_____

Job No._____ Name_____   Location_____ Date_____

Building Type_____ Foundation_____ Frame_____

No. Stories_____ No. Rooms_____ Gross Floor Area_____ Cube_____

Story Hgts:Bsmt._____ 1st Fl._____ Typical_____ Size_____

Areas: Bsmt._____ 1st Fl._____ Typical_____ Rentable_____

	CLASSIFICATION	REMARKS	AMOUNT	
1	EARTHWORK	$		
2	CAISSONS-PILING			
3				
4	CONCRETE WORK			
5	FORM WORK			
6	REINFORCING STEEL			
7	CEMENT FINISHES			
8	STRUCTURAL STEEL			
9	METAL DECKING			
10	FIREPROOFING			
11				
12	MASONRY			
13	ROUGH CARPENTRY			
14	WATERPROOFING			
15	ROOFING			
16	SHEET METAL			
17				
18	WINDOWS			
19	GLASS & GLAZING			
20	METAL WALL FACING			
21	SUN SHADES			
22				
23	MOSAI			
24	GRANITE-STONE WORK			
25	MARBLE			
26	MISC. & ORN. IRON			
27	MILLWORK			
28	METAL DOORS & FRAMES			
29	ROLL UP DOORS			
30	FINISH HARDWARE			
31				
32	LATH & PLASTER			
33	ACOUSTIC WORK			
34	TILE WORK			
35	TERRAZZO			
36	RESILIENT FLOORS			
37	PLASTIC COATING			
38	WALL COVERING			
39	PAINTING			
40	TOILET ACCESSORIES			
41	METAL TOILET STALLS			
	AMOUNTS FORWARDED	$		

(left margin labels: STRUCTURAL, ARCHITECTURAL)

COST CONTROL DEPT.

onstrating how this function is handled in the firm. And the purpose can probably be achieved through description of architectural production alone, if it is kept in mind that engineering production proceeds in a similar manner.

The production process on a job begins with the appointment of the project architect by the director of production at the earliest possible time. While this appointment is the responsibility of the director of production, very often the directors of design and of the office may be consulted, and in some cases the director of business development. In other words, every effort is made to assure not only that the man selected as project architect for a given job will have the best qualifications for seeing the job itself through to a happy conclusion but also that he is the best man available for working with the client. Another consideration is that of compatibility of the project architect and the designer. These questions are worked out in advance between design and production.

In a manner of speaking, the project architect assumes the role that a single architect in a one-man firm would have. To all intents and purposes the project architect is the architect, except that in this case he is backed up by many other people who can help him. And he has another advantage over the lone architect—much of the humdrum detail and paperwork will be done for him by the production administrator and others.

Soon after appointment of the project architect, a job captain is assigned. Together, and with the help of draftsmen, specification writers, cost control experts, and others, they will see the project through production. The job captain reports to the chief draftsman, who comes under the direction of the director of production.

A great deal of attention is paid here to methods for reducing the drudgery of production work. For some years now, Welton Becket and Associates has had a drafting-standards booklet, developed in the production department. This booklet, looseleaf in format, is updated regularly. It is unelaborate and inexpensive to reproduce. All of this because of the belief here that nothing should remain in effect longer than is necessary for efficient work.

A page from the drafting-standards booklet is reproduced opposite, at the upper left. All drawings produced here are expected to carry symbols of the sort shown. This makes it easy to maintain uniformity of such symbolism and easy to train new draftsmen. Drawings are done on sheets in a series of standard sizes with preprinted title blocks. The actual drafting, dimensioning, and lettering are accomplished in accordance with the drafting-standards booklet. For example, the booklet directs that floor plans are to have five strings of dimensions: (1) overall, (2) principal breaks, (3) column grid, (4) partition locations dimensioned from column grid, and (5) masonry openings dimensioned from column grid or masonry wall and the actual masonry opening dimensioned and designated "m.o."

Some of the items covered in the drafting-standards booklet chosen at random to demonstrate its coverage are the following: (1) toilet room wall elevations not to be drawn unless a special condition occurs; (2) concrete to be indicated on plans and sections by shading on the back of the sheet with blue pencil; (3) repetition of notes, dimensions, and reference symbols to be avoided. None of these to be shown on small-scale drawings, except column grid dimensions and references to large-scale drawings when large-scale drawings are part of the set.

The drafting-standards booklet contains a great number of items similar to those cited. All have been carefully worked out to provide ease of drafting, uniformity of drawings, and to lessen the possibility of error. Also included in the booklet are standard symbols to be used for material indications, standard abbreviations which are stocked in decal form, and other matters of importance to the draftsmen.

Every effort is being expended to obtain decals or other reproducibles for every item of the drawings that can conceivably be put into such form. For example, some details that are used often are on plastic that can be adhered to a drawing and reproduced.

In a highly organized firm such as Welton Becket and Associates, it is not surprising to find control forms of various kinds in use. However, it may come as a surprise to some to find such forms so simple, so easy to use, and so few. For example, the working-drawings progress report, shown across-page at the upper right, is one of the key forms. Completed by the project architect for each of his jobs in the working-drawing stage, the form is turned in to the director of production every two weeks. In this way, a continuing record of the progress of each job can be maintained. The form also establishes a control mechanism for assignment of personnel, for anticipating and handling slowdowns of the work, and for billing clients. After a project has been completed, the data from these forms become a sort of diary of its progress through working drawings and can be analyzed at a later date as a lesson for the future.

Another subject that gets considerable attention in the firm is that of the costs of construction. Every effort possible is expended to ensure that realistic budgets are prepared for projects and, once prepared, to stick to them. This entails not just cost estimating but cost control in every sense of the phrase. Elaborate records of costs are kept and analyzed, and experts in the field of costing are employed in the offices.

A typical sequence of cost control steps might be something like this: (1) a budget estimate based on information from the business development people while they are in the process of obtaining the job, (2) very refined budget estimate at the beginning of the architectural services, (3) an estimate at the schematic stage, (4) another at the preliminary stage, (5) a refinement at the working-drawing stage.

And on many projects, there may well be the necessity for additional estimates at intermediate stages.

Two of the forms used by the cost control department are shown across-page at the bottom: the first preliminary description of the project, along with the general construction summary used for succeeding cost estimates.

WELTON BECKET AND ASSOCIATES — ARCHITECTS - ENGINEERS

SPECIFICATION MASTER INDEX (April, '67) — Page 1

JOB _____ JOB NO. _____

Columns: GUIDE SPEC. SECTION REQ'D. | SECTION NO. | WRITTEN | OK TO TYPE | TYPED | PROOFED/S.W. | PROOFED/P.A. | OK TO RUN | PAGES

COVER

TITLE PAGE

TABLE OF CONTENTS

DIV. A – BIDDING DOCUMENTS — A
INVITATION TO BID
INSTRUCTIONS TO BIDDERS — SINGLE PROPOSAL
INSTRUCTIONS TO BIDDERS — TWO PROPOSALS
FORM OF PROPOSAL (NO ALTERNATE BIDS - NO SUBCONTRACTORS)
FORM OF PROPOSAL (ALTERNATE BIDS & SUBCONTRACTORS)
FORM OF PROPOSAL #1 (BASE BID)
FORM OF PROPOSAL #2 (ALTERNATE BIDS - SUBCONTRACTORS - ETC.)

DIV. B – CONTRACT FORMS — B
FORM OF AGREEMENT
FORM OF BOND (PERFORMANCE)
FORM OF BOND (MATERIALS & LABOR)

WELTON BECKET AND ASSOCIATES — ARCHITECTS - ENGINEERS

SPECIFICATION MASTER INDEX (April, '67) — Page 2

JOB _____ JOB NO. _____

DIV. C – GENERAL CONDITIONS — C
GENERAL CONDITIONS (WB&A)
GENERAL CONDITIONS (AIA)
GENERAL CONDITIONS (CLIENT'S)
SUPPLEMENTARY G.C. - Use with WB&A G.C.
SUPPLEMENTARY G.C. - Use with AIA G.C.
SUPPLEMENTARY G.C. - Use with Client's G.C.

DIV. 1 – GENERAL REQUIREMENTS — 1
No.	Item
1.01	SPECIAL CONDITIONS
1.02	SCHEDULE OF DRAWINGS
1.03	MATERIALS
1.04	TESTING
1.05	ALTERNATE BIDS
1.06	UNIT PRICES
1.07	CASH ALLOWANCES
1.08	MANUFACTURERS' INSTRUCTIONS
1.09	INTERIOR COLOR & MATERIAL SCHEDULE
1.10	TEMPORARY CONSTRUCTION
1.11	APPROVED SUBCONTRACTORS

APPENDIX

SECTION 3.01

REINFORCED CONCRETE

1. APPENDIX

(a) The Information and Requirements appearing on the appendix sheets listed in the Table of Contents for this section are hereby established as a part of Section 3.01 for the subject project.

2. PLYWOOD GRADE MARKS

(a) Douglas Fir Plywood for form construction specified under Article 8 - Materials, shall be grade marked with one or other of the following grade marks.

3. REINFORCING STEEL GRADE IDENTIFICATION

(a) Reinforcing Steel shall be identified as to grade with one or the other of the following grade marks rolled into the bar.

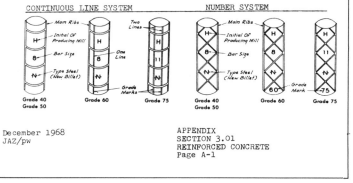

December 1968
JAZ/pw

APPENDIX
SECTION 3.01
REINFORCED CONCRETE
Page A-1

---

4. FORM CONSTRUCTION

(a) Plywood Thickness, depending upon the use of Class I or Class II Plyform, spacing of studs and general construction of forms shall be determined in accordance with the following tables and formulae, and with the requirements of Article 13 - Forms.

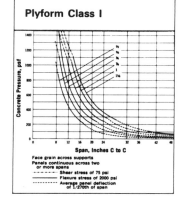 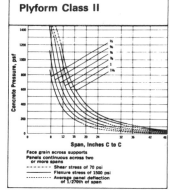

Plyform Class I | **Plyform Class II**

Face grain across supports
Panels continuous across two or more spans
— Shear stress of 75 psi
—— Flexure stress of 2000 psi
······ Average panel deflection of 1/270th of span

Face grain across supports
Panels continuous across two or more spans
— Shear stress of 70 psi
—— Flexure stress of 1500 psi
······ Average panel deflection of 1/270th of span

Suggested Concrete Design Pressures*

Rate of Pour (ft/hr)	Vibrated At 50°F	Vibrated At 70°F	Unvibrated At 50°F	Unvibrated At 70°F
2	510	400	460	360
3	690	530	620	480
4	870	660	780	590
5	1050	790	950	710
6	1230	920	1110	830
7	1410	1050	1270	950
8	1470	1090	1320	980
9	1520	1130	1370	1020

Vibrated Concrete

For R not exceeding 7 ft/hr

$$P = 150 + \frac{9000R}{T}$$

For R exceeding 7 ft/hr

$$P = 150 + \frac{43,400}{T} + \frac{2800R}{T}$$

MAXIMUM — 2000 psf or 150h, whichever is less

Where: P = Maximum Lateral Pressure, psf
R = Rate of Placement, ft/hr
T = Temperature of Concrete in Forms, °F
h = Max. Height of Fresh Concrete in Form, Ft.

*Tabulated values are for concrete of normal density (150 pcf). Test data indicate much variation in concrete pressures. The above values are suggested where better data are lacking. For unvibrated concrete, pressures for vibrated concrete are reduced 10%.

December 1968
JAZ/pw

APPENDIX
SECTION 3.01
REINFORCED CONCRETE
Page A-2

It should be in order, at this point, for a word or two about the climate in Welton Becket and Associates for cost control. First, it should be flatly stated that the philosophy of the firm, as previously pointed out, is to live within construction budgets. And clients have come to expect this of the firm. Project architects and other production people are highly cost-conscious here, as is top-level management. This is not always true of all of the designers all of the time. Considerable pressure may be applied by designers for more money with which to accomplish their projects. This is probably a truism that applies to designers everywhere. And it remains true in this firm. However, the situation here is probably healthier than in some firms. Here, the designers make their demands, and the battles are fought, and the buildings eventually end up within the money. The batting average on costs is very high.

As another attempt toward greater efficiency and lessening of the drudgery of production, Welton Becket and Associates has for some time been involved in automating its specifications. The system in use here stops short of the computer, which the firm feels is not really required so far. However, it would be a fairly simple step to computerize the present system if that should become desirable.

At the present time, the belief among the specification writers in Welton Becket and Associates is that putting their system on a computer would not really help very much and might even make the system less flexible. Be this as it may, the system now being used here seems quite adequate and reasonably flexible.

The most important aspect of the Welton Becket and Associates system is a set of master specifications developed within the firm. For the time being, the people here think that a better way to go than to adopt an outside master specification. The masters have all of the pertinent information needed in each major section of specifications and contain clauses covering all, or most, of the situations that ordinarily occur in the jobs handled by the firm. The masters are stored on perforated paper tape which is prepared with an automated typewriter system that is sophisticated enough to handle the work needed but is actually very simple. It consists, essentially, of regular electric typewriters with attachments that allow punching of tape, editing, and automatic recall of the punched-tape information into typed copy. The equipment also allows deletion of unwanted clauses and insertion of new ones.

Whether or not this system of storing masters and preparing copy from them will prove to be sufficient for the long term is a matter of some conjecture in the firm. As the volume of specifications produced increases, certain problems can be expected to arise. One major problem comes from the necessity of having an operator constantly in attendance of the machines to make deletions and other changes. Another is the relatively slow speed of the machine output compared to that of a computer.

Further experience should allow a more telling analysis of this situation. Also, it should be pointed out that the automated specifications described here are not yet in full use in the offices of the firm. As their use increases, there will be a need for weighing

not only the transposition of the current system to a computer but also the possibility of going to an outside specification system which might make updating the masters considerably easier.

In the Los Angeles office (but so far not in the others) the remainder of the specification reproduction can be accomplished inside the firm. There is a complete printing facility able to do the entire job. The typed copy comes from the automated typewriters ready to reproduce or in need of only moderate changes requiring cutting and pasting.

In the printshop, any required paste-up can be handled. Then the completed copy can be photographed onto paper plates ready to go onto the printing press. Multiple plates can be made by the platemaker and copies furnished to the other offices. Also, the plates themselves can be cut and repasted into new conformations if that is required.

After plates have been made, they go on a small offset press and then are collated and bound into sets ready for distribution. The equipment in the printshop can handle the whole job. Its capacity is such that all Los Angeles specifications can be done here and quite a few handled for the other offices.

It is estimated that some 90 to 95 percent of the architectural specifications can be handled with the automated system, the remainder being so specialized and used so infrequently that they are done by hand each time needed. Some idea of the completeness of the present system may be gathered from the two pages of the specification master index shown at the top, opposite. It will be noted, for example, that three possibilities exist for general conditions: those of AIA, Welton Becket and Associates' own, or those of a client. And also, any of these may be modified with special conditions. It might be asked how a client's general conditions could be automated. The answer is simple when it is remembered that this firm has a number of continuing clients for whom they have done projects over many years. For such clients, depending on volume, a master general conditions may be prepared.

At the bottom, opposite are examples of another important part of the Welton Becket and Associates production process. The pages shown illustrate another attempt to eliminate drudgery and repetitive work in the production process. Here, the purpose is to remove from the drawings all information of a standard, repetitive nature and place it in the specifications. Thus, a great deal of drawing and lettering can be eliminated. Such information can be placed on master sheets that are used over and over, requiring revision only when new information becomes available. And through the use of these sheets, standardization of procedures can be established for all projects when desirable or needed. Of course, the use of these sheets also eliminates or decreases the possibility of errors and misunderstandings.

In the pages immediately following are shown a number of photographs of details, chosen at random, of a few buildings done by Welton Becket and Associates. Perhaps they will serve to demonstrate the kinds of effect the production system here has on the finished product, the building, as well as the effects of the design efforts.

Closeups of details: Left to right, top row; North Carolina Mutual; Gulf Life. Second row; Ford Building, New York World's Fair; Xerox Square. Third row; Automobile Club of Southern California; General Electric Pavilion, 1964–65 New York World's Fair.

152

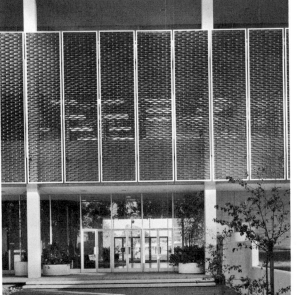

Closeups of details: Left to right, top row; Fashion Island; U.S. Borax Building. Second row; Hotel Sonesta; Automobile Club of Southern California. Third row; Century City.

154

Closeups of details: Cañada College.

156

17
SERVICES DURING CONSTRUCTION

Not every architect would agree with the methods Welton Becket and Associates uses for handling services during the construction phase of projects. But the services work. And clients like the methods.

In the first place, during construction it seems like everyone gets into the act. A job is likely to be visited by the top officers of the firm, by its designer, by other designers, by the engineers, by almost anyone who could conceivably have any interest in it, either directly or indirectly. And in almost all cases, the job visitor will prepare a report which goes to the director of production for his information and analysis. It might be imagined from this that the placement of the responsibility and authority for work under construction might be subject to doubt. Nothing could be further from the truth. These things are spelled out quite specifically. The thing is that neither direct responsibility nor authority for this phase of architectural services is taken here to mean that others in the firm remain neutral to what happens.

Actually, the exact reverse is true. Everyone, it would seem, in this firm believes in the old principle that the building itself is the test of success, not what went before.

It might be expected, however, in view of the dualism that exists on a project between the project architect and the designer that a similar situation might exist in this phase. It does. From the beginning of each project, the project architect retains the responsibility to see the job through to completion, to assure that it is properly processed through construction. As in the preceding phases, in which the

project architect shared responsibility with the designer, so in the construction phase he shares with the field representative. While the project architect retains overall responsibility for the job, his major duty during construction consists of all things that have to do with the client or owner. The field representative takes on the duties that have to do with the construction people. Since both project architect and field representative report to the director of production, problems can be efficiently handled when they arise.

The work of the project architect, in the construction phase, starts with the first moves made that affect the phase, the very straightforward and specific description of architect services during construction contained in all Welton Becket and Associates contracts with clients. This description leaves little or no doubt as to the role of the architect during construction. For example, owner-architect contracts always include words to the effect that Welton Becket and Associates "does not supervise, control, schedule, or regulate the method or means of performance by the contractor or subcontractors. Services are to be distinguished from continuous representation at the site. If desired, a full-time on-site representative may be engaged for your account."

Before construction begins, both project architect and field representative review the owner-architect agreement and the contract analysis made some time previously. After this, the project architect consults with the owner to determine the type of general contract to be used, whether it is to be on the basis

Sketches of the construction process for Xerox Square, Rochester, New York.

of competitive bidding or negotiated, and whether lump sum or some form of cost plus.

At the same time, a determination is made with the owner regarding segregated contracts for foundations, steel, or other construction activities. A decision is reached as to the need for a full-time owner's representative on the job, and the preferences of the owner regarding bidders are determined. Completed contract documents are again reviewed with the owner.

At this point, the project architect, having consulted with others in the firm, prepares the bid list, and often a list of acceptable subcontractors, and oversees the preparation of forms of proposal, invitations to bid, and other required forms and has the required number of sets of documents printed. In a similar manner, the project architect handles all of the remaining steps of bidding. In this sense, as in the preceding phases of services, the project architect acts very much as if he were an individual architect in his own practice.

Any addenda to or clarifications of the set of contract documents are issued by the project architect. And he is the official Welton Becket and Associates representative at the bid opening. It is he who prepares the bid tabulation list and who analyzes the bids and alternates. And he notifies the successful and unsuccessful contractors.

The project architect then advises the client on insurance requirements and consults with him on the owner-contractor contract. It is a well-established principle in Welton Becket and Associates that the architects do not prepare owner-contractor agreements at any time; they only consult, and the agreements are prepared by the owner's attorneys or others. Since Welton Becket and Associates is not a party to such agreement and is not engaged in law practice, the firm feels it is not proper for it to prepare such agreements. And if it did so, the possibilities of errors, omissions, and liability seem so apparent to the management of the firm that it refuses to prepare these agreements.

For years Welton Becket and Associates has had a construction-phase procedure manual which has been carefully revised in the light of experience until most of the usual circumstances are covered by procedures. This manual goes into considerable detail regarding even seemingly innocuous subjects, but the feeling here is that this phase must be accomplished correctly or all of the work that preceded it will be in vain. And there are so many possibilities for mistakes, misinterpretations, and inefficient procedures that the firm believes itself justified in keeping the rules for the sake of the firm as well as that of its clients. One example will serve to illustrate the depth into which this manual delves: when deposit checks are returned to bidders, a transmittal letter prepared by the project architect accompanies them, and the checks themselves are endorsed back to the contractors by two of the three people in each office authorized to do so. No other method is acceptable to the firm.

It was mentioned briefly before that each person from the firm who visits a job site is expected to file a report. He uses a standard form which lists the pertinent data of project name, contractor, date, job number, and so on and has a place for the site visitor to sign his name. The major portion of the form simply provides space for comments, and the visitor fills this in as he sees fit, noting anything he thinks is of importance and which should be brought to the attention of any individuals or departments concerned with the job. One copy is retained by the project architect and another by the field representative; additional copies are furnished to all who have a direct interest in the job.

Just as the project architects and the field representatives make regular visits to their jobs, so do the engineers of various specialties. While the first two named will be making an effort to observe the progress, quantitatively and qualitatively, of the entire job, the engineers for the most part apply themselves only to those portions of the job for which they are responsible. However, as mentioned previously, any Welton Becket and Associate visitor to a job is expected to file a report. Accordingly, an engineer may comment on anything he thinks important. In this firm, where the general rule is for everyone to take the entire job seriously and not just his part of it, the engineers and others can be expected to comment occasionally on things not actually in their province.

Problems on a job that result in relatively minor changes are handled by the field representative. He prepares and issues change orders. It should be noted that Welton Becket and Associates prefers to write owner-architect agreements that allow changes up to agreed-upon dollar amounts to be authorized by the architect rather than bothering the owner with relatively small needs. In such cases, the field representative issues a field change authorization. When clarification of the drawings or specifications is required, this is the province of the project architect. And he is the one charged with requests to the contractor for estimates of relatively major changes and following through on the preparation of change orders by the owner or contractor.

Shop drawings, laboratory test reports, samples, and the like are submitted through the project architect, who routes them to the proper departments for action. In the case of shop drawings, those of an engineering nature are handled by the responsible engineering departments and those that are architectural are usually handled by the job captain of each job or someone he delegates.

Requests for payment from the contractor are carefully reviewed by the field representative, who consults with the project architect, engineers, and others as required. After approval by the field representative and project architect, the request for payment goes to the accounting department, which issues a certificate of payment signed by the director of production administration.

In addition to the duties already discussed, the field representative performs the usual functions on the job, attending contractor's weekly meetings, submitting reports, preparing punch lists, checking progress, interpreting contract documents, and doing the myriad other things that help a project flow smoothly through construction to completion.

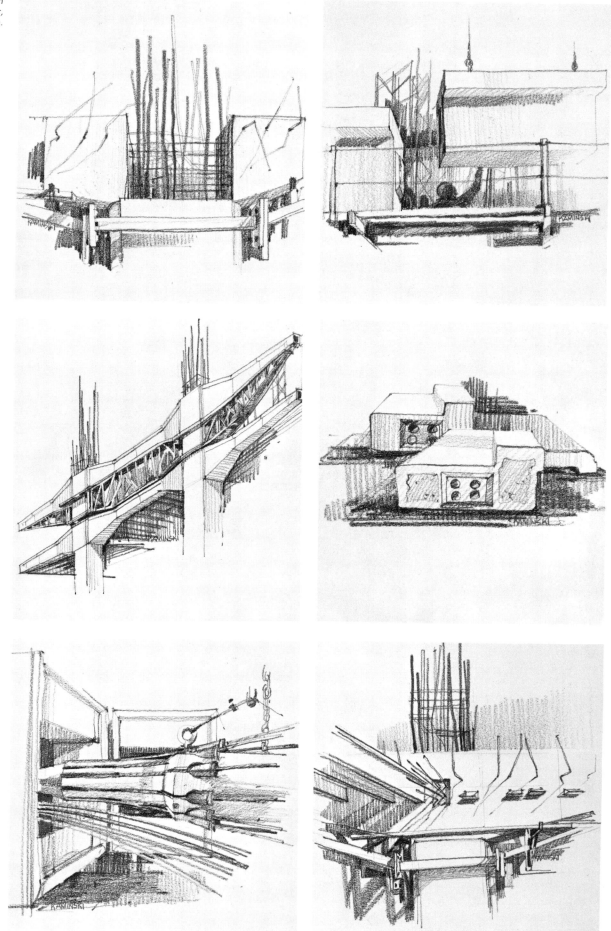

Sketches of the construction process for Gulf Life Tower, Jacksonville, Florida.

160

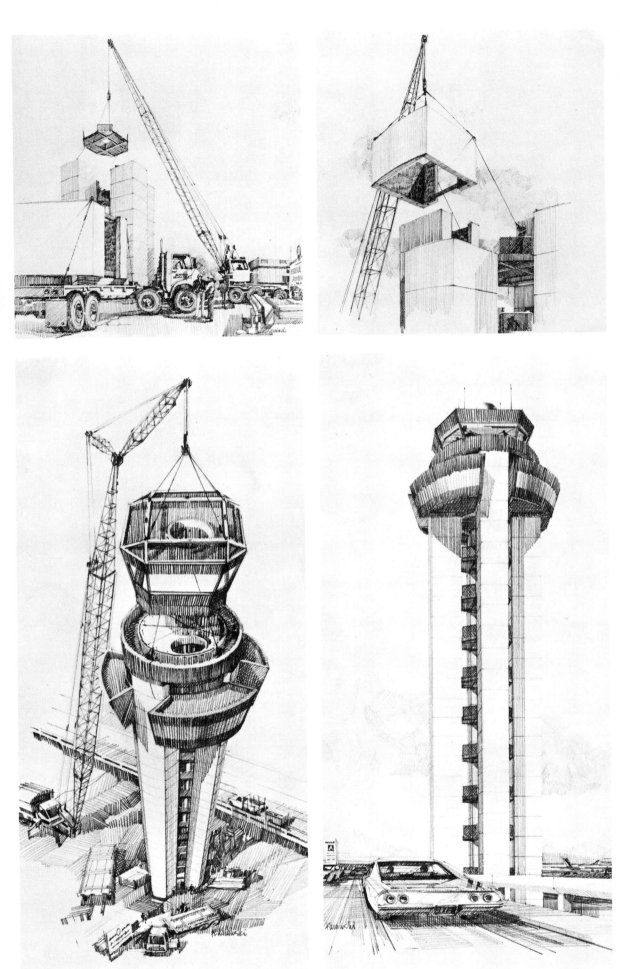

Sketches of airport control tower developed by Welton Becket and Associates as a prototype for the Federal Aviation Administration.

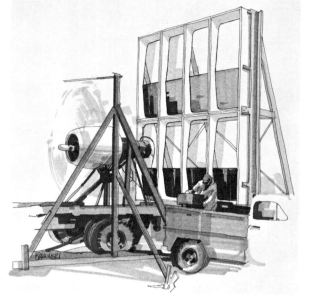

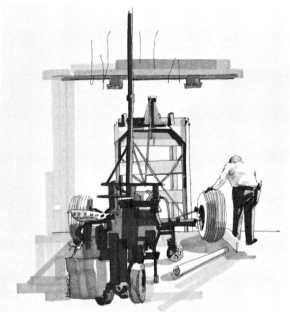

162

OPPOSITE: *Humble Oil & Refining Company, Houston, Texas.*

Part Five

A PORTRAIT OF
A TOTAL DESIGN

Humble Oil & Refining Co.,
Houston, Texas

166

18
THE CLIENTS
AND THEIR PROBLEMS

The central thrust of Welton Becket and Associates is the concept of total design. In the foregoing discussions of the many aspects of the practice, it is this concept that always unifies the many functions and activities of the firm. How total design works has been examined in some detail, but so far only in bits and pieces. At this point, it is time to put it all together. The most useful way to accomplish that is to use one building as a case study, in an attempt to describe what happened when total design was applied to it, how it worked, and the results.

Of course, any of a number of buildings might serve this purpose. The Humble Oil & Refining Company corporate headquarters in Houston has been chosen from among the candidates for a number of reasons. Welton Becket and Associates handled the architectural and related services in all their aspects, from feasibility studies to interiors. The building is a somewhat early example of total design, having been completed in 1962, yet it serves well for a demonstration of the principles of the concept. And the building was well documented during its design and construction.

To begin at the beginning, the commission for the Humble Building came to Welton Becket and Associates in 1958. The client was the Humble Oil & Refining Company, a very large oil-producing, refining, and marketing company, a subsidiary of Standard Oil Company (New Jersey). Organized in 1917, Humble had grown from 541 employees and $8 million in resources at the end of 1917 to 17,000 employees and assets of over $1.5 billion by 1958. Soon after this, a considerable change took place with the merger into this company of five regional affiliates of Standard Oil Company (New Jersey). This reorga-

nization had the effect of bringing all the 41,000 employees of the companies located all over the U.S. under a single top administration, located in Houston. Some years before, the executives of Humble had become aware of the need for a new office building for their corporate headquarters and had begun studies of the possibilities.

As the studies continued within the Humble staff, the acquisition of land in downtown Houston was begun. By 1958, a city block had been assembled as a site for a new office and another block diagonally across from the office site had been acquired for parking.

The studies made by the Humble staff had led to the tentative conclusion that the company should construct an office building of approximately 15 stories to house its 3,300 home-office employees along with a parking garage on the additional site. Some work had been accomplished in the area of space planning and future needs, and a preliminary program had been prepared. The company people assigned to the building project were under the direction of John Craddock, who at the time was the manager of the general service department, a man with considerable experience and knowledge of construction. He had the help of a team of company people with architectural and engineering backgrounds.

As Morgan J. Davis, then president of Humble, put it at the time, speaking of the major reason for the decision to build, "This new building will enable Humble to bring its 3,300 home-office employees together in one central location. At the present time, we are housing various groups of office employees in seven other buildings, some of which are more than four miles from our present home office building. The new building will enable the company to improve efficiency and reduce costs of office space. It will also provide room for expansion in the future."

With a tentative concept of the building, an assembled site, some preliminary space planning and related studies, and a preliminary feasibility report in hand, Craddock and his team started out to find an architectural firm to handle the work. First, they quietly investigated the work of a number of architects who seemed likely to have the capabilities for the job at hand. Then came interviews with the architectural firms that seemed likely candidates.

Eventually, after having interviewed a number of firms, the Humble representatives came to Los Angeles to see Welton Becket and Associates. Welton Becket and several others participated in the first interview. It quickly became apparent that the Humble people, in addition of course to architectural competence, had some other stringent requirements for the architect they would select. They wanted a single organization big enough to handle the whole job, perhaps with the help of consultants. They wanted compatibility with the people in the architectural firm who would handle the building. In fact, they insisted on meeting and getting to know the project architect and designer who would be assigned to the job in advance. They expected efficiency, of course, but they also wanted assurance that the key people assigned would continue on the job until it was completed.

A big order indeed, but there were still further requirements. Humble wanted the architect chosen to reexamine all the preliminary studies and the concepts developed by the company people so far and come up with recommendations to develop these concepts or alternatives to them. And Humble wanted local representation in Houston, a function Welton Becket and Associates could not perform readily since the office there had not been founded at the time.

Finally, after the qualifications of Welton Becket and Associates were reviewed along with those of a number of other architects, the Becket firm was given the commission. To satisfy the Humble requirements for Houston representation, the firms of Golemon and Rolfe and George and Abel Pierce were selected as consulting architects. This was not an architectural association in the usual sense. Rather, the two Houston firms performed certain assigned tasks for Welton Becket and Associates which acted as the architects for the entire building with the exception of the Petroleum Club, located on the forty-third and forty-fourth floors. The interiors of the club were handled by the Pierce firm.

The two consulting architectural firms performed a number of functions. They acted as liaison to some extent with Humble; they attended meetings of importance and advised Welton Becket and Associates on architectural aspects of the building; they handled many of the details of soil tests, code problems, and the like.

Almost immediately upon beginning work on the Humble Building, the people in Welton Becket and Associates discovered another fact of considerable importance: This building was not intended by the client to be a typical corporate headquarters showplace, as might a similar project for a large, successful company. Rather, this building was to be financed by money obtained from the Humble Employee Retirement Fund. And the company expected to occupy only about one-half to two-thirds of the space, with the remainder available for leasing to others. Thus the emphasis was to be placed on a building that would provide a proper rate of return to the retirement fund at normal office rental rates. In other words, this building was expected to correspond more to a so-called investment-type venture with the emphasis on long-range economy than to a corporate symbol with the usual attendant higher costs.

Welton Becket and Associates found itself with an unusually sophisticated client, one with great internal resources and considerable foresight. Humble had researched its own problems in considerable depth and analyzed its own needs. After determining the wisdom of constructing a new building for itself, the company people had come up with some fairly specific ideas of the size and conformation of the structure. They had prepared a fairly detailed program for achieving their needs. They had assigned experienced and knowledgeable people to act as their own representatives. Welton Becket and Associates had what it considered to be a good client, a conviction that lasted throughout the life of this project and into the future after the building had been completed.

Recently, Louis Naidorf, who was the designer of the Humble Oil Building, reminisced about his earliest impressions of the client and its needs: "This was my first real experience with a large corporate client, and I didn't quite know what to expect. I guess it seemed to me somehow that I would be working with the company, as a sort of faceless entity. The exact reverse was true. All of the people at Humble were individuals. They were interesting. They had accomplished things. They had been around, you might say. I remember how surprising it was to all of us who worked on the job to find that we would not be dealing with people who knew little or nothing about architecture, that the Humble team consisted of an architect and engineers led by John Craddock.

"They wanted us to do the total job on their building and they wanted undivided responsibility," Naidorf continued. "They came to us with detailed program requirements and a concept for a building of about fifteen stories that filled its site, a sort of low structure that was highly efficient in cost. And they expected us to be critical of what they conceived. If we had liked their tentative solution, I suppose they would have gone along with our using it for a starting point. But what they really wanted was for us to analyze every single aspect of it and propose alternate solutions. I guess we took this procedure as sort of a test of our architectural integrity. As it happened, we did come up with an alternative that was completely different, and our scheme was built."

On the next page are outlined the essential facts of the building eventually designed and built.

PROPOSED OFFICE BUILDING AND GARAGE
FOR
HUMBLE OIL & REFINING COMPANY
HOUSTON, TEXAS

FACT SHEET

Architects-Engineers: Welton Becket and Associates, Los Angeles & Dallas.

Consulting Architects: Golemon & Rolfe, Houston.
George Pierce and Abel B. Pierce, Houston.

Structural Engineers: Murray Erick and Associates, Los Angeles.

Soils Engineers: McClelland Engineers, Inc., Houston.

Traffic Engineer: Thomas E. Willier, Houston.

Office Building

Location: Block 336 SSBB, bounded by Travis (east), Milam (west), Bell (north), Leeland (south).

Size: 44 stories, concourse, and two basements.

Height: Approximately 600 feet.

Net Usable Area: About 1,000,000 square feet.

Building Population: 5000 – 7000.

Estimated cost: $32 million.

General Description: The office building tower will be about 115 feet by 250 feet and will rise about 600 feet above the block square base which will be set 3½ feet above the sidewalk.

The base will consist of a semi-underground concourse level and two lower basements.

The building will be of high-strength alloy steel frame construction with floors of light-aggregate concrete on metal pans.

Fixed horizontal sunshades of aluminum and porcelain will be an unusual exterior feature.

Special Facilities: Second basement – Stationery and office printing facilities and storage.

First basement – Reproduction and graphics section, mail, file storage, maintenance shops.

Concourse – Cafeteria seating 1200 with kitchen and serving facilities. Auditorium seating 500. Drug store, soda fountain, news stand, barber shop, elevator lobby and lounge. Escalator to main lobby. Air-conditioned tunnel to garage.

Lobby – Glass enclosed, 29 feet high. Automobile entrance on Leeland. Touring Service and information center. Exhibition area. Partial mezzanine over Touring Service and exhibition areas.

Mechanical Floors – Located at about the 10th, 20th, and 30th floor levels will be service or mechanical floors on which will be located the air conditioning and heating distribution systems for the office floors above and below. The mechanical floors will also contain the electrical distribution system and elevator machinery.

Top floors – The two top floors will be glass enclosed and unencumbered by air conditioning cooling towers or compressors which are planned to be located on top of the Garage building.

Garage

Location: Block 353 SSBB bounded by Milam (east), Louisiana (west), Leeland (north), and Pease (south).

Size: 6 stories and two basements.

Gross Area: Approximately 530,000 square feet.

Capacity: About 1300 cars.

General Description: The garage building will be about 250 feet square and will be of reinforced concrete construction. The side walls will be semi-open to allow for full ventilation. The building will have entrances and exits on all four sides. Spiral ramps will serve all floors and basements.

Special Facilities: Lower Basement – Air-conditioned tunnel to office building. Elevator lobby. Storage space.

Street level – Full service station facilities. Space for retail shops. Air-conditioned elevator lobby.

Roof – Boilers, compressors, cooling towers for heating and air conditioning building and garage.

Humble Oil & Refining Co. Building, interiors of the office building and bank.

19
ESTABLISHMENT
OF FEASIBILITY

Soon after Welton Becket and Associates received the commission for the Humble Oil Building in Houston, a series of studies was undertaken by the architects. A reexamination of the program began, along with design studies. These phases are described in the next chapter. Concurrently, two major feasibility studies were started, one into the economic aspects of the project, the other into the problems of traffic flow of automobiles and their parking. In these researches, Welton Becket and Associates was assisted by Thomas E. Willier, Houston traffic and business consultant. The results of these studies were combined into a report delivered to the client in January 1959 and accepted shortly afterward.

The economic report covered a number of major subjects, the existing and future requirements of Humble for its own needs, the existing and future rental market situation in Houston, the future potential demand for building service facilities such as employee cafeteria, company auditorium, television transmission antennas, retail and service shops, and so on. In addition, it contained a budget for the building and a special cost breakdown for the sunshade system that then was proposed and later accepted.

The traffic and parking report was concerned with the practices of company employees and officials at the time and projections of the future situation. Portions of this report were devoted to traffic, accessibility, street capacities, and other items needed for making decisions as to the feasibility of the available site and on the capacities of the proposed parking garage.

Thus it may be gathered that although Humble people had been studying such aspects of their proposed building for some years, they thought it best to have their tentative conclusions verified or disproved by the architects and their consultant. The client wanted a complete new study, in considerable depth, but also wanted to avoid premature publicity on its plans until they could be finalized. This restricted, to some extent, the field investigations possible without giving away what the company was contemplating.

The final report on economics comprised four parts: building facilities, office rental market, projected space needs of the company itself, and financial considerations.

Taking these in order, the building facilities section was developed from studies made by Welton Becket and Associates and its consultant. These included discreet surveys made in Houston.

Studies of the needs for employee dining revealed the fact that facilities of the sort that were of adequate quality and capacity were just about nonexistent within a reasonable distance of the proposed site. Those which were available were either not within walking distance or too expensive for the majority of employees. The conclusion was reached that the building should include a cafeteria, to be operated by the company for the time being, with a caterer rather than an outside operator. The size of the cafeteria was estimated at twelve to sixteen thousand square feet to feed 3,000 to 4,000 people a day in three shifts.

Research indicated that Humble had needed an auditorium seating more than 500 people only once in its whole history. However, there had been a considerable number of meetings attended by up to 500 people. And with a growing number of em-

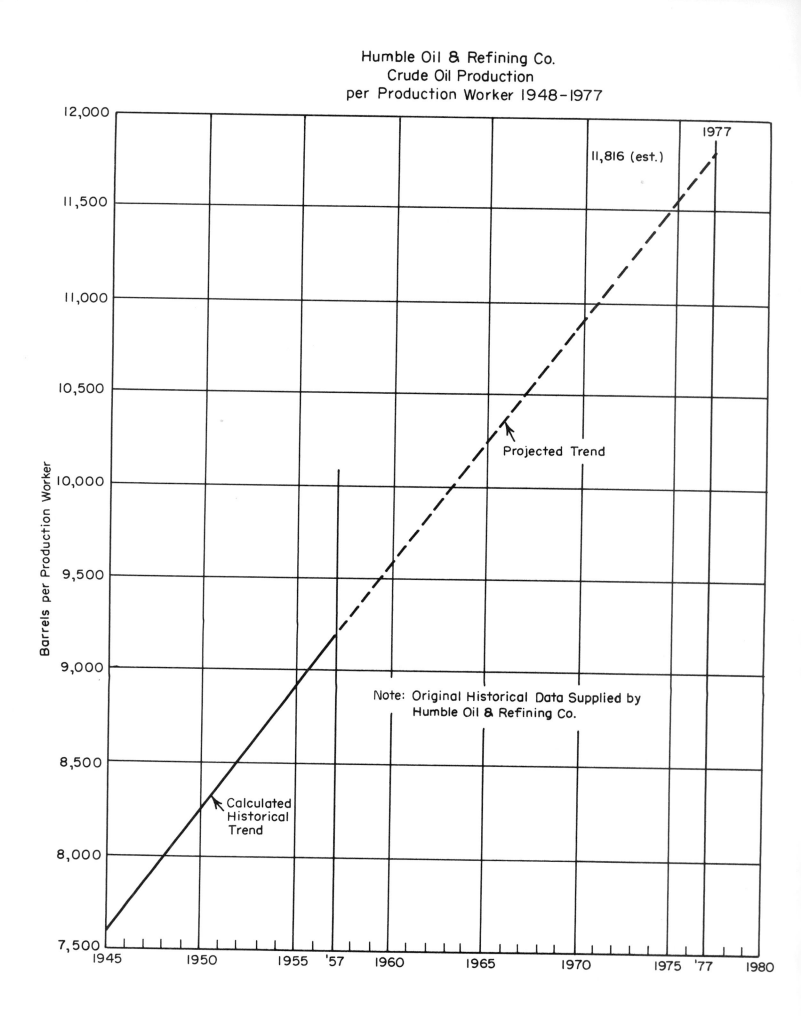

Humble Oil & Refining Co.
Crude Oil Production
per Production Worker 1948-1977

Barrels per Production Worker

1977

11,816 (est.)

Projected Trend

Note: Original Historical Data Supplied by
Humble Oil & Refining Co.

Calculated
Historical
Trend

CONSTRUCTION BUDGET

The Humble Oil & Refining Company has tentatively budgeted the sum of $30 million, inclusive of architect's fees, for the construction of a new home office building. In terms of a building of one million net square feet and 1958 material and labor costs, this figure appears reasonable, although detailed cost analyses cannot be made until preliminary designs are finalized. Some additional allowance should now be made, however, to offset the inevitable inflationary cost increases which will occur before the new building can be completed.

Although the general building contract is scheduled to be let in June, 1960, the general contractor will undoubtedly include in his bid any cost increases anticipated for the year 1961, since a majority of the trades will still be engaged in the work at that time.

During 1958 construction costs nationally rose five per cent on the average, an annual rate not likely to decline in the future. Since contractors' and other fees for professional services are usually figured on a percentage-of-cost basis, the entire original budget should therefore be escalated at the rate of five per cent, compounded annually for a period of three years (1959 through 1961). This results in a total budget estimate for the project, exclusive of land, parking structure, and office equipment, of $34,729,000.

AIR CONDITIONING SYSTEM WITH AND WITHOUT SUNSHADES

Scheme I Building — One Million Net Square Feet

	Without Sunshades (4,252 tons)		With Sunshades (3,870 tons)	
	Total $	$/sq.ft.	Total $	$/sq.ft.
CAPITAL COST:				
Air Conditioning System	$4,415,000	$4.415	$3,870,000	$3.870
Sunshades	----	----	900,000	.900
TOTAL CAPITAL COST	$4,415,000	$4.415	$4,770,000	$4.770
ANNUAL EXPENSES:				
Depreciation of Air Conditioning System (20 yrs. @ 5% per annum)	$ 221,000	$ .221	$ 194,000	$ .194
Depreciation of Sunshades (50 yrs. @ 2% per annum)	----	----	18,000	.018
Utilities	64,000	.064	57,000	.057
Maintenance of Air Conditioning System (2% of Capital Cost)	88,000	.088	77,000	.077
TOTAL ANNUAL EXPENSES BEFORE INSURANCE CHARGES AND REAL ESTATE TAXES	$ 373,000	$ .373	$ 346,000*	$ .346*

*It is assumed that savings in window cleaning costs will offset any sunshade maintenance costs. Therefore, no sunshade maintenance item is included in this analysis.

ployees in the Houston area, with stockholders' meetings, retirement gatherings, and other meetings of the sort, there seemed to be a definite need for an auditorium seating approximately 500. Making such an auditorium available to tenants also seemed likely to attract larger tenants to the building. The architects surveyed larger companies in the surrounding area to determine how they handled this function and came to the conclusion that the 500-seat space would do the job. If larger gatherings were to be held by the company, which seemed unlikely except at very infrequent intervals, the company cafeteria might be used, and several public spaces with adequate seating capacities were available in Houston.

Humble officials wondered if additional revenues might be obtained by placing a television transmission antenna on the roof of their building. The subject was not investigated thoroughly at the time because of the necessity for avoiding publicity on the project. However, it was determined that the existing television stations in Houston had recently built new antennas. For this and other reasons, it was recommended that no antenna be built but that the situation should be investigated again at a later date.

Investigation of the needs for retail space in the proposed building revealed the unfeasibility of including a shopping area in the building at the time of construction, with the few minor exceptions of a drugstore, a barber shop, and a beauty parlor. It was anticipated that no real demand for other retail stores would develop for at least five years. Thus the recommendation was to include space only for those shops mentioned. It was suggested that the barber shop have eight to ten chairs and the beauty parlor ten to twelve booths and that each occupy no more than 2,000 square feet. The drugstore was projected to occupy about 8,000 square feet and was programmed to include a snack bar, a record shop, toy stand, and jewelry and stationery in addition to the drug department. The size and capacity of these three shops was expected to be large enough to cater to the needs of the employees and the tenants.

The Humble Touring Service was investigated. Upon finding that most of its inquiries were handled by mail or telephone, it was concluded that the service could be located in the new building rather than in a more central location downtown. This solution was believed to be the more economical and would allow employees attached to the service to perform other functions such as acting as guides in the building.

The architects felt that the inclusion of an executive dining room or private club within the building was more properly an executive decision than one based on economics. Therefore, no study was made of the subject by Welton Becket and Associates. However, it was suggested that one or more of the top floors would be an ideal location for such facilities if they were thought necessary or desirable.

The projected requirements for crude oil were expected to continue to increase over the coming

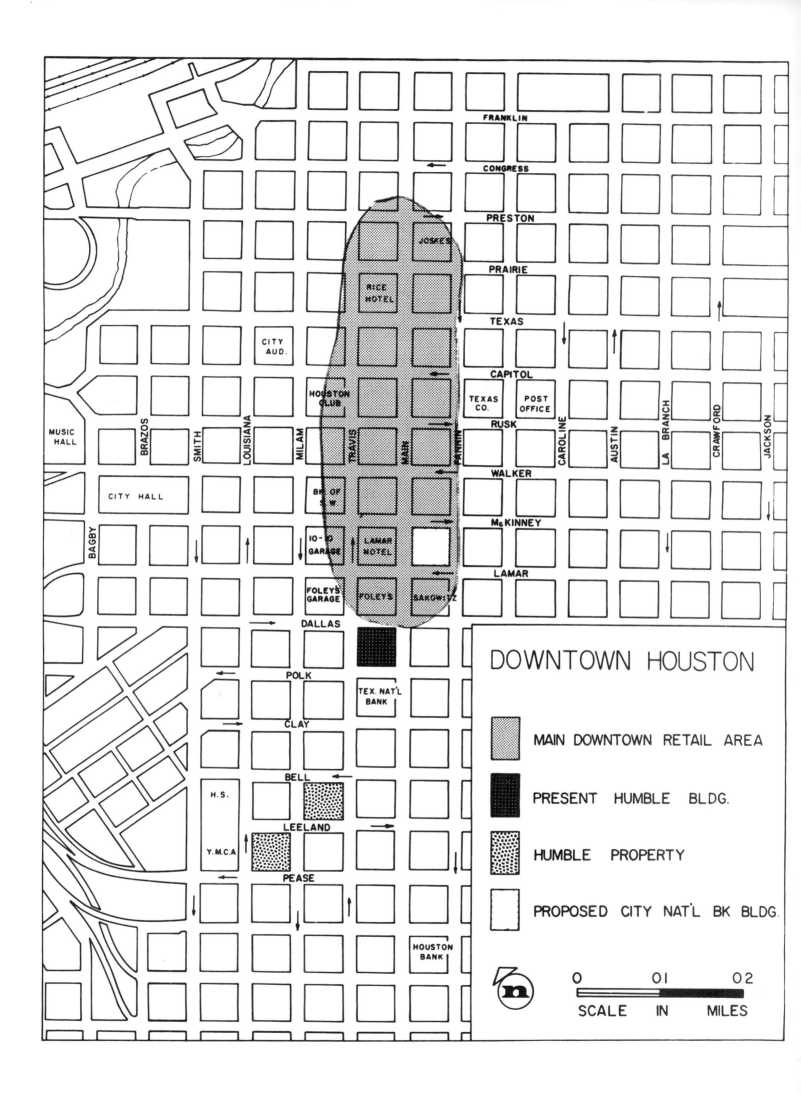

FRANKLIN

CONGRESS

PRESTON

JOSKES

PRAIRIE

RICE
HOTEL

TEXAS

CITY
AUD.

CAPITOL

HOUSTON
CLUB

TEXAS
CO.

POST
OFFICE

RUSK

MUSIC
HALL

BRAZOS

SMITH

LOUISIANA

MILAM

TRAVIS

MAIN

FANNIN

CAROLINE

AUSTIN

LA BRANCH

CRAWFORD

JACKSON

WALKER

CITY HALL

BK OF
S W

McKINNEY

BAGBY

IO-IO
GARAGE

LAMAR
MOTEL

LAMAR

FOLEYS
GARAGE

FOLEYS

SAKOWITZ

DALLAS

POLK

TEX. NAT'L
BANK

CLAY

BELL

H.S.

LEELAND

Y.M.C.A

PEASE

HOUSTON
BANK

DOWNTOWN HOUSTON

MAIN DOWNTOWN RETAIL AREA

PRESENT HUMBLE BLDG.

HUMBLE PROPERTY

PROPOSED CITY NAT'L BK BLDG.

0   01   02

SCALE   IN   MILES

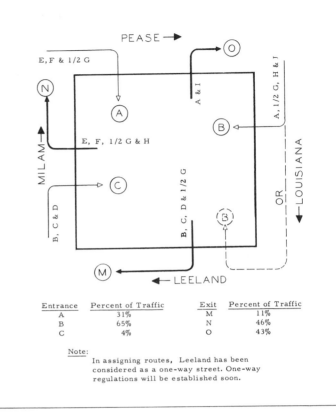

years at a rapid rate. For the economic study, figures on total crude production were related to Humble's share and this then related to the barrels per production worker, as shown in the chart on page 172. Then the proportion of production workers to office workers was determined and projected into the future. Finally, the estimated number of office workers was multiplied by space allowances per worker to arrive at net floor area required. In short, this describes the method used by Welton Becket and Associates to project space required in the new building.

The method used by the architects for projecting space needs was quite different from that previously used for Humble's own projections. While Welton Becket and Associates based its projections on a study of pertinent external factors, primarily the expected growth of crude oil production per worker and its results, those of Humble were primarily based on an extrapolation of past experience. A Humble estimate, made in 1956, envisioned a space need in 1975 of between 660,000 and 1 million net square feet. This was based on an average of about 170 square feet occupied by each employee.

The projections made by Welton Becket and Associates were made on the basis of a 1977 office population of 6,144, the figure derived from the crude oil study. Using 160 square feet average per employee, the architects projected a need for approximately 1 million net square feet. According to Humble's 1958 study, the population would be about 7,320 by 1977 and the study envisioned an average of about 135

square feet per employee. Here again, the net usable space was about 1 million. The two projections appeared to agree with each other, even though the assumptions and methods were different. Therefore, the recommendation was for 1 million net square feet.

The projected rental market in Houston seemed, at the time of the architects' economic study, to be healthy and well able to absorb the rental space Humble would have available when the building was completed. Estimates of the time envisioned the absorption of newly available office space in Houston at a rate of about 300,000 square feet a year. At the time there were about 550,000 square feet under construction that would be ready within the four years needed for planning and construction of Humble. Together with the approximately 250,000 to be put on the market in the new building and the 450,000 to be vacated by Humble when it moved, the total to be made available during the four-year period seemed to be just about what the growing market could be expected to absorb.

On page 173 are shown two of the actual pages from the Welton Becket and Associates economic report, the one on the left giving the generalities of the overall budget for the office building with projections of the escalation to be expected before completion. The illustration on the right projects the effect of the sunshade system, finally accepted for the building, on the capital expenditures and the operating costs. These budget figures were based on detailed budget estimates prepared at the time.

On these pages and those following are shown some of the pages of the feasibility studies made by Welton Becket and Associates for the Humble Oil Building.

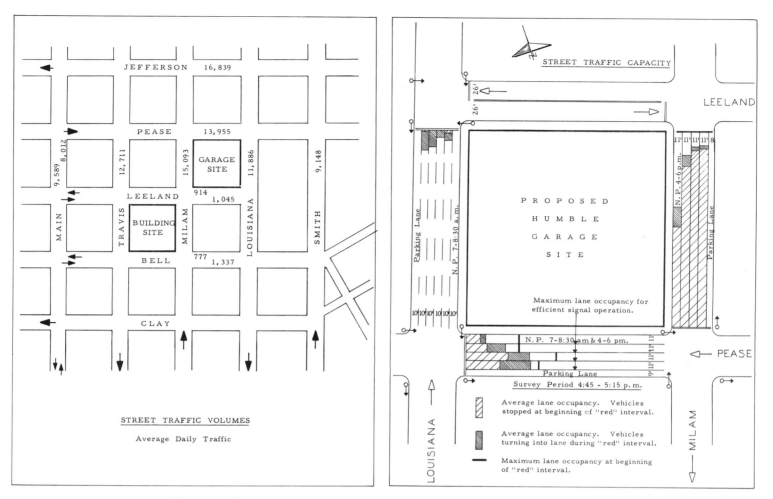

STREET TRAFFIC VOLUMES

Average Daily Traffic

The second portion of the report submitted by the architects and their consultant in January 1959 was concerned with traffic and parking. As may be gathered from the pages of the study reproduced here and on the pages immediately preceding and following, this study was quite complete.

Handled in the main by the consultant, Thomas E. Willier, under the direction of the architects, these studies were conducted by the use of field surveys and analyses. The most important survey was one conducted to determine the transportation and parking habits of all who would move to the new building. For simplicity, it was decided to ascertain what these people did on a single day in September 1958. On the same day, all visitors to the various Humble office locations were also surveyed.

The results of this survey revealed little or nothing startling to anyone familiar with Houston, an automobile-oriented city. However, they did reveal the sort of information needed for decision making related to transportation and parking for the new building.

On the day of the survey, of the 3,300 employees of the company, some 2,900 came to work. The others were sick, on vacation, or away on business trips. Of those who came to work that day, some 1,600 drove and about 1,100 rode with the drivers. Only 187 took buses and 38 walked. The study further reported where employees lived on that day indicating that almost none lived in the vicinity of the central business district or of the site for the new building. Fees for parking ranged from about $11 to

$15 per month, on the average, although about 200 had free parking of one kind or another and some 70 people paid more than $15 a month. In fact, there were 2 who managed to pay over $25.

On the day of the survey, 231 employees drove company cars to work, but they are included in the totals given before. Visitors to the various Humble offices of the time revealed a daily total of about 265, with only 10 percent at any one time for a total minimum of 27 visitors' spaces.

Projections of the parking needs from the figures determined in the survey revealed a need for 1,600 spaces at the time of the survey and an estimated 3,500 or so by 1975. Also, projections were made of charges that might be feasible for parking by the month and recommendations included in the report.

Studies were also made of traffic flow, one-way streets, and related subjects. The general recommendations were that a parking garage to house some 1,000 or more spaces should be constructed on the available site diagonally across from the new building. The garage was to be for self-parking, and the monthly rate would be $20. It was further recommended that consideration be given to assembling another site farther away from the office building for a garage that would contain another 1,000 spaces at $15 each a month. A pedestrian tunnel should connect the first garage with the office building.

At the time of presentation to the client of the economic and parking study, a design brochure was also presented showing very complete schematics of the new building.

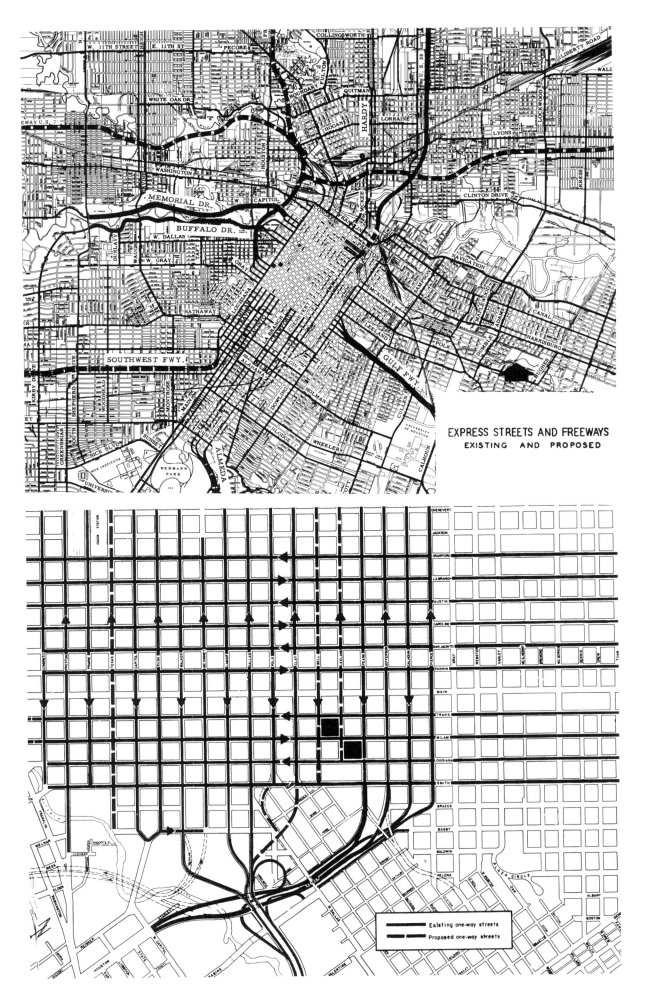

EXPRESS STREETS AND FREEWAYS
EXISTING AND PROPOSED

Existing one-way streets
Proposed one-way streets

PLACE OF WORK AND PLACE OF RESIDENCE OF HUMBLE EMPLOYEES

The place of work and place of residence data, obtained in a survey of Humble employees, are summarized in the following Table B-1. Areas of residence indicated in the Table are delineated on the Questionnaire map, reproduced in Appendix A. Boundaries of the residence areas were selected so as to provide specific areas tributary to major travel routes serving the Central Business District.

TABLE B-1

PLACE OF WORK VS PLACE OF RESIDENCE

Department	A M	A F	B M	B F	C M	C F	D M	D F	E M	E F	F M	F F	G M	G F	H M	H F	I M	I F	J M	J F	Totals M	Totals F	Total
Humble Building																							
Adv. & Pub. Rel.	6	1							1	5	1	2	10		9	7	7	12	1		35	27	62
Controller	64	33		2	8	5	2	1	59	45	23	24	62	15	42	25	72	56	8	6	340	212	552
Credit Union												2			1			1			4	1	5
Crude Oil	1	5				3		1	4	2	1	3	8		3	3	6	9		1	23	27	50
Eco. & Stat.	1	1										1	3				2	1			6	4	10
Empl. Rel.	8	14			1		1	1	2	8	4	5	6	6	7	14	23	23		5	51	77	128
Exec. Secy.						1						2				5		1			0	9	9
Exploration	22	25			5	1	2	1	28	27	7	15	25	21	31	29	36	33	5	7	161	159	320
Gas & Gas Prod.									2	2	1	1	4	1	2	1	5	4			14	9	23
Gen. Service	65	40	4		14	12	2		20	20	5	10	9	2	7	6	15	18	8	1	149	109	258
Humble Pipe Line	15	13	1					1	18	8	5	5	19	1	22	4	25	8	3	4	108	44	152
Law	6	1	1	2	1			2	1	5	2	8	9	3	6	3	15	14			41	38	79
Manufacturing	2	6						2	3		2	3	4		4	2	11	7	9		35	20	55
Marketing																			1		1	0	1
Production	7	10						3	19	12	8	16	37	11	25	9	53	32	4	2	154	96	250
Purchasing	5	7						2	5	1	1	1	8	1	7	5	7	9	2	2	35	28	63
Research																	1	1			1	1	2
Treasury	13	17			1	4		1	2	12	2	2	4	3	5	6	8	12	3	5	38	62	100
Total	215	173	6	5	30	27	7	15	165	147	62	96	210	66	171	120	286	241	44	33	1196	923	2119
1st. City Nat'l Bank																							
Aviation									4	1	1				1			1			6	2	8
Exploration	1	1							2	2			1		1		2	4	2	1	9	8	17
Gen. Service												1						1			0	2	2
Law		2							1	1	1		3	1	1	1	2	3			8	8	16
Marine		2								1			1				1	2			2	5	7
Traffic	1	1			1	1			3		1	1	2		3	1	6	2			17	6	23
Total	2	6			1	1			10	5	3	2	7	1	6	2	11	13	2	1	42	31	73

a-2

MODE OF TRAVEL OF EMPLOYEES

The Questionnaire Survey revealed that the automobile provided transportation to work for 93% of Humble's employees. Six percent reported using bus transportation and 1% walked or used other means of transportation. A summary of the mode of travel is submitted in Table C-1.

CENTRAL BUSINESS DISTRICT

	Drove Personal Car		Drove Company Car		Passenger in Car		Bus		Walked & Other		Total
Male	745	50%	193	13%	438	30%	90	6%	20	1%	1486
Female	422	41%	3	(-)	505	49%	94	9%	13	1%	1037
Total	1167	47%	196	8%	943	37%	184	7%	33	1%	2523

PRUDENTIAL & FANNIN STATE BANK BUILDINGS

	Drove Personal Car		Drove Company Car		Passenger in Car		Bus		Walked & Other		Total
Male	85	56%	33	22%	32	22%	1	(-)	1	(-)	152
Female	143	58%	2	1%	96	39%	2	1%	4	1%	247
Total	228	57%	35	9%	128	32%	3	1%	5	1%	399

Of the 2,523 Humble employees who reported working in the Central Business District only 7% used bus transportation, as compared to a 22% usage of buses by all workers in the C.B.D. Less than 1% of the 399 Humble employees who reported working at the Prudential Building and the Fannin State Bank Building indicated use of bus transportation. The indication that less than 1% of the employees at Prudential and the Fannin State Bank Buildings use public transportation may be attributed to less satisfactory bus service outside of the C.B.D. and to the availability of free employee parking. Trends in transit use in the City of Houston indicate that the percentage of Humble employees using public transit will probably continue to decline.

A relatively high percentage of female employees drive personal cars to work, 41% to the Central Business District and 58% to the Prudential and Fannin State Bank area. Of the 2,922 employees who reported transportation use, 1,626 or about 56% revealed that they drove a car to work on the day of the survey.

a-4

TABLE C-1.

PLACE OF WORK VS MODE OF TRAVEL

Department		Humble Building d/p	d/cc	P.	B.	W.	Texas Nat'l Bank d/p	d/cc	P.	B.	W.	1429 Travis d/p	d/cc	P.	B.	W.	Prud. & Fannin State d/p	d/cc	P.	B.	W.	First City Nat'l Bank d/p	d/cc	P.	B.	W.
Adv. & Pub. Rel.	M	18	6	9	2																					
	F	16		10		1																				
Aviation	M																					4	1		1	
	F																					1		1		
Controllers	M	187	2	125	19	7	2		3								52	20								
	F	67		122	20	3			1								104		77	1	1					
Credit Union	M	3		1																						
	F			1																						
Crude Oil	M	11	1	9	2																					
	F	11		13	3																					
Eco. & Stat.	M	2		4																						
	F			2	2																					
Emp. Rel.	M	27	11	11	1	1	1	4																		
	F	40		32	4	1	1		4																	
Exec. Sec.	M																									
	F	7		2																						
Exploration	M	81	25	49	6		23	52	12	2		1										5		3	1	
	F	66		78	15		14	1	17	2												4		3	1	
Gas & Gas Prod.	M	6	2	4	1	1																				
	F	4		5																						
Gen. Service	M	83	2	40	17	7	2					17		6	1		2									
	F	48		42	19				2			2		3										1	1	
Humble P. Line	M	55	12	33	7	1	17	9	6	3																
	F	19		20	3	2	1		2																	
Law	M	26	13	1		1		10									2					2	2	1	3	
	F	16	1	18	3		4		3								3					4		2	1	1
Manufacturing	M	12	7	13	3																					
	F	9		10	1																					
Marine	M																							2		
	F																					2		2	1	
Marketing	M		1														31	33	12	1	1					
	F																34	2	19	1	3					
Production	M	75	7	57	15		17	20	18	2																
	F	40	1	45	7	3	14		9	2	1															
Purchasing	M	17		17		1																				
	F	7		16	4	1																				

(continued)

a-5

TABLE E-1.

PLACE OF WORK VS TYPE OF PARKING FACILITY

Department	Meter M	F	Curb M	F	Lot M	F	Garage M	F	Other M	F
Humble Building										
Adv. & Pub. Rel.			1		18	15	5	1		
Controllers	1		20	4	140	49	13	12	15	2
Credit Union					3					
Crude Oil			2	1	7	8	1	2	2	
Eco. & Stat.					1		1			
Emp. Rel.			7	1	21	36	5	2	6	
Exec. Secy.					4		3			
Exploration			8	6	74	54	13	6	11	
Gas & Gas Prod					4	4	3			
Gen. Service	26	7	31	8	27	28	4	2	3	3
Humble P. Line			14		39	15	12	3	2	1
Law				1	32	11	6	3	1	2
Manufacturing			1		8	8	9	1	1	
Marketing							1			
Production			9		63	39	5	1	5	2
Purchasing			3		13	4	1	3	1	
Research									1	
Treasury			6	1	15	19	5	3		
Total	27	7	102	22	465	294	84	42	49	10

Department	Meter M	F	Curb M	F	Lot M	F	Garage M	F	Other M	F
1st City Nat'l Bank										
Aviation					4	1	1			
Exploration			2		3	4				
Law						3			2	2
Marine					1		2	1		
Traffic			1		9	2				
Total	--	--	3		17	10	5	1	2	2

Department	Meter M	F	Curb M	F	Lot M	F	Garage M	F	Other M	F
Prud. & Fannin S.										
Controllers					42	98	7	6	3	
Gen. Service					2					
Law					1	3			1	
Marketing			1		36	28	2		25	8
Total	--	--	1	--	79	131	9	6	29	8
Male			1%		67%		8%		24%	
Female						90%		4%		6%

Department	Meter M	F	Curb M	F	Lot M	F	Garage M	F	Other M	F
Texas Nat'l Bank										
Controller			1		1					
Emp. Rel.							5			1
Exploration			6	1	52	12	14	2	3	
Gen. Service					2					
Humble P. Line	1		6		6		12	1	1	
Law					3	4	5		2	
Production			4		11	10	22	4	6	1
Total	1	--	17	1	75	26	58	7	6	1

Department	Meter M	F	Curb M	F	Lot M	F	Garage M	F	Other M	F
2001 Commerce										
Controllers			3						2	

Department	Meter M	F	Curb M	F	Lot M	F	Garage M	F	Other M	F
1429 Travis										
Exploration					1					
Gen. Service	1		7		2	8	1			
Total	1		7		3	8	1			

Department	Meter M	F	Curb M	F	Lot M	F	Garage M	F	Other M	F
Humble Garage										
Gen. Service			9		3		1		1	

Department	Meter M	F	Curb M	F	Lot M	F	Garage M	F	Other M	F
C.B.D. Offices										
Total	29	7	141	23	563	338	149	50	60	13
Male	3%		15%		60%		16%		6%	
Female		2%		5%		78%		12%		3%

a-9

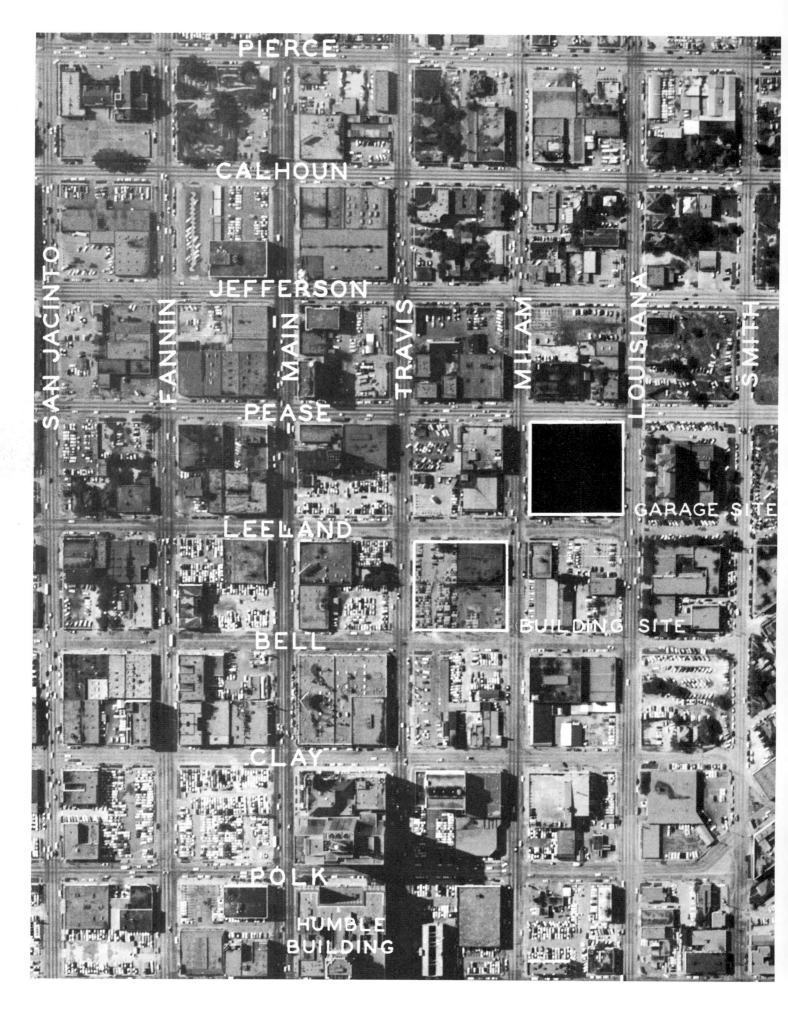

PIERCE

CALHOUN

SAN JACINTO

FANNIN

JEFFERSON

MAIN

TRAVIS

MILAM

LOUISIANA

SMITH

PEASE

GARAGE SITE

LEELAND

BUILDING SITE

BELL

CLAY

POLK

HUMBLE
BUILDING

Humble Oil & Refining Company, Houston, Texas.

20
STUDIES AND
THE PROBLEMS SOLVED

The first major presentation of schematics for their new building to the executives of Humble took place early in 1959. This was the culmination of many long months of study and design by Lou Naidorf, the designer, who stayed with the project from beginning to completion, and by the entire team that assisted him.

In early meetings, the Humble people had stated emphatically that they wanted a building that they could point to with pride, one that would reflect the large and imposing size of the company. But they also wanted a building with human, not superhuman, scale—one that would have bearing but not be overbearing.

The Humble team had studied the needs of the company and analyzed methods of translating these into a building. The site had been assembled and the program written. The architects had gone over the studies made by the company, rechecking Humble's data and concepts, analyzing everything all over again, testing the first data and concepts against newer research and ideas. All of this led to the actual design of the building that came to be built.

A project architect had been named for the building at the beginning of architectural services, and he too was to see the project through to completion. This was what Humble had requested when they asked for continuity of personnel while interviewing architects before awarding the commission. Later a job captain would be named who would be a project architect in his own right, and he would also continue with the project to completion. And in this case, he would even move to Houston to be present at the site during construction and to start a new office for Welton Becket and Associates in that city. For a job of this size and scope, for which Welton Becket and Associates would perform total design, a job captain of unusually high ability was thought to be needed. And when the construction phase began, it seemed very natural to have him move to Houston to be on the job.

In the beginning phases, through programming, schematics, and design, the project architect performed his functions in the usual manner of project architects in this firm. He was the Welton Becket and Associates contact with the client. He worked closely with the design department. He handled the administrative duties required. He directed the work in the production department. As time went on, the administration of the project grew in scope to the point where the project architect needed to spend almost all his time handling this part of the work. The presence of a highly qualified job captain on the job made it possible for the project architect to concentrate on administration while the job captain assumed most of the responsibility for production of working drawings and specifications. This then was the composition of the leadership of the Welton Becket and Associates team for Humble.

During the early months, the studies made by the architects were not really studies of buildings at all but were confined to functions. The volume of building space needed to house the various divisions of the company was worked out. The divisions and departments themselves were researched to determine schematic types of floor plans needed to house their functions. Studies of elevators were made: the distances to the elevator bank, the possibilities of housing a large department on more than one floor and the effects of that solution on its functions, and on the elevator requirements. Would it be preferable to house a large department or several smaller ones on one large floor, thus making savings in cost? Or would it be better to go to a smaller floor which would increase the window area? Should there be windows in the offices at all? Could the windows be eliminated by a high level of efficiency in air conditioning and lighting? And what effect, if any, would this have on those working here?

One of the important studies made early during architectural services entailed a very detailed look at how Humble actually operated within its offices. The architects were somewhat surprised to find that, in spite of the great size of the company, individual departments were relatively small. There were no large loft spaces occupied by huge engineering or accounting departments, for example. The rule in Humble was to keep departments small and house them in individual offices. Thus, there was a tradition in the company not of large spaces occupied by numbers of people but of private office spaces occupied by single employees and of small adjacent spaces occupied by only a few.

As the earliest studies of the Humble Oil Building proceeded, the designer began to examine the effect of the building mass on the city and on the immedi-

ate vicinity of its site. As it happened, all the taller buildings in Houston were located at some considerable distance from the site. And it appeared that no new high-rise buildings seemed likely in the immediate vicinity for some time to come.

Very rough mass models were developed showing the possibilities for the further development of the studies of the building into widely varied conformations.

Study models were made on the basic low-rise block building concept that had been developed by Humble before engaging the architects. This scheme provided an adequate amount of space needed by the company, in an almost cubical building that occupied almost every inch of its site.

Other study models were prepared indicating what happened when that scheme was changed to ones in which various portions of the site were left open to be developed in plaza or courtyard fashion. As time went by, the conformation of the building changed from that of a rather low building filling its site to a relatively tall building tower resting on a base structure that almost filled the entire site, to a high-rise tower with a considerable amount of the site area left open.

These early mass models were studied in great detail, individually and as they related to each other. Photographs of them were made and then superimposed on aerial shots of the city, and on others in larger scale showing only the site itself and its close environs.

As the studies of the massing of the building

Shown here are three versions of the earliest study models of the Humble Oil Building. One indicates the original idea of the Humble people for a block building that filled the site; others are further developments.

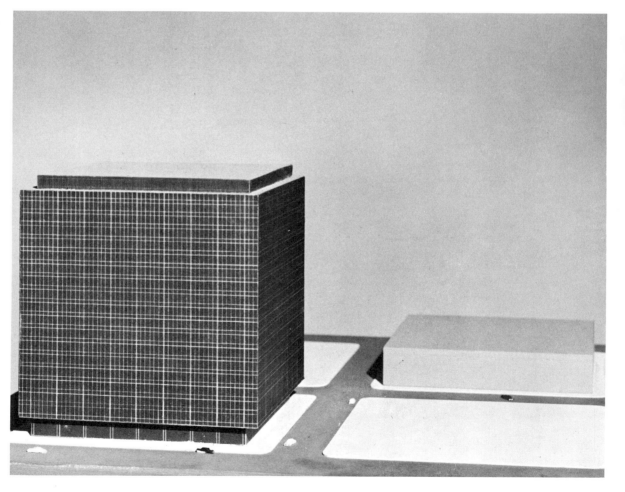

proceeded, those concerned with space needs, floor areas, functional requirements, and the like also went forward.

It began to become apparent to the designer and to the others working on the Humble Oil Building that the requirements for the building seemed to call for a high-rise tower on a relatively open site.

From a planning and functional standpoint, the sizes of departments, their organization, and the need for many private offices all seemed to call for smaller floor areas than a low-rise building would have. This seemed to dictate a tower approach. In the studies of superimposed mass models on aerial views of the city and site, it also became apparent that the site occupied a very prominent location in Houston. If the building placed on it were handled correctly, it could become a landmark visible for miles not only to an air traveler approaching the city but also to those approaching by automobile and to people in almost any location within the city.

When typical floor plans had been developed in various sizes, here again it seemed apparent that a scheme for a smaller floor and larger number of stories seemed better than one with larger floors and fewer stories. As time went on, the floor plans were developed more fully and their size divided into the total area required to determine the exact number of stories needed in the building. The designer now admits he was surprised to find this simple arithmetical calculation had produced a scheme which could be further developed into a building of very fine proportions. But he also recognized the necessity of

considerable further study of the floor plans, the conformation, and the detailing in order to achieve the design goals that had been set for the building.

Accordingly, when the first rather informal presentations of the early schematics were made to the client, they took the form of rough floor plans and mass models. The high-rise schemes began to find favor with the client. And finally, the low-rise scheme was discarded once and for all.

Neither the earliest mass models nor photographs of them have survived, but some idea of what they were like can be gathered from the model of the block building shown across-page, though it was made somewhat later. This scheme did not remain a serious possibility for the building beyond the very early informal presentations to the client. It was superseded by an early decision to develop a high-rise tower of some kind. Two of the rough models of the high-rise scheme, made at the time, are shown on this page. It will be noted that they vary somewhat in the shape of the floor plans. Other than that, they are quite similar except for the lesser number of stories in the version on the left and its pedestal structure, which provides a considerable amount of the floor area required.

At this point in the history of the design of the building the Humble people had not yet been sold on the inclusion of sunshades. However, as may be seen in the illustrations on the page preceding, the architects had started to work on these at an early stage. At the time, the architects felt that a considerable amount of detail should be developed on the

exterior of the building in order to avoid another slick, curtain-wall scheme. And they were also beginning to think about the effects of the strong Texas sun on the air conditioning loads and on the comfort of the occupants of the building. As time went on, the sunshades were to become one of the dominant elements of the design of the building.

The later models shown here indicate the directions which the development of the design took. After the decision had been reached in favor of a high-rise tower with open space at its base, the designer worked on two widely varied exterior solutions simultaneously. One took the form of a quite conservative treatment of a building enclosed by a curtain wall, dominated by a strong expression of the exterior columns. This scheme seemed adequate but unsatisfactory in many ways. It looked very much like a number of other buildings around the country. It seemed to have no individuality, or very little. Worst of all, it did not express the climate of Houston, the level plains of the area. It was felt that some kind of sunshading for the building would make such an expression.

By this time, the conformation of the building had become quite apparent. It would be a quite tall tower, some 600 feet in height and only about 250 feet in the wider dimension of its plan. As the designer, Louis Naidorf, puts it, "We had conceived a cliff and we felt we needed some way to break up its sheer height. Horizontal layers seemed a good way to break up the cliff. And sunshades at the heads of the windows seemed a good way to achieve the

horizontality. This was going to be a costly solution, we knew.

"We also knew that we were going toward sunshades only partially on the basis of function, the rest of it was feeling or intuition. And we knew, worst of all, that the client very likely might not buy this solution. In any case, we went ahead with this scheme."

As shown in the photographs of models here, the sunshade scheme had become dominant. Of the four versions of the building shown, only one deviates from this scheme. In the other versions, the only major differences are to be found in the treatment at the tops of the office building and the garage.

As the designer said, the decision to pursue the sunshade scheme was composed of part function and part feeling or intuition. Some aspects of the actual functioning of the sunshades are discussed in the next chapter, along with drawings illustrating some problems to be overcome in this respect and the details used to overcome them. The architect's feeling or intuition about the sunshades is harder to explain or illustrate. Louis Naidorf remembers this phase of his work in this way, "We had tried all sorts of tricky screens and grilles in the past, but we immediately recognized the need here for the simplest kind of treatment. We believed that horizontal sunshades would make the space much more habitable or comfortable for the occupants of the building. We were convinced that the exterior of the building needed some sort of special treatment in order to avoid monotony or boredom. But perhaps

The illustrations of the models of the Humble Oil & Refining Co. Building shown on these pages indicate the results of studies made after the time of the early models shown previously. By the time of the models shown here, the major decision to leave a large portion of the site open had been made and the office building had taken on a high-rise conformation.

the most important thing that drove us toward the sunshades was the feeling that we wanted to achieve a vital, living building that would continuously change as the sun moved over and around it, a building that would vary inside and out as the seasons changed and the days went by."

The design work progressed and the building began to take shape in the designer's mind and in drawings and models. In the pages following, a number of sketches serve to illustrate what was happening. A great variety of things were tried and discarded or developed more fully. The sunshade idea was tested again and again, as were other concepts of the building and its elements. Early in June 1959, the architects were ready to make a complete presentation of the design of the building to the full Humble Board.

Two schemes had been developed for this presentation, one a simple tower without sunshades, the other with sunshades. The architects expected to do everything in their power to sell the sunshade scheme. They had prepared a very full set of mounted drawings and a very finished model.

The presentation team consisted of Welton Becket; Maynard Woodard, the director of design; Louis Naidorf, the designer; the project architect; and Arthur Posner, the interior designer. In the middle of the night before the presentation, the team members went to the Humble offices where they carefully set up their exhibit in a small auditorium.

The members of the presentation team admitted later to a considerable amount of nervousness. They were to recommend a $32 million dollar building scheme, one that would cost considerably more than the other alternative. They had heard that the members of the Humble Board and the officers of the company were extreme individualists and might react in unpredictable ways. This was borne out by their experiences with the Humble people with whom they had been working closely. But the team felt that it had done its homework and had the answers ready. And they decided that working with individualists who might or might not be predictable served to keep the architects from putting together a canned presentation. Altogether they expected to get a fair, impartial, and realistic hearing from those who must approve the building.

Louis Naidorf recalls the presentation, "We gave them a rigorous, almost mathematical, logical presentation. They asked good questions. We answered them in a thorough fashion. At one point, after we had almost finished and had recommended the sunshade building, the Humble treasurer said that he understood the sunshades would cost $1 million, but would recover their costs by reducing the price of the air-conditioning plant and its operational costs. We told him that was only partially true. The next question was why we were advocating the sunshades. We replied that it was our conviction that the sunshades would make the building more comfortable and they would make it better looking. At this point, the treasurer said that he considered those very sensible reasons. Soon afterward, they approved the design and authorized working drawings."

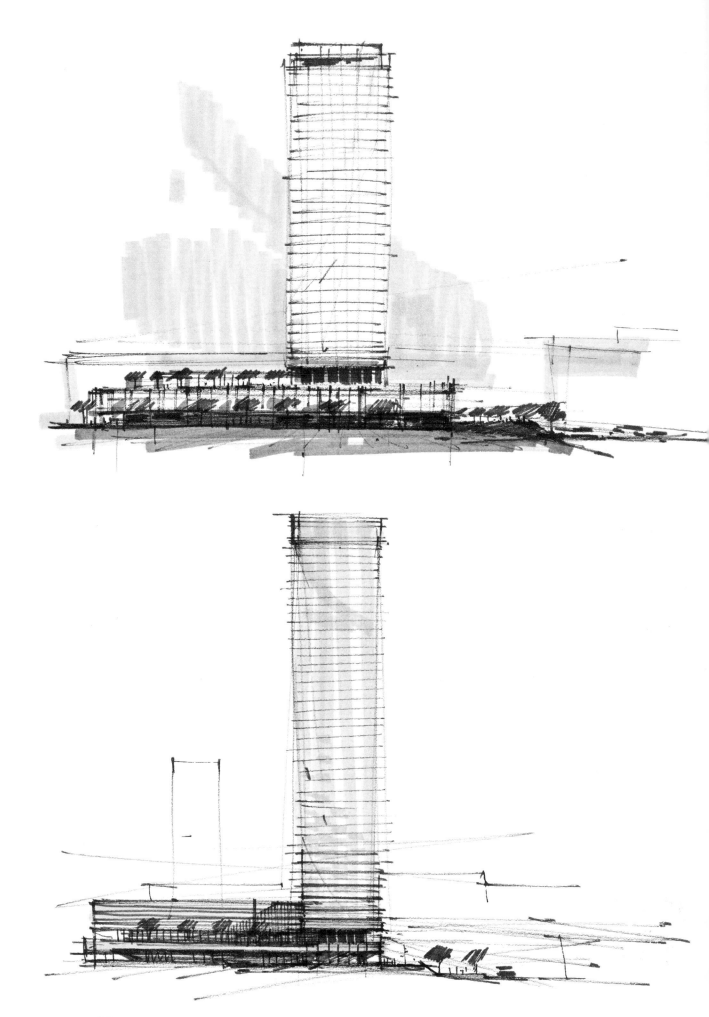

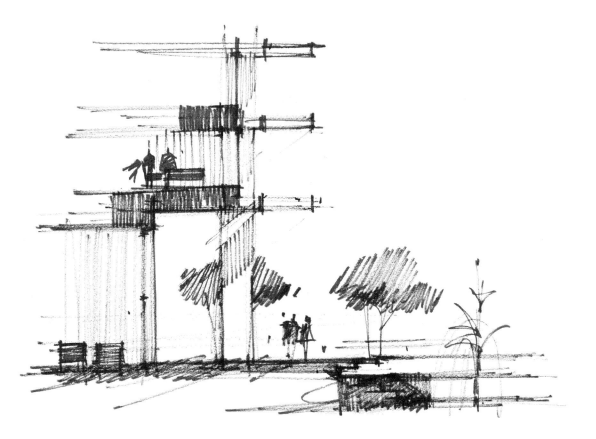

Design sketches of various aspects of the Humble Oil Building indicate the attention to the details and the attempts to develop schemes without sunshades as well as with them.

189

As design studies proceeded, the sunshade scheme began to become entrenched as the most desirable solution for the Humble Oil Building.

190

191

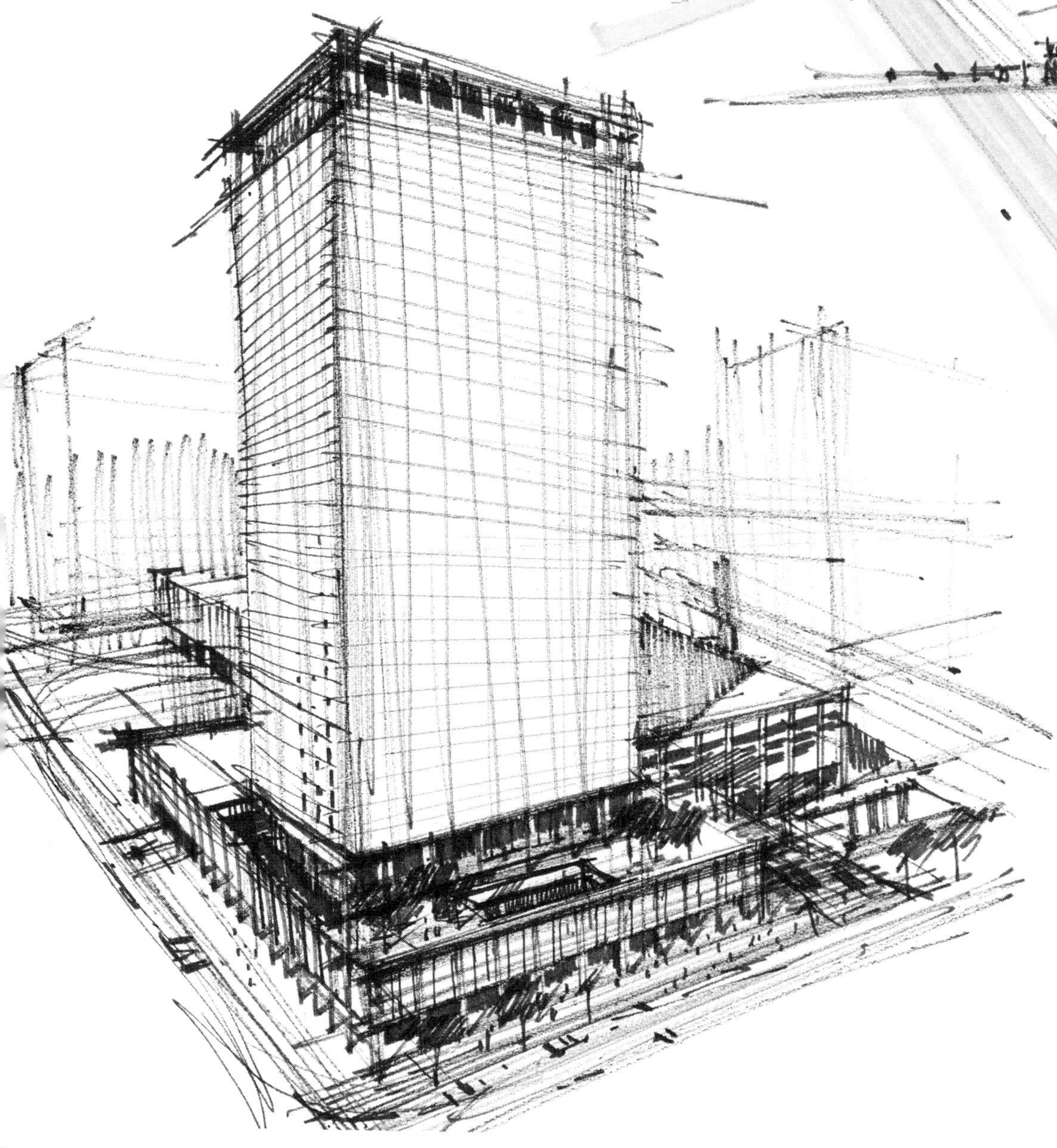

Literally thousands of sketches were made of various aspects of the Humble Oil Building and of its smallest details. The sketches shown here and in the preceding pages give some idea of the amount of attention given by the designers.

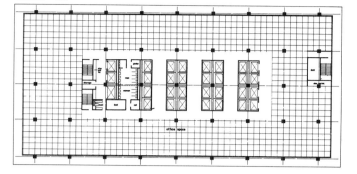

FIRST ELEVATOR RISE OF OFFICE BUILDING
Gross area   27,535
Net rentable   20,492
Floor efficiency   74.5%

office space

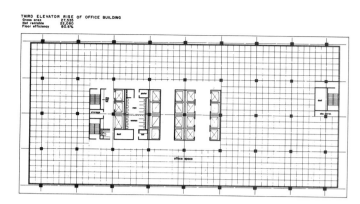

THIRD ELEVATOR RISE OF OFFICE BUILDING
Gross area   27,535
Net rentable   22,080
Floor efficiency   80.5%

office space

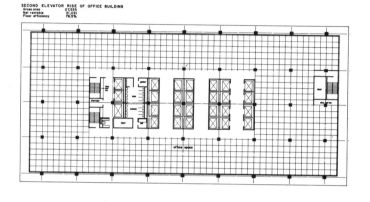

SECOND ELEVATOR RISE OF OFFICE BUILDING
Gross area   27,535
Net rentable   21,021
Floor efficiency   76.5%

office space

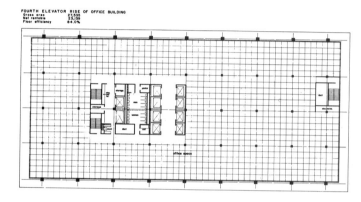

FOURTH ELEVATOR RISE OF OFFICE BUILDING
Gross area   27,535
Net rentable   23,139
Floor efficiency   84.0%

office space

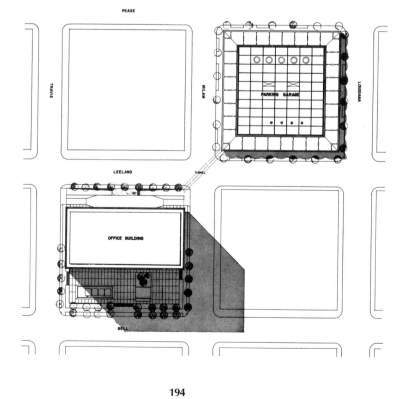

SITE PLAN OF OFFICE BUILDING AND PARKING GARAGE

PEASE

TRAVIS

MILAM

LOUISIANA

PARKING GARAGE

LEELAND

TUNNEL

OFFICE BUILDING

BELL

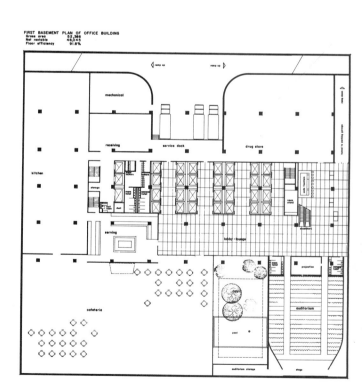

FIRST BASEMENT PLAN OF OFFICE BUILDING
Gross area   52,386
Net rentable   48,045
Floor efficiency   91.8%

ramp up   ramp up

mechanical

receiving   service dock   drug store

kitchen

storage

serving

lobby - lounge

projection

cafeteria

auditorium

auditorium storage   stage

194

Three photographs made at the time of the major presentation of the Humble Oil Building to company officials are shown here. At the time of this presentation, the major design aspects of the building as it was to be constructed had all been made and it was at this time that top company officials approved these aspects. Across page are shown the major drawings that were part of this presentation; top photograph shows (left to right) John Croddock and Roy Horton of Humble, Welton Becket and Consulting Architects Albert Goleman and George Pierce: center shows same individuals who are joined in the bottom photograph by other Humble officials.

195

Shown here are three of the interior sketches presented to top Humble officials as part of the major presentation discussed in this chapter.

The final model of the Humble Oil Building, after all modifications had been made, is shown here. It will be noted that extreme changes had taken place since the first original study model illustrated on page 184. A glance at the photographs of the actual building on page 164 and elsewhere will indicate how little the building changed from this point on through construction.

197

Humble Oil & Refining Co.,
Houston, Texas.

Humble Oil & Refining Company,
Houston, Texas.

21
PRODUCTION OF DRAWINGS AND SPECIFICATIONS

On July 25, 1959, the Humble Oil & Refining Company issued a press release announcing that it had authorized Welton Becket and Associates to proceed with working drawings and specifications for its new $32 million headquarters building in Houston. The architects had received the commission in 1958, had performed the feasibility studies and programming, and now had a design which had been accepted.

What was envisioned was an office building of forty-four stories and three basement levels, approximately 600 feet in height, and about 225 by 115 feet in floor dimensions, with a gross floor area of 1.4 million square feet, of which about 1 million would be net usable. At the time, Humble expected to move 3,300 employees into the building upon its completion and lease out about half of the space. In addition, there was to be a parking garage for approximately 1,300 cars diagonally across the street from the offices. The two buildings would be connected by a pedestrian tunnel.

In addition, the Humble announcement pointed out that the building would have a concourse level beneath the lobby which would contain a cafeteria seating 1,200 people, a 500-seat auditorium, lounges, and space for several small shops. All service facilities, including elevators and restrooms, were to be grouped in a central core, allowing offices to be placed on all four sides of the building. A landscaped plaza, with sculptured fountains and pools, would occupy a large space in front of the building.

The announcement went on to say that the build-ing was planned on the basis of a module 4 feet 8 inches square and that each module would have access to electrical, air-conditioning, and telephone connections. A feature of the building would be its sunshade system that would shield the building from direct sunlight, with an aluminum and porcelain enamel shield, allowing only filtered light to strike the windows. Working drawings and specifications were expected to be complete within six months.

The Humble press release thus confirmed what has already been discussed in previous chapters. The building was to be quite different from what had been originally visualized by the Humble people. But it was one that they had approved and it was one they felt would work well and that they could be proud of.

As the building moved into production, the job captain came to perform more of the functions of directing the actual drafting work and the project architect began to spend more time on the adminis-tration of the project. Since it was envisioned that all the architectural and engineering production would be completed within six months, allowing the building to be put out for bids early in 1960, an unusually large number of draftsmen were assigned to work under the direction of the job captain. All the production work, except structural engineering, was handled in the Los Angeles office of the archi-tectural firm.

One factor that helped immeasurably in speeding up the work was the high state of development of the presentation drawings and other materials that had been shown to the Humble Board of Directors and which they had accepted. A comparison of the floor plans shown here and on the following page with the earlier versions on page 194 demonstrates the fact that the preparation of working drawings was concerned with refinement of what had already been developed rather than great changes. Examination of the models presented to the Humble Board together with the photographs of the actual building also serve to demonstrate this fact.

One change that did take place was that the longer dimension of the office tower grew somewhat, from 225 feet to about 250 feet. Not seemingly a change of great moment, this did add almost 3,000 square feet of floor area to each floor. This was thought necessary and was to contribute quite a bit to a rise in the budget for the building.

As will be noted in the plan of the concourse shown here as compared with that on page 194, some changes were made on that floor, notably the increase in the size of the kitchen and serving rooms for the cafeteria. Also some of the elevator banks were blanked off on this floor and the handling of the ramps for trucks to the loading dock was re-

studied. Adjacent to the cafeteria is a sunken garden with a pool, as shown on the plan of the concourse. In this way light would be admitted to the cafeteria and a view created for those using this level of the building. Also it will be seen that the company auditorium is located on this level.

There are two additional basement levels beneath that of the concourse. On these levels are located storage, printing, and duplicating facilities, other service functions, and the barber and beauty shops.

As may be seen in the plan of the lobby or ground-floor level, opposite, the building proper occupies slightly less than half of the site. The remainder is devoted partially to ramps that allow automobile access to this level for special purposes. However, most of the space outside of the building has been developed into a plaza with potted shrubbery, a reflecting pool with three sculptured fountains, and a light well open to the sunken garden on the concourse level one story below. These elements have been worked out to provide a setting for the building itself and an outdoor place for employees and visitors to stroll or relax. All in all, the plaza has proved to be quite a success, except for the fountains: the water tends to be sprayed all over the plaza by the

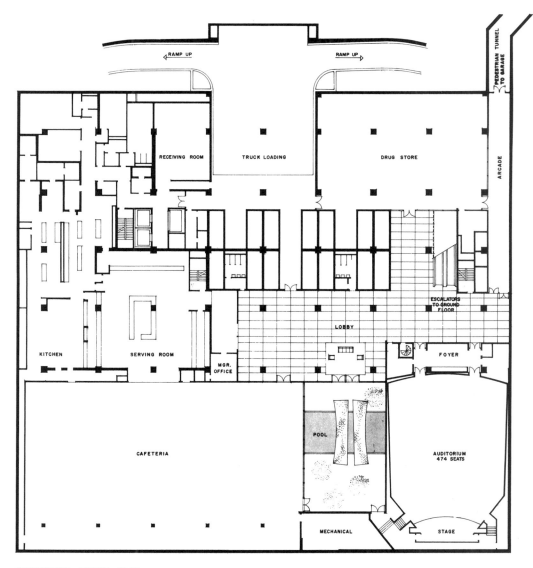

CONCOURSE FLOOR PLAN

frequent Texas winds, and they are therefore now shut down. As designer Louis Naidorf admits, "We should not have handled the fountains as we did."

The ground floor of the Humble Oil Building contains the lobby of the building, or rather two lobbies since there is a main entrance on one side of the building and an automobile lobby on the opposite side. These lobbies range along the length of the building and are separated only by the elevator and service core. Of importance on this floor is the Humble Touring Service Center, which is located at one end. This service handles requests for information about routes of travel and related matters for anyone who inquires. In addition, the people who staff the service act as guides to the building for visitors.

Commenting on the overall design of the building Welton Becket said at the time, "The Humble Company's requirements for a high percentage of private offices and its desire for a significant structure that would be a contribution to the community led to the design of a high-rise tower using only 40 percent of the site. This resulted in an open, landscaped plaza that assures the community that the area will never become a dark skyscraper canyon." After it had been

completed, Becket continued to point to the Humble Building with considerable pride, and he was the one who first suggested that it be used in this book as a case study of the total aspects of total design.

As production of the architectural portions of the working drawings proceeded, so did the engineering. The structural engineers were Murray Erick & Associates, succeeded by Stacy & Skinner, who usually handled the major part of the structural engineering for buildings done by the architectural firm. Later, this structural firm was to be merged in Welton Becket and Associates.

Stacy & Skinner engineered the Humble Oil Building for hurricane stresses, using a high-strength steel frame with adequate wind bracing for the loads envisioned. The structure was fireproofed with formed, poured-in-place concrete on the exterior columns, sprayed concrete on interior columns and girders, and vermiculite plaster on intermediate beams. Floors were designed with cellular metal decking through which electrical and communications cables were run. On top of the decking, $2\frac{1}{2}$ inches of lightweight concrete was placed. The foundation was a 7-foot-thick concrete mat.

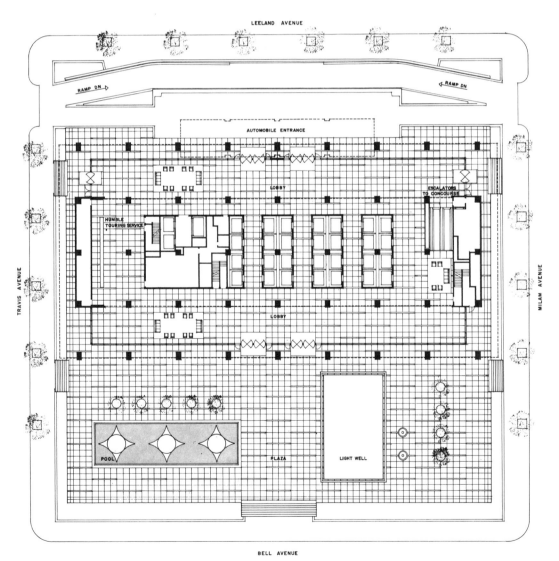

GROUND FLOOR PLAN

The plans shown here and the section and plan shown on the pages immediately following indicate very accurately the actualities of the Humble Oil building, as constructed. It will be noted that these plans have changed somewhat from the earlier versions shown on page 194.

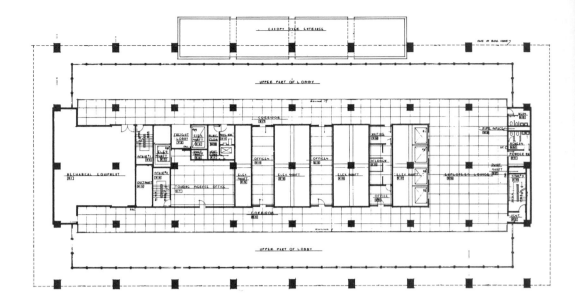

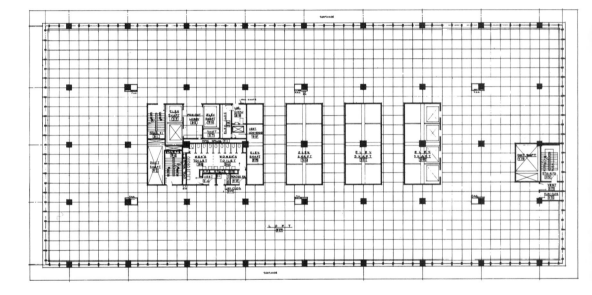

Studies of the requirements for mechanical and electrical phase of the Humble Oil Building began early in the architectural process. Paul Sessinghaus, of Welton Becket and Associates, began to discuss the needs and how to provide for them with John Craddock of Humble. As time went on, their conversations and further studies led to a decision to use cellular steel decking for all floors, thus providing a flexible, but quite conventional, distribution system for electrical and communications services. The direction they took in the heating and air conditioning of the building was anything but conventional. They decided to provide basement and roof levels for the

building that would be completely free of mechanical equipment. And they set out to find ways of accomplishing this.

The researches they carried on at this time led to a decision to locate all boilers, compressors, and cooling towers on the roof of the parking garage to be located diagonally across the street from the offices. A service tunnel would deliver heating and air conditioning to the office building. This decision made it possible to place an observation tower on the office building and to utilize the basement levels for purposes other than equipment. Through reduction of the loads such equipment ordinarily places on the roof structure, the structural system of the office building could be lightened, reducing its cost. Four floors of the office building, the ninth, twenty-first, thirty-third, and forty-fifth, were utilized for mechanical distribution.

As the architectural and engineering production for the Humble Oil Building progressed, the interior designers were also at work. As is usual in the Becket firm, this work did not consist merely of selecting furniture, fixtures, colors, and finishes. Instead, two important major design functions were being handled: that of the architectural interiors—the mass, form, texture, color, and so on of the building itself—and that of the furniture and furnishings to be placed inside the building. These two major design functions were carried forward together.

Studies were made of the architectural features of the interiors, the use of materials, and their form. Studies of furniture and related needs were begun. As time went on, a rationale for the interiors began to emerge from the work of the interior people and the architectural designers. Patterns and themes began to develop for the interiors as they related to the exterior. It began to become apparent that the building exterior might well be light in tone, with considerable pattern in its walls from the sunshades and considerable elegance in its white marble-sheathed columns, its open landscaped plaza, and its walls of natural aluminum and dolomite. Concurrently with the design work on the exterior, which would eventually lead to the materials and appearance described here, the work on the interiors progressed in the same direction. The materials of the exterior could be continued into the lobby; the textures and forms outside made part of the surroundings inside. The colors outside and inside could be made to blend with and complement each other. The entire building could be all of a piece, without the distraction in many other buildings caused by a lack of correlation between exterior and interior. This was to be total design, as conceived and practiced by Welton Becket and Associates.

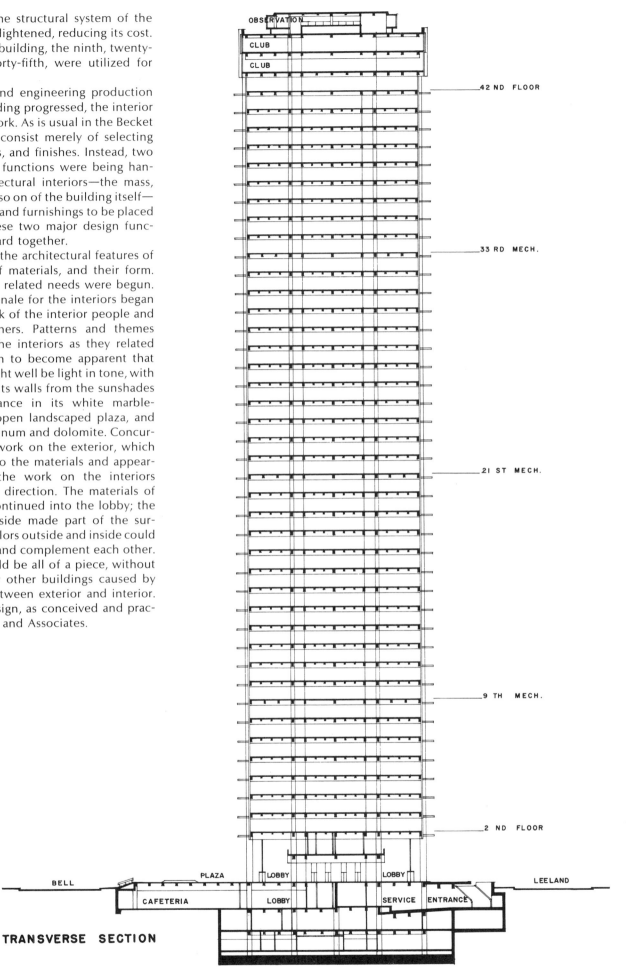

TRANSVERSE SECTION

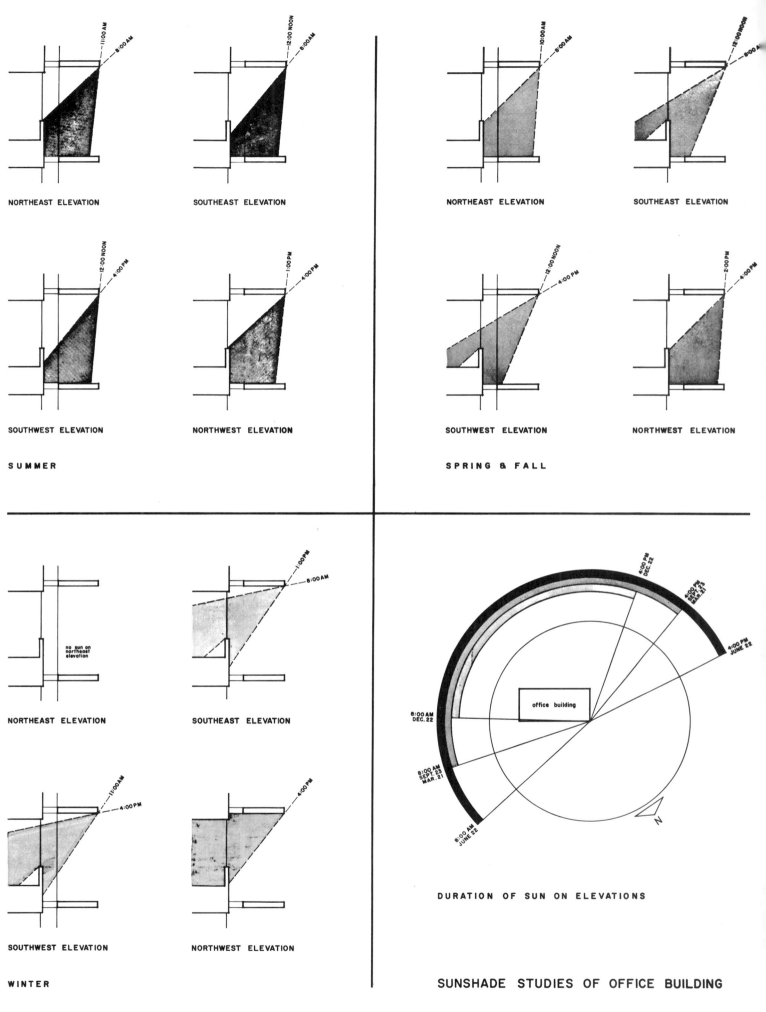

NORTHEAST ELEVATION

SOUTHEAST ELEVATION

SOUTHWEST ELEVATION

NORTHWEST ELEVATION

SUMMER

NORTHEAST ELEVATION

SOUTHEAST ELEVATION

SOUTHWEST ELEVATION

NORTHWEST ELEVATION

SPRING & FALL

no sun on northeast elevation

NORTHEAST ELEVATION

SOUTHEAST ELEVATION

SOUTHWEST ELEVATION

NORTHWEST ELEVATION

WINTER

office building

DURATION OF SUN ON ELEVATIONS

SUNSHADE STUDIES OF OFFICE BUILDING

206

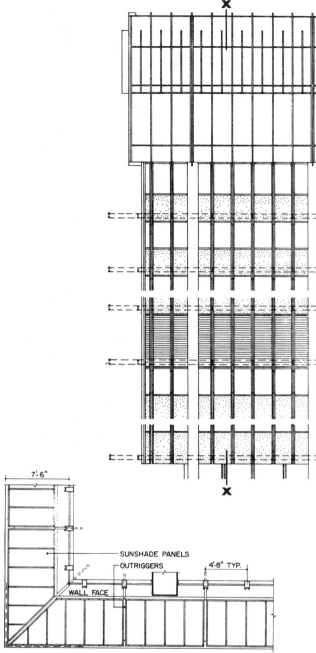

As discussed in the text and as indicated in the illustrations of the Humble Oil Building, the horizontal sunshades became a major feature of the design. The two studies shown here were part of the presentation to officials mentioned earlier.

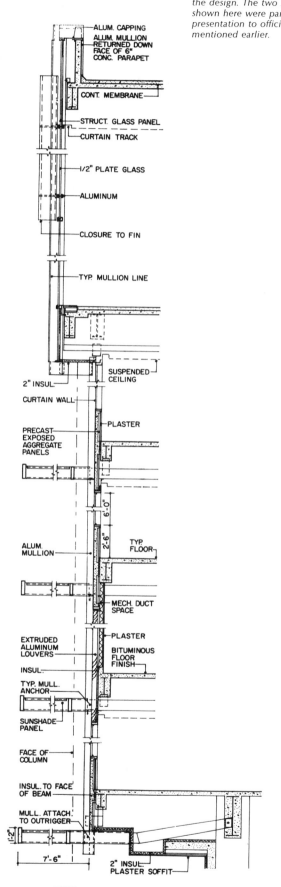

- ALUM. CAPPING
- ALUM. MULLION RETURNED DOWN FACE OF 6" CONC. PARAPET
- CONT. MEMBRANE
- STRUCT. GLASS PANEL
- CURTAIN TRACK
- 1/2" PLATE GLASS
- ALUMINUM
- CLOSURE TO FIN
- TYP. MULLION LINE
- SUSPENDED CEILING
- 2" INSUL.
- CURTAIN WALL
- PLASTER
- PRECAST EXPOSED AGGREGATE PANELS
- ALUM. MULLION
- 6'-0"
- 2'-6"
- TYP. FLOOR
- MECH. DUCT SPACE
- PLASTER
- EXTRUDED ALUMINUM LOUVERS
- BITUMINOUS FLOOR FINISH
- INSUL.
- TYP. MULL. ANCHOR
- SUNSHADE PANEL
- FACE OF COLUMN
- INSUL. TO FACE OF BEAM
- MULL. ATTACH. TO OUTRIGGER
- 1'-2"
- 7'-6"
- 2" INSUL. PLASTER SOFFIT

SECTION X-X

PLAN OF SUNSHADES

- 7'-6"
- SUNSHADE PANELS
- OUTRIGGERS
- 4'-8" TYP.
- WALL FACE

Continuous horizontal sunshades are cantilevered a distance of 7 feet from 41 of the building's 44 floors. They control solar radiation, reduce the air-conditioning load and create changing patterns of light and shade on the facades. Supported on aluminum outriggers, the aluminum panels are covered with a light gray porcelain enamel on the top surface to reduce glare, and white porcelain enamel on the bottom surface to harmonize with the facade. The panels are held at the line of the projecting white-marble-sheathed structural columns, a distance of approximately 1 foot 6 inches from the curtain wall. Air thus can circulate freely up the face of the building and warm air pockets are avoided. The shades support maintenance men when they wash the structure's 6,241 fixed glass windows. They are designed to carry a 200-pound dead load and to withstand wind velocities up to 150 miles per hour. The 4-foot 8-inch-wide precast spandrel panels of the curtain wall have an exposed Texas dolomite facing which is self cleaning. Aluminum mullions are natural finish

*Humble Oil & Refining Co.,
Houston, Texas.*

208

22
DESIGN TRANSLATED
INTO A BUILDING

At one point during the work on the Humble Oil Building, the president, Morgan J. Davis, asked in a meeting with the architects where the sign saying Humble Oil would go. First on his feet to answer was Maynard Woodard, Director of Design for Welton Becket and Associates, who pointed out that in the opinion of the architects there would be no need for such a sign, since the entire building would say Humble Oil. To this the president replied that he thought so too. So the building did come to be built without a sign on top or anywhere else.

Perhaps this incident may serve to illustrate the tenor of the relationships between architects and clients for this building. The architects were impressed with the caliber of these clients and with their knowledge and ability. They were to be even more impressed when the building was put out for bids. The bids were to be submitted as a base bid with prices on a series of alternates, but there was also a provision that each contractor must submit a method for handling extras that might arise during construction. And the extras method must include the amount the contractors required in profit on this work.

As it happened, the low bidder on the base bid, W. S. Bellows Construction Corporation, was also low after some of the alternates had been accepted. However, the architects felt that the profit expected by the low bidder on extras might be a bit high and suggested to the clients that they might negotiate this point with Bellows. The Humble people would not negotiate, stating that they felt the base price with alternates was favorable to Humble while the extras were favorable to the contractor. And that, after all, seemed to them to be a reasonable state of affairs.

The results of the total design services performed by the architects, the reasonableness and ability of the clients, the good site, and the entirely adequate budget would best be seen in the Humble Oil Building itself, of course.

As a substitute, the attempt made in these pages is to portray a few of the attitudes and actions that went into the concepts of the Humble Oil Building and their development into a design, into production documents, and finally into a completed and occupied building. A glance back through the preceding few chapters might give some indications of the results of the decisions to handle the portrayal of the building in this manner. In any case, the portrayal certainly reveals much more of the character of the building than would have been possible in fewer pages made into relatively static layouts.

The photographs of the Humble Oil Building shown in the preceding chapters portray some of the things that went a bit awry as well as those which went right. The wind problem with the fountains has already been pointed out. And there are other things the architects might change now if they had another chance at them, for example, the rather exhaustive development of the detail of the exterior walls. Strong and bold from a distance, these walls seem a bit fussy and overdetailed close up. In this respect, the designer of the building now feels that he may have been a bit carried away with the design cleverness of multiple intersections of elements of small size in the walls and sunshades and that he should have simplified the details.

But to criticize in this manner is to be very finicky indeed and really does not lead very far. The building is there; it exists; it functions; the owners like it; and it has attracted considerable attention from those in the architectural and other design professions as well as from the great numbers of others who have seen it. As architects are sometimes apt to say when they are feeling certain emotions, the building does make a statement. Not all would agree exactly as to the strength of the statement or to its validity or success. But most would agree—at least to an extent—as they browse through the many pictures of it in this book, that the building has an interesting, everchanging quality—that it in fact has character.

The changing characteristics of the exterior are well illustrated by the exterior shown across-page, made from a photograph taken in late afternoon of a windy summer day. Contrast this to any of the other exterior photographs shown in this and the preceding chapters.

In the illustrations shown previously, and especially in those in the pages immediately following, the results of the concepts of total design can be clearly seen. The results of handling architectural, engineering, interior, and landscaping together are clearly discernible. Design decisions were made to relate to all of the elements of the building, inside and out; they do not occur in one place, to be replaced by another quite different decision in another. As an obvious example, the design motif used on the doors shown on the following page is to be found repeated in the light fixtures of the conference room to which they admit. And the same motif can be found in many other places, in varying forms, all over the building.

How much of the work of total design did the Becket firm perform? The simple answer is *all of it*, with the exception of the structural engineering. But even in this, the consulting firm was closely associated to Welton Becket and Associates and eventually was to be merged into the architectural firm. Other than the usual architectural and engineering services, what else was accomplished? Without overcomplicating the answer, Welton Becket and Associates designed all of the interiors and landscaping, selected all of the furniture and furnishings, including carpets and accessories, except that a relatively large number of such items were actually designed by people in the firm and then companies were found to produce them. In addition, Welton Becket and Associates designers commissioned almost $500,000 in art work in the name of their clients, and Becket staff people executed additional art for the building.

How did the building project emerge financially? The original budget for the office building was $32 million. With the addition of a considerable amount of floor space and the acceptance of a number of alternates by the clients, the final cost was $39 million. The parking structure cost an additional $4 million which was just about equal to the original budget for its construction. The timing of the building was exactly as had been projected. It was completed late in 1962 and occupied shortly afterward.

What is the building actually like? What is the atmosphere, which cannot really be imagined from the photographs? No doubt it would appear quite different to each observer. To this observer, it presents a quite impressive, interesting, warm exterior when viewed from a distance. As one approaches it, this feeling persists, but the overall effect changes considerably as one gets closer. The effects of the small detail, for example, are not apparent at all from a distance but grow in importance as the observer approaches. The plaza is pleasant, not overdeveloped, sparsely furnished with shrubbery, a bit monumental—an aspect the building itself, large as it is, successfully avoids.

Entering the main lobby, the observer is struck with the richness of the materials, travertine marble on the elevator core walls, bronze-formed panels above the mezzanine, handsome furniture arranged into relatively small conversation groupings. Approaching the elevator, the observer notices the quality of the detailing everywhere; it is highly developed and quite precise.

Downstairs, the view into the sunken garden, which contains plantings and a small pond with a bridge, creates a very warm and human effect; and the light coming down from the opening above is welcome. The garden seems a trifle small and perhaps a bit precious. This feeling disappears upon entering the door of the cafeteria, where a 6-foot-high 100-foot-long tapestry mural by John Smith absolutely dominates the space with its bright colors, composition, and texture. Other elevator rides to some of the office floors reveal a great spaciousness, warm colors, and natural woods, an atmosphere of considerable elegance mixed with efficiency of space use. Perhaps it really is not necessary to go on. This is a well-designed building that fits its occupants and functions in the way a well-designed building should. Everything is not perfection here, but then it never is.

Upon completion of the building, C. E. Reistle, who had succeeded Morgan J. Davis as president of the company announced, "The 3,700 home office employees of Humble will occupy 60 percent of the building, which will provide us with expansion space up to the year 1977." To this, Davis, by then board chairman of the company, expressed the feelings of the owners, "Casting a long shadow over Houston, the Southwest, and our nation, our new building serves as a focal point for company progress and reflects our confidence in the future of the petroleum industry and in the city of Houston."

And what of the reactions of client representative, John Craddock? Five years later, when Humble Oil's parent firm, Standard Oil Company (New Jersey) was ready for its own corporate headquarters building in Rockefeller Center, Craddock was given the task of coordinating that job as he had the one in Houston. Craddock chose Welton Becket and Associates to space-plan Standard Oil's 1.3 million square feet of office space and to act as the company's architectural consultants.

Humble Oil & Refining Co.,
Houston, Texas.

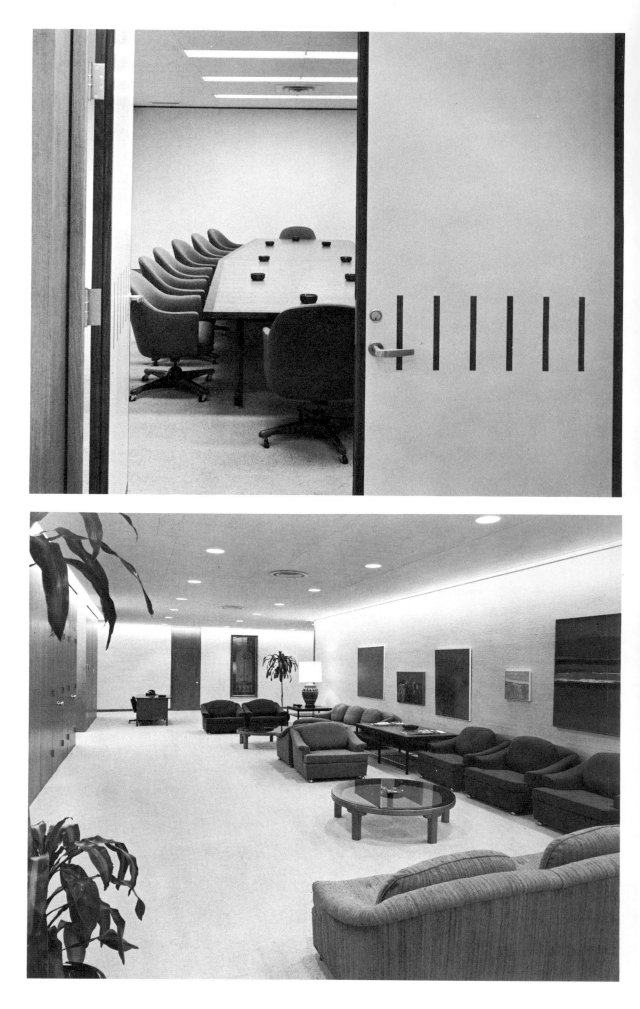

Humble Oil & Refining Company,
Houston, Texas.

OPPOSITE: *Pittsburgh National Building, Pittsburgh, Pennsylvania.*

Part Six

THE FUTURE OF TOTAL DESIGN

*Cadet Activities Center,
United States Military Academy,
West Point, New York.*

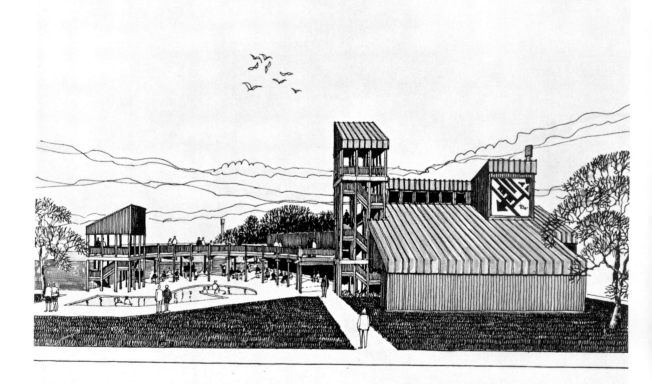

*Plaza Del Oro,
Houston, Texas.*

220

23
A LOOK AHEAD
AT TOTAL DESIGN

For some time now, the young (early forties) president of Welton Becket and Associates, MacDonald Becket, has been giving much of his time and thought to the future of architecture and that of his firm. His concern parallels that of the other top people of Welton Becket and Associates. Meetings, seminars, top-level conferences are held within the firm with increasing frequency. Becket has found himself drawn into speaking engagements on the subject and into writing articles. At this juncture, he is apt to expound on the subject to anyone who exhibits interest. The deep concerns of Becket and the other Welton Becket and Associates staff members reflect their convictions that architecture holds the key to future environmental progress unequaled by any epoch of the past. And they expect to be ready for what they believe will be a major participation by their firm.

At this point, it seems appropriate to examine some of the directions Becket and his confreres see in the future of total design and, in Chapter 24, what they see in the future of Welton Becket and Associates.

To say that the Becket management sees great change in the future is a considerable understatement. The belief in future change is, of course, not very startling among architects or others concerned with the directions in which man and his world are headed. However, MacDonald Becket and others in this firm have perhaps a clearer vision than some and are certainly doing more than most to prepare themselves for the changes they foresee. In any case, the

future course of Welton Becket and Associates described in the next chapter will be more meaningful if put in the context of what the Becket people believe will happen to the building industry, to architecture, to total design, and to the world in which accomplishments of this sort will be made. Therefore, the remainder of this book will be devoted to the projections of MacDonald Becket and the other Welton Becket and Associates top people.

In the first place, as Becket has been saying frequently in articles and speeches, the construction industry finds itself facing two considerable phenomena in the coming years. In Becket's opinion, these will revolutionize the construction industry. The first consists of the great changes taking place in technology, economics, politics, and the behavioral sciences. Technological progress, in tune with scientific progress, has been increasing in geometric proportion for many years. It will continue to do so, but it can also be expected that sociology and the other behavioral sciences, which have lagged behind, will accelerate.

New political situations will arise. Governmental bodies may be expected to play increasingly larger roles in the construction industry as they become more involved in housing, in codes, and other statutory controls, especially in environmental controls.

The behavioral sciences will increasingly point the way toward more humane solutions of environmental problems, toward greater emphasis on the needs and desires of people in their environment.

A prototype enclosed suspended stadium, researched and designed by Welton Becket and Associates in an effort to solve problems of future enclosures for large athletic and other events.

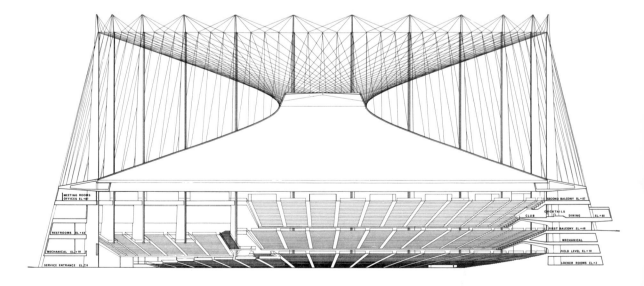

The soaring costs of land, the even more steeply rising costs of labor, the increasing costs of materials will all deeply affect the future of the construction industry and of architecture.

The second major phenomenon facing the construction industry, as seen by Welton Becket and Associates, is that of the need to spend the equivalent of 3 trillion present-day dollars in building construction during the last third of this century. This is the amount necessary to replace buildings that will become obsolete and to provide for the needs of a population expected to double its present size in the next forty years. Coupled with the great amounts of money needed for building construction during the last third of the century will be the needs, increasing at a similar rate, for transportation, disposal, and other systems. Existing cities need rebuilding; new cities will be founded and built. And all on a scale and of a complexity never before faced by architects or any others involved in the construction industry.

What will happen to the building industry as the pace of change quickens and the volume of construction grows? The staff of Welton Becket and Associates are convinced that each element of the industry—the contractors, the product manufacturers, the engineers, the architects and all other disciplines—must change radically to be prepared for the work to come. And they must change radically to prepare to meet the needs of all clients to come, clients who will change as much as any other factor in the process.

Taking a look at clients first, it is apparent that they are becoming more sophisticated in the area of architecture. Clients are becoming more demanding of their architects. Clients are tending to become larger. They are entering the development field and becoming involved in large numbers of buildings rather than just a few. They are beginning to expect better performance in meeting time schedules and budgets. They are beginning to become deeply involved in the complete process of construction, in the tax and legal questions, in the real estate considerations, in the complete financial picture for the life of buildings.

One of the most important aspects of the changes taking place in clients has to do with their size. Client organizations are growing in size rapidly. MacDonald Becket expanded upon this theme in a recent speech when he said, "We are looking toward an era of ever larger clients acquiring ever larger parcels of land and approaching architects to design ever larger developments integrating a variety of building types."

What about architectural firms? Becket went on, "To meet the needs of such clients and their projects, ever larger architectural capabilities must be developed, and this will require the creation of ever larger architectural firms." To these factors, add that of the increasing complexity of projects and Becket believes, "All these factors will have to be dealt with by the architect in the face of sharply rising land, labor, and material costs. There is no reason to believe that the current 10 percent per year increase in construction costs will level off in the foreseeable future. All of this must inevitably lead to an entirely new kind of architectural practice."

In the Becket view, architectural practice in the future will be considerably more akin to that of his firm than to most others. In addition to architectural firms becoming ever larger, as he has put it, they will become more involved with newer services needed by the clients of the future. The emphasis is on service as the function of the professional architect to the exclusion of any other endeavors such as manufacturing, sales, or construction.

A list of typical services that would be offered by architectural firms of the future would include project administration; project scheduling; site selection; land use; economic feasibility; master planning; development and project programming; space programming and planning; function and flow studies; architectural design; special studies in such areas as acoustics and traffic; structural, mechanical, and electrical engineering; interior design including furnishing, decorating, and graphics; cost control; construction document preparation; and services during construction. It will be noted that the list above is intended to be suggestive of the scope of comprehensive services envisioned by Welton Becket and Associates for the future but cannot be considered complete. Rather, the philosophy of the firm would indicate that such a list might well grow considerably if the needs of clients warranted it. The only other restriction would be that additional activities be in the area of service to the client.

What of the future of cities, particularly of their central cores? In the opinion of those in the Becket organization, the central cores will be saved and the cities themselves revitalized, largely by architects. The first step will be the development of more workable plans for the cities than at present, and the key to this will be found in mass transit. With the advent of reliable, inexpensive mass transit, the major problems of the city core, traffic, parking, sprawl, and orientation to human needs can all be solved.

As the central cores of cities become revitalized, they will not only function better for facilities with single functions such as corporate headquarters' office buildings, but they will also function better for what Welton Becket and Associates terms one-of-a-kind facilities, governmental offices of various types, as employment centers, and as central points for transit systems. Each firm, institution, or function will take strength from, and lend vitality to, all others. In this way, the decay of the central core will be stopped and a growth trend started.

The people at Welton Becket and Associates believe the central cores of cities will become more pedestrian-oriented than automobile-oriented in the future. This trend will make possible many amenities not really feasible in cities as they are today. Open space around buildings will become more common. Pedestrian malls will be developed, as will the overpasses, for people, at levels above streets. As costs of land go up, so will building heights. And mixed uses for buildings will increase, office buildings being combined with hotels, apartments, and other uses. Single-purpose office buildings that function only from nine to five will be replaced by multifunction

Theme Office Building Project for Century City, Los Angeles, California—a pioneering design which was never built.

Tempo Building for General Electric Company—another precedent-setting design that was never built.

224

buildings that will include shops, theaters, and other activity centers so that the buildings will be in use for longer periods of time thru the normal working day and even on weekends.

In the Becket view of its world, architects will be deeply involved in the future of cities, including their central cores. In order to handle projects of the magnitude that will be required, architectural firms will have to provide a complete range of services to their clients. Firms will have to be large enough and diversified enough to perform this work, which will be larger, more complex, and more demanding than ever before.

MacDonald Becket and the others of Welton Becket and Associates believe that individual buildings themselves will also change radically as the years go by. For example, many office buildings in the not too distant future will house people in only half of their space, the other half being utilized for computers and other automated equipment and filing. As time goes on, the portion devoted to people may decrease even more. It is even conceivable that a new building type will evolve to take the place of many office buildings of today, a building housing almost entirely equipment, such as computers, that is communicated with by people at locations remote from them.

Prefabrication will become widespread in the future, not only of small, simple units but of complete systems and even of complete rooms and larger units. A beginning is being made in residential work, particularly in such elements as bathrooms. But the Becket firm sees this trend spreading to hotel rooms, hospital rooms, and into other building types.

Based on the considerable amount of research being performed by the Becket firm, some other trends in building seem apparent. For example, the trend in hospitals is seen to be toward single bedrooms for greater patient privacy and hospital efficiency, shorter corridors, "clean corridors" in surgical suites, and larger operating rooms to allow for the developing of new surgical procedures.

A trend is seen toward enclosed stadiums and another toward grouping for economy of cultural activities of various sorts into complexes. Department stores are to be designed to provide more dramatic settings for the merchandise; in a sense they will be like theaters for the presentation of goods. Government buildings will tend more toward the functional than the monumental, without losing the desirable attributes of the latter. Airports will be planned in the context of the communities in which they exist, with better land use and transportation systems on the ground. Shopping centers will make greater use of covered malls, and their interior spaces will be better utilized for a great variety of functions, integrating the retailing functions with theaters, apartments, hotels, offices, and other uses. Shopping centers in the suburbs then will follow the trend toward multiuse functions, remaining usable over longer periods of the day. These then are a few examples of the trends in buildings foreseen by the Becket firm.

The answers to the demands of the clients for these buildings and for cities were put by MacDonald Becket in a recent speech: "Continually challenged by the new clients and the new projects, the architect must be able to refine his ability to create massive, multibuilding, multifunction developments within strict time and cost budgets and also improve his ability to provide innovative planning and imaginative design concepts. Only a good architect, with a top-flight organization, working as a free agent, can produce the quality of results needed in the future."

What do the people at Welton Becket and Associates think about the practice of architecture in the future? In analyzing the firms of today, from which the firms of the future will evolve, the Becket group often refers to the fact that there are three major types of firms in existence now. In their view, one such firm is that of a master or "form-giver" architect with a relatively small staff. This is a man who mainly through his own design talents has been able to establish a personal style of architecture. A second type, also with a small staff, concentrates on smaller work in residential, commercial, and institutional areas, usually within a very limited radius of its office. In each of these cases, the management of the firms is in the hands of one principal or of a few partners. The third type today consists of the larger architectural firm, often a corporation, that offers more complete services on more of a variety of buildings of larger scale and which operates on a much broader geographical base.

As seen by the Becket people, the first two types of firms have very limited potential for growth in the size and complexity of the work they can handle, in the scope of services they are able to perform, and in their ability to operate over large areas of the country or the world. The third type of firm, the more or less full-service office, is the only one of the three with the capability of growth in every way as an independent architectural firm. The future of the smaller firm and the form-giver is seen by the Becket firm as precarious. It is believed here that both will continue to exist but that they will receive ever decreasing shares of the available work and the single and smaller multifamily residential buildings and commercial buildings will come more and more from the assembly line. And the larger work will increasingly go to the larger full-service architectural firms.

In competition with the independent, privately owned architectural firm will be two newer operations, that of the firm that handles design and construction and the architectural firm owned by a company in some other business, either related or unrelated to the construction industry. Some design-construction firms will build for their own account; some will not. Some may well become developers in their own right. The Becket people believe the major portion of the architectural work will go to independent architectural firms if they prepare themselves for the services they will be called upon to perform.

As MacDonald Becket puts it, "Building and urban projects of the future will be so highly complex that it will take an architectural firm concerned with architecture to accomplish them properly. Architecture must be first, not second or third, on the total services priority list."

Clinton Square,
Syracuse, New York.

State Street South,
Quincy, Massachusetts.

226

24
A LOOK AHEAD
AT THE PRACTICE

Almost ten years ago, Welton Becket, the founder of Welton Becket and Associates, made a speech to an American Medical Association Congress, outlining what he believed at that time to be the overriding problems of architecture and of cities. The speech of that time turned out to be highly prophetic and remains valid today as a description of the ills of cities which architects must play a major role in curing. It might be in order to quote a portion here.

In speaking of the cities, Welton Becket said, "Let's take a look at the environment in which our urban population dwells. The evidence of poor planning, or of no planning, is all too obvious. A tour through any of America's metropolitan centers will show congestion, both of persons and vehicles, clogged streets, dark skyscraper canyons, foul air, poor transit, severe noise conditions, and high density. Such a tour will show a lack of industrial controls, insufficient and ineffective zoning, uncontrolled signing, and inadequate sanitation."

Welton Becket went on to comment to the doctors in the audience about the escape to the suburbs, in progress then as now, the beginnings of the process of decay even there. He spoke about pollution of the air and the water and the effects of noise. He dwelled at some length on the effects of pollution and the other ills of the environment on people and generally painted a quite dismal picture of what we have brought upon ourselves in our surroundings on this earth. After calling upon the doctors to

pledge themselves to the goal of correcting the environmental ills he had described, Welton Becket pledged to them that his firm, Welton Becket and Associates, would continue to improve its abilities to develop tomorrow's environment properly.

Maybe this short recap of that speech of almost a decade ago will serve as an introduction to this, the last chapter of a book about the total design of Welton Becket and Associates. The dedication of the firm today, and looking forward to tomorrow, is to the proposition of "preparing itself to develop tomorrow's environment properly." And today's.

How will the firm go about this? Welton Becket and Associates expects to expand its capabilities, expand its size, expand the services offered, expand its geographical base. And the firm expects to improve its services, improve the caliber of its staff, improve its performance for clients and for society.

What services? Elsewhere in this book, the services have been outlined in some detail. There is probably no need to enumerate them again here. But, very simply, what is intended by this firm is that it will have full services of the kinds needed by its clients across the country. This means mechanical, electrical, and structural engineering in every office of Welton Becket and Associates. It means interior design in every office. Naturally, it means the full range of the usual or basic architectural services in schematics, design development, production of construction documents, and services during construction. It

227

Park Plaza, Oshkosh, Wisconsin.

Project D for a Midwestern City.

228

means providing services in graphic design, programming, feasibility studies, master planning, and a myriad of other activities. All of these are within the services of the firm at present.

To gain an insight into what the firm is thinking about for the future, the area of what the Welton Becket and Associates people call "project administration" might be taken as an example. A project administrator, in the sense meant here, would be assigned to oversee an entire building project from idea to completed building. He might represent the client's interests in everything from the site selection through the direction of segregated contracts during construction. Related to this is the expectation that Welton Becket and Associates will become more involved in site assembly, in financial analyses of various types, and related activities.

A considerable departure from the thinking of most architects lies in an investigation being made by the firm of the possibilities of its getting into the function of lease negotiation on behalf of its clients. And surprisingly perhaps, Welton Becket and Associates is also thinking about the possibility that it might also take on the actual management of buildings the firm has done for clients. As MacDonald Becket sees it, "Who could be more qualified to manage a building than the man who has lived with it from its inception, who knows all about it, including all of the hidden things not shown on the drawings or named in the specifications?"

Another idea of interest to the firm, and one which it is investigating, is that of handling purchasing of interior furniture and furnishings for its clients. The thought here begins with the possibility of obtaining for clients better products of this kind at more economical prices. In this case, if the firm goes in this direction, a national purchasing office will probably be established to handle this function for all Welton Becket and Associates offices across the country. Another advantage of such a department would be the possibility of affecting the design of such products by the manufacturers themselves and also within the Becket organization. Through the exercise of the considerable purchasing power that would result from such a national department, Welton Becket and Associates feels its clients could benefit from improved quality, lower prices, and better delivery schedules and checking methods.

As has been pointed out previously, the Becket organization is one of the few architectural firms in the country with an actual research arm. Of the many benefits expected to be forthcoming from this function perhaps the greatest is that of providing research services for clients when required. Another benefit, of course, is that Welton Becket and Associates has within itself the capabilities for performing specific research of its own that will tend to make the firm progress faster than might otherwise be the case. The volume of this work that can be handled may be considerably extended by joint ventures with other research organizations or by commissioning other groups to perform work for the Becket organization. Another benefit that Welton Becket and Associates expects eventually will come from the research operation will be in the form of patentable products or systems, which produce additional income for the firm.

Perhaps the attitudes of Welton Becket and Associates toward expansion of services can be derived from the specific examples of subjects of investigation noted so far. But it probably should be added that their thinking does not end with what has been discussed here. Rather, they are giving some thought to such things as the possibility of their own wholly owned subsidiary that would do blueprinting and perform other related functions such as reproducing specifications. And on their minds are thoughts of adding such activities as traffic analysis and specific environmental planning, and major civil engineering.

What will the Welton Becket and Associates firm be like if it expands its services in the directions described above? Perhaps the best place to start is to say that the firm will be truly national in scope, the first architectural office that can properly make that claim. One of the dimensions of this is that the firm expects to have an office within an hour or so flying time of all of the major population centers of the U.S. Analysis has shown that the present Los Angeles office serves an area, within that span of time, of some 11 million people, the New York office about 33 million, Chicago some 22 million, San Francisco about 5 million, Houston approximately 4 million. Thus the firm now is in a position to serve, within an hour's time, any client among some 40 percent of the nation's population.

It should be noted that in the areas occupied by these 75 million people, the vast majority of all buildings of considerable size are commissioned—and built. The addition of an office in the Southeast would add about 3 to 4 million, or more, people to the total served. Beyond that step, further expansion of the number of offices would come very slowly if at all. If the flying time to clients were extended to an hour and a half or so, the present offices plus one in the Southeast could serve almost every square mile of the United States.

Nothing has been said here about foreign projects, but it should be pointed out that Welton Becket and Associates has always done a considerable amount of work overseas and will continue to do so. It can be reasonably expected that such work will grow in volume. Although the people in the firm expect to handle this work in their domestic offices, the possibility of foreign offices always exists.

Now it may come as a surprise to some when they learn how the Becket organization views the next few years regarding the expansion of the firm in size. Remembering that the organization put $209 million of construction in-place in 1969 and raised that total to $225 million in 1970, it may be unexpected that the figures for 1971 are running almost exactly parallel to those of the previous year in spite of the sad state of the economy. Of course, one of the reasons 1970 was better than the preceding year was the acquisition of the firm that became the Becket Chicago office. Otherwise total construction put in place would have been down somewhat, because of the down trend in business in the country. However, the Becket firm has been able to hold its own in 1970 while many firms have suffered considerably.

The Resource Center,
Century City,
Los Angeles, California.

Westchester County Courthouse,
White Plains, New York.

At the present time, the projection being made by the firm envisions doubling the 1970 billings, approximately, by 1975. Thus the projection would give the firm more than $400 million per year of construction in place at the end of the five-year period. To accomplish this volume, the firm will have to grow to almost double its size in personnel. This constitutes one of the major problems faced: how to find talented people in adequate numbers to maintain this sort of growth rate. In the past, such people have been found and the firm feels it can continue to attract people of high caliber.

It should be pointed out that doubling the size of the firm's billings to represent $400 million of construction in place each year will entail a total employment of roughly 1,100 people in the firm's offices. It should be noted that this estimate is quite conservative, and its basis should be established here. The assumptions on which the 1,100-employee base were established include these: one more office would be established of approximately seventy-five to a hundred people; the existing offices would all have structural, mechanical, and electrical engineering in the house, while only Chicago and Los Angeles have these functions at present; all offices would have interior design; none of the more esoteric functions such as purchasing and the like have been included in making these projections. Thus, after allowing for the necessary people to staff the engineering and interior design functions in those offices that do not have them, for seventy-five to a hundred in the Southeast or another new office, the projection calls for an increase in architectural, management, and corporate level people of only about 15 percent in the next four years. A modest proposal indeed.

In the organization of the firm, the Welton Becket and Associates people feel they have one of the strongest factors pointing toward growth. The reorganization some time ago of the firm into a corporate structure under which complete, full-service offices operate in strategic locations around the country seems to lend itself to growth in service and size in a manner similar to that of any growth-minded corporation in any industry. Each office will eventually have all of the major departments required for full practice, and the corporate office can supplement these everyday services in special areas such as project administration, research, purchasing, and so on. The firm is strongly acquisition-minded and is on the lookout for other firms that might strengthen the overall output. The Southeast has already been mentioned as a likely spot for a Becket office, either by acquisition or other means. But this area is not the only possibility. Offices will be located wherever it seems to make sense and good business. It should be mentioned, however, that the firm feels itself under no pressure to expand willy-nilly. It believes its present offices can continue to produce good profit ratios, expand their volume, and do a good job for clients. And Welton Becket and Associates will establish new offices only when convinced it is for the good of the company and that there are top-flight people to man them.

In some large firms, in any given industry, the fact of growth, of bigness, often seems to become a fetish. Bigness breeds bigness; growth breeds growth. And if anyone stopped to analyze the worth of what was happening, the values being produced, he might be surprised to find that these things had become ends in themselves with little additional meaning or increase in profits.

The Becket firm is dedicated to growth and to the values that come from being a large architectural organization. They do not preach bigness and growth for their own sakes. Rather, the great size of this firm and the size to which it will grow in the future are closely allied to the scope of the accomplishments the people in the firm wish to make.

Many examples have already been cited of activities or services only a large architectural firm could reasonably provide: purchasing for its clients, a complete research department, nationwide service to clients within an hour or so flying time.

Other activities could be cited. A random list might include the fact that the Becket firm is deeply involved with computers and other forms of automation. Accounting systems are computerized. More and more, engineering calculations are being handled with the aid of computers. Studies are under way of automated drafting methods. Welton Becket and Associates has its own printshop in Los Angeles for the reproduction of specifications. Cost control activities are being automated. Much of the drudgery of these activities is being eliminated, but more importantly, perhaps, the services to clients are being overwhelmingly improved.

Another area of activity in Welton Becket and Associates lies in systems analysis. Only an embryo beginning so far, but one that holds great promise as a future source of information for the Welton Becket and Associates staff, as a vehicle for problem solving, and as a service to clients.

Without going into a multitude of detail, one example may serve to illustrate how the size of this firm contributes to the quality of its services and to the profitability of the operations. As has been pointed out, specifications here are being put on an automated system, employing paper punched tapes. At the present time, the system is almost complete. Only a firm of considerable size, doing a large volume of work, could afford its own system of this sort.

The results are spectacular. The quality of the specifications has been vastly improved. The time required has been considerably reduced. And the cost per page of specification has been cut to less than half what it was before automation.

All in all, what the plans of the Becket firm add up to is a dedication to improvement of the excellence of its design and broader scope for the design services offered to its clients. It is of interest that the staff, from top to bottom, are now talking more of aesthetic excellence than ever before. They dwell on the needs for a unique combination of services and aesthetics which they are busy developing.

Welton Becket and Associates has prepared itself for the future. Its president, MacDonald Becket, and those around him, believe they can foresee enough of that future to partake deeply of all that future will offer in architecture—in total design.

Garrett Corporation,
Torrance, California.

Contemporary Resort Hotel,
Walt Disney World,
Orlando, Florida.

232

Bullock's Department Store,
Northridge, California.

Nassau Coliseum, Mineola,
New York.

233

Plaza Del Oro,
Houston, Texas.

Grand Ole Opry House,
Nashville, Tennessee.

234

John F. Kennedy Educational, Civic and Cultural Center, Mineola, New York.

Aerospace Education Center, Air Force Academy, Colorado Springs, Colorado.

INDEX OF BUILDINGS

Aerospace Education Center   107, 235
Colorado Springs, Colorado
Air Force Academy Foundation,
  Colorado Springs, Colorado
In design.

Aetna Life & Casualty Building   25, 110, 155
San Francisco, California
Crocker-Aetna Co., Subsidiary of
  Aetna Life & Casualty Co. and
  Crocker Estate Co., San Francisco, California
Completion: 1969.

Airport Traffic Control Tower   161
Dallas-Fort Worth, Texas
Federal Aviation Administration, Washington, D.C.
Under construction.

Almaden Fashion Plaza   118
San Jose, California
Emporium-Capwell Co., San Francisco, California
Completion: 1969.

Automobile Club of Southern California   44, 152, 154
  Beverly Hills-Westwood Office
Century City, California
Automobile Club of Southern California,
  Los Angeles, California
Completion: 1965.

William Beaumont General Hospital   137
Fort Bliss, El Paso, Texas
Department of the Army, Washington, D.C.
Under construction.

Bethlehem Steel Building (now ISI Building)   20
San Francisco, California
Bethlehem Steel Co., Inc., Bethlehem, Pennsylvania
  (now owned by Insurance Securities)
Completion: 1960.

The Beverly Hilton   13
Beverly Hills, California
Hilton Hotels Corp., Beverly Hills, California
Completion: 1955 (first phase).

Bullock's
  La Habra, California   109
  Bullock's Inc., Los Angeles, California
    (Division of Federated Department Stores)
  Completion: 1969.

  Lakewood, California   109
  Bullock's Inc., Los Angeles, California
  Completion: 1965.

  Northridge, California   233
  Bullock's Realty Corp., Los Angeles, California
  Completion: 1971.

  Pasadena, California   109
  Bullock's Inc., Los Angeles, California
  Completion: 1947.

  Sherman Oaks (San Fernando Valley), California   109
  Bullock's Inc., Los Angeles, California
  Completion: 1963.

  Westwood, California   109
  Bullock's, Inc., Los Angeles, California
  Completion: 1950.

Cadet Activities Center   220
West Point, New York
U.S. Military Academy, West Point, New York
Under construction.

California Federal Savings and Loan Building   13
Los Angeles, California
California Federal Savings and Loan Association,
  Los Angeles, California
Completion: 1960.

California Teachers Association State Headquarters 76, 153
Burlingame, California
California Teachers Association, Burlingame, California
Completion: 1959.

Cañada College 67, 156
Redwood City, California
San Mateo, California, Junior College District
Chan/Rader Associates, San Francisco, California
  (joint venture)
Completion: 1969.

Canyon Village 68
Yellowstone National Park, Wyoming
National Park Service, Washington, D.C.
Completion: 1957.

Center Plaza 95, 97, 146, 153
Boston, Massachusetts
Center Plaza Associates, Boston, Massachusetts
Completion: 1966, 1967, 1969 (three phases).

Century City 100, 103, 154
Century City, California
Aluminum Company of America, Pittsburgh, Pennsylvania
Original master plan completed 1958.

Century City Theme Office Building 224
Century City, California
Century City, Inc., Los Angeles, California
Never constructed.

Clinton Square 226
Syracuse, New York
New York State Urban Development Corp. and
  Beacon Construction Co., Boston, Massachusetts
Under construction.

Com-Ed West 143
Carmel Valley, California
Del Monte Corp., Monterey, California
Never constructed.

Contemporary Resort Hotel 120–121, 232
Walt Disney World, Florida
U.S. Steel Corp., Pittsburgh, Pennsylvania and
  WED Enterprises, Glendale, California
Completion: 1971.

Cullen Center 22
Houston, Texas
Cullen Center Inc., Houston, Texas
Completion: 1962–1963.

Downtown Office Building 144
Los Angeles, California
Cabot, Cabot & Forbes
Boston, Massachusetts
In design.

Equitable Life Building xii
Los Angeles, California
Equitable Life Assurance Co., New York, New York
Completion: 1969.

Esco Building 142
Los Angeles, California
In design.

F & M Center 138
Richmond, Virginia
First & Merchants National Bank, Richmond, Virginia
Carneal & Johnston, Associate Architects
Under construction.

Fashion Island 56, 154
Newport Beach, California
The Irvine Co., Newport Beach, California
Completion: 1967.

Federal Office Building 107
Los Angeles, California
General Services Administration
Washington, D.C.
Albert C. Martin & Associates and Paul R. Williams (joint
  venture)
Completion: 1966.

First State Bank 44
Clear Lake City, Texas
Del E. Webb Corp., Los Angeles, California and
  Humble Oil & Refining Co., Houston, Texas
Completion: 1966.

500 Jefferson Building 162
Houston, Texas
Cullen Center, Inc., Houston, Texas
Completion: 1962.

Ford Division General Office Building 14
Dearborn, Michigan
Ford Motor Co., Detroit, Michigan
Albert Kahn, Associate Architect
Completion: 1956.

Ford Motor Company Pavilion 152
1964–1965 New York World's Fair
Ford Motor Company
Dearborn, Michigan
Completion: 1964.

Garrett Building 232
Torrance, California
The Signal Companies, Los Angeles, California
Never constructed.

Gateway Buildings 103
Century City, California
Century City, Inc., Los Angeles, California
Completion: East, 1964; West, 1962.

General Electric Attraction 22, 152
New York World's Fair, 1964-65, New York, New York
General Electric Co., Schenectady, New York
Completion: 1964.

General Electric Tempo Building 224
Summerland, California
General Electric Co., Schenectady, New York
Never constructed.

General Petroleum Building 12
Los Angeles, California
General Petroleum Corp., Los Angeles, California
Completion: 1949.

Goetz Residence 10
Los Angeles, California
William Goetz

Grand Ole Opry House 234
Nashville, Tennessee
WSM Inc., Nashville, Tennessee
Under construction.

Gulf Life Tower ii, 23, 152, 160
Jacksonville, Florida
Gulf Life Investment Co., Jacksonville, Florida
Kemp, Bunche & Jackson, Associate Architect
Completion: 1967.

Hampshire Plaza 139
Manchester, New Hampshire
Spaulding & Slye Corp., Boston, Massachusetts
Under construction.

Hartford National Bank Building 27–28
Hartford, Connecticut
Hartford National Bank & Trust Co., Hartford, Connecticut
Jeter & Cook, Associate Architect
Completion: 1967.

Hawaiian Village   7
Honolulu, Hawaii
Henry J. Kaiser, Oakland, California and
   Fritz B. Burns, Los Angeles, California
Edwin L. Bauer, Associate Architect
Completion: 1957.

Hoffman Medical Research Center   38
Los Angeles, California
University of Southern California, Los Angeles, California
Completion: 1969.

Hotel Sonesta   154
Houston, Texas
Cullen Center, Inc., Houston, Texas
Completion: 1963.

House of Tomorrow   11
Los Angeles, California
Fritz Burns, Los Angeles, California
Completion: 1946.

Humble Oil Building   20, 164-217
Houston, Texas
Humble Oil & Refining Co., Houston, Texas
Goleman & Rolfe and
   George Pierce & Abel Pierce, Associate Architects
Completion: 1963.

Inter-Continental Hotels   106
New York, New York

   Antigua, West Indies
   Schematic studies.

   Buenos Aires, Argentina
   Schematic studies.

   Kinshasa, Republic of the Congo
   Under construction.

   Lisbon, Portugal
   Schematic studies.

   Oberai, Bombay, India
   Schematic studies.

   Phnom Penh, Kingdom of Cambodia
   Schematic studies.

   Saigon, South Vietnam
   Schematic studies.

   Singapore
   Schematic studies.

Jai Alai Auditorium   11
Manila, Republic of the Philippines
City of Manila
Completion: 1940.

Kaiser Center   17, 18
Oakland, California
Kaiser Center, Inc., Oakland, California
Completion: 1960.

John F. Kennedy Education, Civic & Cultural Center   233
   (*Nassau Coliseum*)
Mineola, Long Island, New York
County of Nassau, New York
Under construction.

Los Angeles International Airport   22, 130-136
Los Angeles, California
City of Los Angeles, California
Pereira & Luckman and Paul Williams,
   Los Angeles, California (joint venture)
Completion: 1962.

Los Angeles Memorial Sports Arena   14, 62, 153
Los Angeles, California
Los Angeles Coliseum Commission
Completion: 1959.

The Manila Hilton   24, 70-72
Manila, Republic of the Philippines
Delgado Brothers Hotel Co.,
   Manila, Republic of the Philippines
C. D. Arguelles, Associate Architect
Completion: 1968.

The Meadows   2, 153
San Rafael, California
C. Wheeler and S. Weiss, San Rafael, California
Completion: 1964.

Medical Field Service School   107, 141
   Brooke Army Medical Center
Fort Sam Houston, Texas
Department of the Army, Washington, D.C.
Under construction.

Middlesex Bank Building   142
Burlington, Massachusetts
Middlesex Bank, Burlington, Massachusetts
Under construction.

Montgomery Residence   10
Los Angeles, California
Robert Montgomery

Morgan Residence   10
Los Angeles, California
Henry Morgan

The Music Center of Los Angeles County   xi, 23, 78-91
Los Angeles, California
Music Center Lease Co., Los Angeles, California
   Ahmanson Theatre
   Completion: 1967.

   Dorothy Chandler Pavilion
   Completion: 1964.

   Mark Taper Forum
   Completion: 1967.

Mutual Benefit Life Building   73
San Francisco, California
Walter H. Shorenstein, San Francisco, and
   Mutual Benefit Life Insturance Co, Newark, New Jersey
Completion: 1969.

Nassau Coliseum   233
Mineola, Long Island, New York
County of Nassau, New York
Under construction.

New Queens High School   138
Queens, New York, New York
New York City Board of Education
In design.

The Nile Hilton   14
Cairo, United Arab Republic
Completion: 1959.

North American Rockwell Building   139
El Segundo, California
North American Rockwell Corp., Los Angeles, California
Never constructed.

North Carolina Mutual Life Building   21, 145, 152
Durham, North Carolina
North Carolina Mutual Life Insurance Co.,
   Durham, North Carolina
Marion A. Ham, Associate Architect
Completion: 1965.

Northgate Shopping Center   56
San Rafael, California
Draper Shopping Centers Inc., San Rafael, California
Completion: 1966.

239

Northrop Building 140
Century City, California
Century Park Associates, Century City, California
Completion, 1970.

Olive View Hospital Medical Treatment & 25, 38
  Care Facility
Los Angeles, California
County of Los Angeles, California
Charles Luckman Associates (joint venture)
Completion: 1970.

Orange Civic Center 8
Orange, California
City of Orange, California
Completion: 1963.

Pan Pacific Auditorium 10–11
Los Angeles, California

Park Lane Apartments 163
Monterey, California
Stanford Weiss, Los Angeles, California
Completion: 1967.

Park Plaza 228
Oshkosh, Wisconsin
The Miles Kimball Co., Oshkosh, Wisconsin
Completion: 1970.

Pauley Pavilion 62
University of California at Los Angeles
Board of Regents, University of California
Sacramento, California
Completion: 1965.

Phillips Petroleum Building 21
Bartlesville, Oklahoma
Phillips Petroleum Co., Bartlesville, Oklahoma
Completion: 1964.

Pittsburgh National Building 218
Pittsburgh, Pennsylvania
Pittsburgh National Bank, Pittsburgh, Pennsylvania
Under construction.

Plaza del Oro 220, 234
Houston, Texas
Shell Oil Co., Houston, Texas
(Master plan).

Pomona City Hall 112
Pomona, California
Civic Center Corp., Pomona, California
B. H. Anderson, Associate Architect
Completion: 1968.

Pomona Library 112
Pomona, California
Civic Center Corp., Pomona, California
Everett & Tozier, Associate Architects
Completion: 1965.

Project D 228
Location confidential
Designed 1969.

Prototype Stadium 222
Research study.

Prudential Square 12–13
Los Angeles, California
Prudential Insurance Co. of America,
Newark, New Jersey
Completion: 1948.

Resource Center 128, 230
Century City, California
Henry Adams and Century City Inc.,
San Francisco and Los Angeles, California
In design.

Santa Monica Beach Facilities 68
Santa Monica, California
City of Santa Monica, California
Completion: 1958.

Security Pacific Bank Building 6
  (Tishman Airport Center)
Los Angeles, California
Tishman Realty & Construction Corp.,
New York, New York
Completion: 1963.

Seibu 5
Los Angeles, California
Seibu, Inc., Tokyo, Japan
Completion: 1962.

Shell Information Center 140
Houston Texas
Shell Oil Co., Houston, Texas
Under construction.

Sheraton Hotel 143
Tehran, Iran
Sheraton Design & Development Corp.,
Boston, Massachusetts
In design.

Southland Center. 15
Dallas, Texas
Southland Life Insurance Co., Dallas, Texas
Mark Lemmon, Associate Architect
Completion: 1959.

State Street Bank Operations Center 141
Quincy, Massachusetts
State Street Bank, Boston, Massachusetts
Under construction.

State Street South 226
Quincy, Massachusetts
State Street Bank, Boston, Massachusetts
(Master planning).

Stern Brothers 99
Wayne Township, New Jersey
Allstores Realty Corp., New York, New York
Completion: 1970.

Stonestown Shopping Center 13
San Francisco, California
Stoneson Development Co., San Francisco, California
Completion: 1951.

Tishman Airport Center 105
Los Angeles, California
Tishman Realty & Construction Co.,
  New York, New York
(Master planning).

U.S. Borax Building 154
Los Angeles, California
The Carter Co., Los Angeles, California
Completion: 1963.

U.S. Embassy 107
Warsaw, Poland
U.S. State Department, Washington, D.C.
Completion: 1963.

U.S. Exhibit 107
Moscow, USSR
U.S. Department of Commerce, Washington, D.C.
Completion: 1959.

U.S. Naval Postgraduate School 107
  Academic Building
Monterey, California
U.S. Naval Postgraduate School
Monterey, California
Completion: 1968.

U.S. Naval Postgraduate School Library   107
Monterey, California
U.S. Naval Postgraduate School,
Monterey, California
Under construction.

UCLA Center for the Health Sciences   13–14, 25, 108
University of California at Los Angeles
Regents of the University of California,
   Berkeley, California

   Institute for Chronic Disease
   Completion: 1965.

   Jules Stein Eye Institute
   Completion: 1966

   Marion Davies Children's Clinic
   Completion: 1962.

   Neuropsychiatric and Brain Research Institute
   Completion: 1961.

   Reed Neurological Research Center
   Completion: 1970.

   School of Public Health
   Completion: 1968.

Valley Center   122–125, 236
Phoenix, Arizona
Valley National Bank, Phoenix, Arizona
Guirey, Arnold & Sprinkle, Associate Architects
Under construction.

Veterans Administration Hospital   107
Palo Alto, California
Veteran's Administration, Washington, D.C.
Completion: 1961.

Walt Disney World   120–121, 232
Walt Disney World, Florida
WED Enterprises, Inc., Glendale, California
Under construction.

Wells Fargo Bank   146
San Rafael, California
Wells Fargo Bank
San Francisco, California
Completion: 1965.

Welton Becket and Associates Building   30, 37
Los Angeles, California
Welton Becket and Associates, Los Angeles, California
Completion: 1960.

Westchester County Courthouse   230
White Plains, New York
County of Westchester, New York
Under construction.

White Plains Mall   137
White Plains, New York
Benerofe Associates, White Plains, New York
Under construction.

Willowbrook Shopping Center   98
Wayne Township, New Jersey
Rouse Co., Newark, New Jersey
Completion: 1970.

Worcester Center   51–55
Worcester, Massachusetts
Worcester Center Associates, Boston, Massachusetts
Completion: 1971.

Xerox Square   27, 74, 152, 158
Rochester, New York
Central City Holding Co., Rochester, New York
Completion: 1968.

INDEX OF PHOTOGRAPHERS

B-bottom   T-top
C-center   R-right
L-left

Amiaga, Gil, 43 (T), 52, 53, 54

Banks, Peter, 36 (second down)

Cabanban, Orlando, 41, 48, 59 (T), 66 (all but bottom)

Checkman, Louis, 51, 141 (B), 233 (B)

Cross, Herbert Bruce, 100, 186, 187, 197, 222, 224

Disney, Walt Productions, 120

Eyerman, J., 23 (T)

Freiwald, Joshua, 2, 153 (bottom left)

Hedrich-Blessing, 14 (T)

Kaminsky, Robert, 158, 160, 161, 162

Koch, Richard, 107 (bottom right), 135, 140 (T), 144, 232, 233 (T), 235, 236

Korab, Balthazar, II, XI, XII, 17, 20, 21, 22, 23 (B), 25, 37, 38, 44 (T), 56, 62 (T), 73, 80, 82 (T), 83, 90, 91, 95, 97, 108 (upper left), 109, 110, 145, 146 (B), 152 (top left, center left and bottom right), 153 (bottom right), 154 (center left), 155 (top left and bottom), 164, 166, 170, 181, 182, 199, 200, 208, 211, 212, 213, 214, 215, 216, 217

Miller, Charles, 11 (C)

Molitor, Joseph, 24 (T), 27, 28, 74, 98, 99, 152 (top right and center right)

Moulin Studios, 13 (T)

Nadel, Leonard, Dedication page, 15 (T)

Nelson William, 108 (third row right)

Partridge, Rondall, 14 (C), 67, 153 (center photos), 155 (top and center right), 156

Payne, Richard, 234 (T)

Rand, Marvin, 5, 6, 8, 12 (B), 14 (B), 17, 18, 22 (C), 44 (B), 62 (B), 68 (T), 81, 83 (lower three), 84, 85, 86, 87, 103, 105, 107 (top left and second row left), 108, 112, 146 (T), 152 (bottom left), 153 (top right), 154 (top, center right and bottom), 163

Ratto, Gerald, 76, (153 top left)

Rogers, John, 15 (B)

Shulman, Julius, 9 (L), 11 (B), 12, 13 (B)

Simmonds, Douglas, 13 (C)

Sturdevant, Roger, 20 (T)

Thom, Wayne, 118

United Press International, 71

Vanguard, 184, 185

Wasser, Julian, 33, 34, 35, 36, 40, 42, 43 (B), 46, 47, 49, 50, 58, 59 (all but top), 60, 61, 64, 65, 66 (B)

Wenkam, R., 7

Williams, Harry, 9 (R)

Wright, Wayne, 68 (B)

INDEX

Accounting, procedures for, 36, 42
Administration, Welton Becket and
    Associates:
    Department of, 20, 33–36
    Production, 39, 42–43, 58–61, 113–117
Agreements, owner-architect, 59, 113–114
    with consultants, 59
Airports:
    hypersonic, study of, 70, 122, 126–127
    Los Angeles International, 22
      new terminal for United Air Lines,
        130–136
Analysis, contract, 114–115
Andrews, Carl, 36
Architects, project, 58–60, 149–151
Architectural firms, future types of, 225
Architectural services, 4, 21
Architecture:
    future of, 221–231
    general versus specialized practice,
      20–21, 129–136
    philosophy for, 3–8, 23, 129–130
Arguelles, Carlos, 70, 72
Awards, architectural, 15, 23

Beardwood, Jack, 20, 22, 33–36, 94, 96, 104
Becket, Bruce, 19, 33, 35, 58
Becket, Evro, 9
Becket, MacDonald, 19, 22, 31, 33–36, 96,
    119, 221–222, 225, 229–230
Becket, Welton David, 9–16, 21, 23, 26,
    33–34, 104
    on conflicts of interest, 21
    death of, 16, 19, 31
    early years of, 9
    on the future, 227
    and the Humble Oil Building, 168, 187,
      195
    organization of Welton Becket and
      Associates, 14

Becket, Welton David (*Cont.*):
    partnership: with Charles Plummer and
      Walter Wurdeman, 10–11
      with MacDonald Becket and Maynard
        Woodard, 31
      with Walter Wurdeman, 9–14
    proprietorship, 14
    as a story teller, 10, 12, 15, 26
Becket, Welton M., 19–20
Beer, David, 49
Behavioural sciences, 221
Bela, Jack, 48
Bellows, W. S., Construction Corporation,
    209
Blair, Henry, 46
Board, Project Review, 34, 39
Breidert, O. H., 41
Brennan, Henry, 43, 58
Brower, Martin, 36, 96
Bullock's Inc., work for, 12, 25, 109, 233
Burns, Fritz, and the House of Tomorrow,
    11
Business:
    architecture as, 75–111
    new, developing, 94–96
Business Development, 22, 93–96

Cabrol, Pierre, 35, 40
California, University of, at Los Angeles,
    13, 14, 25, 108
    Center for the Health Sciences, 14, 25
    Environmental Design Workshop,
      School of Architecture, 119
    supervising architect for, 14
    work for, 13, 14, 25, 108
Chappell, William, 47
Cities, changes taking place in, 223
Clients:
    attitudes of firm toward, 24, 46
    changes taking place among, 223

Clients (*Cont.*):
    development of, 93–96
    education of, in architecture, 24
    importance of, 24
    repeat, 23–25, 104–109
Codes, building, writing of, 69–70
Committee:
    coordinating, 40–41
    executive, 33–34, 39
Computers, 115, 120, 231
Construction, services during, 58, 60, 157,
    159
    procedure manual for, 159
Coordinating committee, 40–41
"Corporate Architects," Welton Becket and
    Associates as, 21
Corporate practice, 14, 22, 31–38, 78, 82
Cost control, 58, 60, 149–150
Costs, soaring, of land and construction,
    223
Craddock, John, 167–168, 195, 204
Craig, Robert, 49

Davis, Morgan J., 167, 195, 209–210
Davis, Noel, 46
Design:
    architectural: definition of, 22–23, 46
      directors of, 48–49
      organization of, 45–50
      philosophy of, 23, 129–130
      principles of, 19–29
      and schematic development, 129–136
      style, Welton Becket and Associates
        and, 47
    graphic, 49–50
    of the Humble Oil Building, 183–199
    interior, 49
    total: business of, 76–111
      concepts of, 2–29
      framework for, 30–75